LBJ AND VIETNAM

AN ADMINISTRATIVE HISTORY OF THE
JOHNSON PRESIDENCY SERIES

LBJ AND VIETNAM
A Different Kind of War

BY GEORGE C. HERRING

UNIVERSITY OF TEXAS PRESS, AUSTIN

LIBRARY OF CONGRESS CATALOGING-IN-PUBLICATION DATA

Herring, George C., date.
    LBJ and Vietnam : a different kind of war / by George C. Herring.—1st ed.
        p.   cm.—(An Administrative history of the Johnson presidency series)
    Includes index.
    ISBN 0-292-73085-3 (alk. paper)
    1. Vietnamese Conflict, 1961–1975—United States.   2. United States—
Politics and government—1963–1969.   3. Johnson, Lyndon B. (Lyndon Baines),
1908–1973.   I. Title.   II. Series: Administrative history of the Johnson
presidency.
DS558.H454   1994
959.704′3373—dc20   93-36793

TO THREE GREAT TEACHERS:

.

VIRGINIA HUMMEL, C. HOMER BAST, EDWARD E. YOUNGER

CONTENTS

FOREWORD ix

PREFACE xi

ONE "A Different Kind of War" 1
*The Johnson Administration and the Conduct
of Limited War in Vietnam*

TWO No More MacArthurs 25
*Johnson, McNamara, the Military, and the
Command System in Vietnam*

THREE The "Other War" 63
Management of Pacification, 1965–1967

FOUR The Not-so-secret Search for Peace 89

FIVE "Without Ire" 121
Management of Public Opinion

SIX "Fighting while Negotiating" 151
The Tet Offensive and After

SEVEN   Conclusion   178

NOTES   187

INDEX   221

FOREWORD

This book is the eleventh in a series called "An Administrative History of the Johnson Presidency." Taking a broad view of administration, the series was designed first to present the infrastructure of presidential management—the structure, personnel, and operating relationships for decision making and policy administration: Emmette S. Redford and Marlan Blissett, *Organizing the Executive Branch: The Johnson Presidency* (University of Chicago Press, 1981); Richard L. Schott and Dagmar Hamilton, *People, Positions, and Power: The Political Appointments of Lyndon Johnson* (University of Chicago Press, 1983); Emmette S. Redford and Richard E. McCulley, *White House Operations: The Johnson Presidency* (University of Texas Press, 1986); and David M. Welborn and Jesse Burkheard, *Intergovernmental Relations in the American Administrative State* (University of Texas Press, 1989). These books are paralleled by another on the exercise of the appointive power for judicial positions: Neil D. Mc-Feeley, *Appointment of Judges: The Johnson Presidency* (University of Texas Press, 1987).

A second group of books has dealt with the presidential management of the policy-making and implementation process in particular areas. This book fits generally into this category. Other studies include W. Henry Lambright, *Presidential Management of Science and Technology: The Johnson Presidency* (University of Texas Press, 1985); James E. Anderson and Jared E. Hazelton, *Managing Macroeconomic Policy: The Johnson Presidency* (University of Texas Press, 1986); Harvey C. Mansfield, Sr., *Illustrations of Presidential Management: Johnson's Cost Reduction and Tax Increase Campaigns* (Lyndon B. Johnson School of Public Affairs, 1988); Paul Hammond, *LBJ and the Presidential Management of*

Foreign Relations (University of Texas Press, 1992); and David M. Welborn, *Regulation in the White House: The Johnson Presidency* (University of Texas Press, 1993). The second group of the series is completed with the publication of this volume.

A third group was planned with a more specific concentration on implementation. We confess that money and performance fell short, but we still anticipate a volume on the implementation of civil rights legislation.

This series of studies has been financed by a grant from the National Endowment for the Humanities, with additional aid from the Lyndon Baines Johnson Foundation, the Hobitzelle Foundation, and the Lyndon B. Johnson School of Public Affairs of the University of Texas at Austin.

The findings and conclusions in the various works in this series do not necessarily represent the view of any donor.

Emmette S. Redford
Project Director

James E. Anderson
Deputy Director

PREFACE

Drawing parallels with his illustrious predecessors Woodrow Wilson and Franklin Roosevelt, Lyndon Baines Johnson, on the eve of his momentous decisions for war in July 1965, lamented that "every time we have gotten near the culmination of our dreams, the war bells have rung." "If we have to fight," he added, "I'll do that." "But I don't want . . . to be known as a War President."[1]

Whatever his wish, Johnson *is* remembered as a war president, and among America's commanders-in-chief he generally rates with the least effective. He is popularly viewed as the only president to lose his war, something he greatly feared and on more than one occasion vowed he would not let happen. He was attacked by the antiwar left as the stereotypical, shoot-from-the-hip Texan, the warmonger who destroyed Vietnam to save his own ego and political fortunes. He has been scored by the political right as a timid, all-too-political war leader who refused to do what was necessary to win an eminently winnable war.

Such criticisms tell a great deal about the way Johnson fought the war, but they do not get at the fundamental problems of his war leadership. To be fair, of course, limited war is extraordinarily difficult to fight, especially within the American system, and Vietnam was a war that probably could not have been won in any meaningful sense. Still, the deficiencies of Johnson's leadership contributed to the peculiar frustrations of the Vietnam War and to its outcome, and these deficiencies derived to a considerable extent from his personality and leadership style.

This book will analyze LBJ's management of the Vietnam War. It will look at the way limited war theory and Johnson's own leadership style influenced his conduct of the war. Through close scrutiny of the command system, it will examine the way in which strategy was formulated and implemented. It will seek to explain in the process the curious phenomenon of why, although there was near universal dissatisfaction among Johnson's advisers with the way the war was being fought and the results that were being obtained, there was no change of strategy or even substantive discussion of a change. By looking at the administration's management of pacification programs, its handling of scores of private and third country peace moves, and its perception and manipulation of public opinion, this book will examine some of the diverse facets of an extremely complex war. It will also attempt to show how they interacted with each other and to explain why they were rarely brought into harmony. It will analyze the period after Tet and especially the little-studied period after Johnson's March 31, 1968, speech, when the administration's efforts to implement a complex strategy of fighting while negotiating starkly exposed the deficiencies of Johnson's war management.

America's failure in Vietnam challenged as perhaps nothing else has one of the nation's most cherished myths—the notion that we can accomplish anything we set our collective minds to—and partisans of many points of view have sought in its aftermath to explain this profoundly traumatic experience. Many of those seeking to explain why the United States failed are in fact arguing that an alternative approach would have succeeded. Such arguments are at best debatable on their own terms. They are also dubious methodologically. Much more can be learned by focusing on why the war was fought as it was without reference to alternative strategies, without presuming that it could have been won or was inevitably lost. This study tries to do that.

Like most books, this one has a story of its own. In January 1985, when I was completing research at the Lyndon Baines Johnson Library for a revision of *America's Longest War*, Professor Emmette Redford approached me about doing a book on Johnson's management of the conflict. I hesitated, at least a bit fearful of getting into an area of analysis I was only dimly familiar with and also because I was committed, I thought, to leaving Vietnam after more than a decade of study. Eventually, I consented, in part because I had already accumulated mountains of material I could not use in the revision of my earlier book and did not want to "waste," in part because I found it difficult to resist the lure of a subject that continued to fascinate and disturb me. The book took far longer to complete than I had anticipated. It was put aside numerous times for other projects and for most of the three years that I chaired the University of Kentucky history department. There were times when I despaired (even more than is ordinarily the case in the writing of a book) that it would ever get done.

That I have completed it is in part attributable to the many people who have assisted and encouraged me along the way. Financial support for the research was provided by the Lyndon Baines Johnson Foundation, the Lyndon Baines Johnson School of Public Affairs, the U.S. Army Military History Institute at Carlisle Barracks, and the University of Kentucky Research Foundation. Perhaps most important, a Fulbright award to New Zealand provided me the escape from administrative duties and distance from other intrusions that made it possible for me to get going again. I am grateful to Laurie Cox of the New Zealand–United States Educational Foundation and to the University of Otago for making this possible. My colleagues at Otago provided a most congenial atmosphere in which to work, and Rob and Kathie Rabel, in particular, were the most delightful of hosts. A sabbatical leave supported by the University of Kentucky enabled me to complete a long-delayed project.

Those historians who do "traditional" research depend on archivists. I am especially grateful to the staffs of the Manuscript Division, Library of Congress, the Federal Records Center, Suitland, Md., the Marine Corps Historical Center, Washington, D.C., and the Air Force Historical Research Center, Maxwell Air Force Base, Ala., for assistance rendered with this project. Richard Sommers and David Keough of the U.S. Army Military History Institute provided indispensable help during my several research trips to Carlisle Barracks.

This book relies heavily on the resources of the Lyndon Baines Johnson Library, and a special word of thanks goes to Harry Middleton and his staff. I have been making research trips to Austin since 1977 and have found every one a genuine pleasure, not simply because of the richness of the materials but also because of the hospitality and helpfulness of the people. I am also grateful to Tom Johnson for permission to use his invaluable notes on top-level 1967–1968 meetings, notes that provide quite remarkable insights into Lyndon Johnson's leadership and management style. I am especially grateful to David C. Humphrey of the LBJ Library. David is truly the historian's archivist, a professional who brings to his work an incomparable knowledge of the documents and a very special eagerness to help researchers. Those of us who study this period are in his debt.

My students Clarence Wyatt, Bruce Smith-Peters, Robert Hodges, and Robert Brigham helped with the research. Don Higginbotham, Gen. Bruce Palmer, Maj. Earl Tilford, and Richard H. Kohn read chapters and offered invaluable suggestions. The warm response to my Harmon Lecture at the U.S. Air Force Academy in October 1990 provided a great stimulus to completing this work, and I am grateful to Col. Carl W. Reddel and his colleagues for providing me that opportunity. Professors Emmette Redford and James Anderson have been the most patient and supportive of editors, never giving up on me (even, perhaps, when they should have). They have also been astute critics, providing extensive commentary on several drafts of the manuscript. Dottie Leathers could not at first understand why I had to complete the book but supported and assisted me anyway, and for this I am grateful. When the U.S. mail let me down, she came through, searching through hopelessly disorganized files and sending me halfway across the world huge volumes of urgently needed notes and drafts.

It is a very special pleasure for me to use the publication of this book to thank three teachers who greatly influenced my choice of a career and contributed immeasurably to whatever success I have attained. Virginia Hummel, my high school English teacher, inspired me to write. C. Homer Bast sparked an interest in history while I was a first-year student at Roanoke College and nurtured it over the next four years. The late Edward E. Younger was more than a teacher to those of us whose work he supervised at the University of Virginia. He was a mentor and a friend. He taught us to be historians but always reminded us by his own warm personal example that we were foremost human beings. Placement of the names of these truly great teachers on the dedication page of this book represents a small and altogether inadequate expression of my appreciation for their inspiration and assistance.

George C. Herring   *Lexington, Kentucky*
                                                    January 1993

LBJ AND VIETNAM

"A Different Kind of War"

ONE

*The Johnson Administration
and the Conduct of
Limited War in Vietnam*

At 12:34 P.M. on July 28, 1965, President Lyndon Baines Johnson strode into the East Room of the White House and positioned himself before the two hundred reporters already assembled there. Standing behind a strange, Rube Goldberg–like contraption that served as a teleprompter and deflected the television lights from his eyes, easing the worry lines in his face, the president spoke in somber tones. He began by explaining why Americans were fighting and dying in Vietnam. He went on to outline U.S. goals in that faraway land. He revealed that he was dispatching an additional 50,000 troops, raising the total number to 125,000, and he affirmed that more would be sent later as requested. In the face of communist aggression, he pledged, the United States would not surrender and it would not retreat.

Despite its solemnity, Johnson's "war message" was curiously ambivalent. Insisting that "this is really war," he went on to reassure his listeners that it would not be necessary to call up the reserves or declare a national emergency. In the same breath that he spoke of war, he spoke of peace, expressing his nation's willingness to negotiate and its hopes for a peaceful solution. He called upon the United Nations to employ all its "resources, energy, and immense prestige" in search of peace in Vietnam.

The president's ambivalence no doubt in part reflected the heavy burdens of his office. "I do not find it easy," he admitted, "to send the flower of our youth, our finest young men, into battle." But it also reflected the nature of the war he and his top advisers were committed to fight and indeed their strategy for waging it. "This is a different kind of war," he noted in the opening lines of his statement, words pregnant with meaning but generally overlooked in the commentary that followed. "There are no marching armies or solemn declarations." [1]

Johnson's war message was received by the media in much the spirit it was delivered, seriously, but without any sense of urgency or impending crisis. The *New York Times* gave it a modest, five-column headline. The headline and the story that followed placed the president's appeal to the UN on equal footing with his commitment of an additional 50,000 troops. A related front-page story indicated that Congress was relieved by the president's course, and still another story reported that the decisions were not expected to harm the booming domestic economy. In an editorial, the often critical *Times* praised Johnson's restraint and his apparent commitment to a controlled and carefully limited operation. [2]

The newsweeklies responded in a similar vein. *Time* portrayed a pensive and obviously troubled Johnson on its cover, but it would go no further than to state that "last week unquestionably marked a turning point in U.S. policy toward a war in Viet Nam." As for the future, *Time* safely predicted that more U.S. troops would be sent and more would become involved in combat. In terms as low-keyed and off-handed as those of the president, it also raised the possibility that the war might be "long drawn out." But the cover story went on to talk about LBJ's dramatic achievements at home and provided a "scorecard" of what was touted as the most historic week of legislative accomplishment in U.S. history. [3]

Johnson's speech fell between *Newsweek*'s deadlines. Its August 9 cover story thus dealt with the twentieth anniversary of the dropping of the atomic bomb. A brief account commented that the president's Vietnam decisions were as "dramatic for what they rejected as for what they proposed," permitting the nation "an almost audible sigh of relief." Reflecting the mood of the moment, *Newsweek* noted the absence of "hot tides of national anger" and remarked on the "strange, almost passionless war" the United States was fighting in Vietnam. "There are no songs written about it," the magazine concluded, "and the chances that any will seem remote," a prediction that turned out to be tragically off the mark. [4]

July 28, 1965, might therefore be called the day the United States went to war without knowing it, and it is now clear that this was no accident. Johnson's July 28 press conference culminated six weeks of deliberation and an intensive week of meetings resulting in a decision for an open-ended military commitment in Vietnam. The press conference was also part of a carefully orchestrated strategy for waging limited war. The Johnson administration set out to fight this "different kind of war" in "cold blood," in Secretary of State Dean Rusk's words; that is, without mobilization and without arousing popular emotion. Fighting such a war, as it turned out, divided the nation as nothing since its own civil war a century earlier and eventually destroyed the administration that tried to do it. In a broader sense, it raised complex and still unresolved problems about the management of limited war and indeed its viability as an option, problems the Johnson administration perceived only belatedly and struggled unsuccessfully to resolve.

I

Johnson and his advisers brought to their war in August 1965 a set of assumptions about, principles of, and rules for limited war drawn from the Korean experience and academic writings on the subject in the 1950s and 1960s. Indeed, a veritable cult of limited war had developed in these years in response to the institutionalization of the containment policy, the popular frustrations caused in the United States by the Korean War, and the Eisenhower administration's New Look defense policy and strategy of massive retaliation.

Limited war was not, of course, exclusively a twentieth-century phenomenon. After the carnage and destruction of the Thirty Years' War, European rulers in the late seventeenth and early eighteenth centuries had deliberately set out to restrict the means and ends of combat. They had seen the dangers of unleashing the passions of their own people. They had made huge investments in their armies, needed them to maintain domestic order, and thus were loath to risk them in battle. Once involved in war, as a consequence, they sought to avoid major battles, employed professional armies in cautious strategies of attrition, used tactics emphasizing maneuver and fortification, and adopted unwritten rules protecting civilian lives and property. The aim was to sustain the balance of power rather than destroy the enemy. Wars were to be conducted with minimal intrusion into the lives of the people. Indeed, that master practitioner of limited war, Frederick the Great, once observed that a war was not a success if most people knew it was going on.[5]

Although the United States came into being in the age of limited war, that type of conflict proved incompatible with the American experience and character. Native Americans were not familiar with the rules of "civilized" warfare applied in Europe, and the recurrent conflicts on the frontiers of the New World took a very different shape. The homes of the colonists were often their fortresses and all men and women were soldiers. The wars were for survival, "the urgent defense of the hearth by everybody against an omnipresent and merciless enemy." To be sure, the United States, out of weakness, fought essentially defensive wars against Britain in 1776 and 1812 and wisely avoided the pursuit of total victory against Mexico in 1846. Still, in seeking the elimination of British power from much of North America, revolutionary leaders foreshadowed what historian Russell Weigley has called the "American way of war." As the nation's power grew, that approach became entrenched. The Civil War set the pattern by suggesting that "the complete overthrow of the enemy, the destruction of his military power, is the object of war." In the first and second world wars, the United States, once committed, mobilized superior forces in a total war setting for total victory and in World War II unconditional surrender.[6]

The exigencies of the nuclear age brought a revival of limited war in the mid-twentieth century. During the Korean "police action" President Harry S Truman had rejected Gen. Douglas MacArthur's more traditional and aggressive strategy and imposed limits on ends and means to avoid an expanded war with the Soviet Union in an area of marginal strategic importance. The Eisenhower administration's emphasis on nuclear weaponry and massive retaliation seemed a return to total war concepts. Once the Soviet Union had developed effective delivery systems for nuclear weapons, however, it was obvious to theorists such as political scientist Robert Osgood that massive retaliation could not work. With nothing but nuclear weapons as a deterrent, the United States in responding to Communist challenges in marginal areas would face the unthinkable choice of nuclear war or acquiescence.

To escape that dilemma and find a means of containing Communist expansion while minimizing the risks of a nuclear holocaust, Osgood and others advised limited war. Such a strategy would harness the nation's military power more closely to the attainment of its political objectives. A variety of military instruments, including conventional forces, would be readied to respond to different threats at different levels. The amount of force employed in any situation would be limited to that necessary to achieve political aims. The objective would be not to destroy opponents but to persuade them to break off the conflict short of achieving their goals and without resorting to nuclear war.[7]

Osgood's classic 1957 study provided a set of broad guidelines for the conduct of limited war. Leaders must "scrupulously limit" their political objectives and clearly communicate those objectives to the enemy. They must make every effort to keep open diplomatic channels to terminate the war through negotiations on the basis of limited objectives. They must restrict to the area and amount consistent with the attainment of the desired political objectives the geographic locality of the war and the instruments used. Limited war must be directed by the civilian leadership. The special needs of the military should not affect its conduct, and indeed the military must be a controllable instrument of national policy.[8]

Subsequent writers such as Thomas Schelling, Henry Kissinger, and Herman Kahn refined limited war theory, focusing on the use of military power to persuade an adversary to act in the desired way by conveying threats of force. Military action was less important for the damage it did than for the message it sent. War became a sort of bargaining process through which force was employed to persuade enemies that persisting in what they were doing would be too expensive to continue. "The object," Schelling wrote, "is to exact good behavior or to oblige discontinuance of mischief, not to destroy the subject altogether."[9] The implicit assumption was that the use of force could be orchestrated in such a way as to communicate precise and specific signals and that an opponent would back down in the face of such threats and pressure.

Limited war theory had numerous flaws. It was primarily an academic, rather than a military, concept, and it drastically misunderstood the dynamics of war. Both Osgood and Schelling seemed to say that since limited war was mainly about bargaining and diplomacy, it required no knowledge of military matters and indeed military considerations should not affect its conduct. Despite the popular frustrations caused by fighting a limited war in Korea, they were also grandly indifferent to the domestic political problems it posed. Osgood conceded that this type of conflict ran counter to the American tradition in war and that Americans might not easily accept the "galling but indispensable restraints" required by it. But he neatly dodged the problem with platitudes, calling for candor and courage on the part of leaders and surmising that if Americans were treated as adults they would respond as such.[10]

The limited war theorists devoted more effort to explaining *why* their type of war should be fought rather than *how* it was to be fought. In terms of bargaining theory, moreover, they assumed a greater capacity than was warranted on the part of a gigantic bureaucracy like the U.S. government to send clear, precise signals, and they reduced the behavior of potential adversaries to that of laboratory rats.

Johnson and his top advisers shared the major tenets of limited war theory. They saw their primary task in July 1965 as persuading the North Vietnamese to stop support of the insurgency in South Vietnam, and they set out to accomplish that goal by gradually escalating the application of air power and ground forces without threatening the destruction of North Vietnam itself. Veterans of the Cuban missile crisis, certain that a nuclear exchange would be an "unspeakable calamity," they were determined to keep control of the war in their own hands and to hold the military on a tight rein. They were committed to limiting as much as possible the geographical area of the conflict and the volume of force used. The heavy emphasis on negotiations in Johnson's

July 28 statement conveyed the administration's determination to keep open the prospect of a diplomatic settlement and end the war short of total victory. The low-key tone of Johnson's "war message" and his refusal to arouse the emotions of the nation reflected the administration's determination to fight the war in "cold blood," as dispassionately as possible and with minimal disruption of the lives of Americans. Rusk and Secretary of Defense Robert S. McNamara were both certain that this was the only way war could be fought in an era when the Communist threat was so pervasive and nuclear weapons so destructive. They were also persuaded that the American people must become accustomed to fighting in this manner since, as McNamara put it, this was the type of war the United States would likely fight for the next half-century.[11]

II

To fight this "different kind of war," the Johnson administration relied on decision-making machinery already in place. When he assumed the presidency in November 1963, LBJ inherited John Kennedy's top foreign policy advisers and his system for using them. Rusk and McNamara were, of course, nominally the president's top advisers on military and foreign policy issues. Distrustful of the established bureaucracy, however, Kennedy had added a layer between the White House and the executive departments. He scrapped Eisenhower's cumbersome National Security Council apparatus, the object of much criticism by 1960, and appointed Harvard dean McGeorge Bundy special assistant for national security affairs with an office in the White House basement. There, Bundy assembled a small staff of experts and created the White House's own Situation Room, installing equipment providing direct access to Defense Department, State Department, and Central Intelligence Agency cable traffic. Kennedy preferred ad hoc, informal meetings to Eisenhower's regular, highly formalized National Security Council meetings. Bundy's job was to organize those meetings, see that the right people and papers were there, and report results back to the departments and agencies. Washington gossips made much of the rivalry between Rusk's State Department and Bundy's office, and some of it was merited. The latter in fact often went beyond its role as a clearinghouse and became an active advocate of specific policy positions. At the same time, the NSC was also useful to State, giving it a point of contact and means of access to the White House that it would not otherwise have had.[12]

Johnson adapted the Kennedy system to his own management style. Sensitive to his lack of experience and expertise in foreign policy and eager to maintain continuity with his predecessor's policies, he retained McNamara, Rusk, and Bundy. A more orderly administrator than Kennedy, he generally preferred to deal directly with his cabinet officers. Fearful to the point of paranoia of leaks and disagreements within his official family, a man who made a fetish of loyalty and consensus, he preferred small intimate meetings of top officials—the "principals"—to Kennedy's larger, more freewheeling affairs.

Still, the NSC staff of some forty-eight people remained in operation and performed essentially the same functions. Three experts tracked regional issues and crises, while others maintained liaison with the Joint Chiefs of Staff and the CIA. The NSC staffed interdepartmental committees and task forces. It kept the White House informed of what was going on in the departments and agencies and the latter apprised of the president's needs and thinking. It remained a "message center" for the White House, "a service," Bundy advised Johnson, "which we could turn back to the State and Defense Departments and to the CIA, but only at the price of losing our own grip on the flow of information."[13]

Between his accession to the presidency and the decision for war in Vietnam, Johnson's personal ties with McNamara and Rusk deepened. Both shared their president's concept of unswerving loyalty. Like him, each was a workaholic, regularly putting in twelve-hour days and seven-day weeks. "He is the first one at work and the last one to leave," Johnson boasted of McNamara. "He is there every morning at 7:00 A.M. including Saturday. The only difference is that on Saturday he wears a sportcoat." Rusk worked the same schedule, and by his own count took off but twelve days in eight years in office.[14]

McNamara carried an especially heavy load during the transition and assumed the role of a virtual desk officer on Vietnam. Johnson leaned heavily on him and, at least in the early years, stood in awe of his genius as an organizer and his drive and persistence. "He's like a jackhammer," the president proudly exclaimed. "He drills through granite rock until he's there."[15]

Johnson and Rusk became especially close and remained so to the bitter end. Both were southern boys of modest origins who had made good, and both had been outsiders in Kennedy's Camelot. During the painful days of LBJ's vice-presidency, Rusk had treated him with courtesy and respect, taking special pains to insure that he was regularly briefed on major foreign policy issues. The secretary of state described himself as "one hell of a staff officer"; others labeled him an "ideal lightning rod," the "perfect number two." "He's a damned good man," Vice-President Johnson admiringly told his brother. "Hard-working, bright, and loyal as a beagle."[16]

As president, LBJ instinctively turned to his secretary of state, and although the two treated each other with the reserve that was Rusk's style, their relationship was intimate and based on genuine mutual affection. The president especially appreciated Rusk's caution and his ability to see several sides of an issue, once describing him as the "just a minute man around here." "He has the compassion of a preacher and the courage of a Georgia cracker," Johnson told Max Frankel of the *New York Times* in July 1965. "When you're going in with the Marines, he's the kind you want at your side. . . . He's the kind you'd entrust your daughter to." [17] In fact, the longer they occupied the same foxhole on Vietnam, the closer they became, and they were much closer when they left office in 1969 than when Johnson assumed the presidency in 1963.

Among LBJ's top advisers, Bundy, by any standard, appeared the odd man out. Scion of the eastern establishment, Ivy League, the very embodiment of the elite Johnson feared and despised, Bundy's relationship with the president was necessarily more awkward and mutually uncomfortable than those with Rusk and McNamara.

At the same time, Bundy had carved out a position in the Kennedy White House that made him even more valuable to Johnson. As manager of the flow of information, expediter, and watchdog of the labyrinthine federal bureaucracy, he was closer to the president than any cabinet officer. He was usually the first to see Johnson on an issue and the last to see him before a decision was made. During the months when the commitment in Vietnam was steadily escalating, Bundy and McNamara were the key figures. The national security adviser was in Vietnam when the National Liberation Front (NLF) struck Pleiku on February 7, 1965, and he came back a firm advocate of escalation. In addition, during the summer of 1965, he became the chief public spokesperson for and defender of the increasingly controversial Vietnam policy. In time, his presumed indispensability became a liability in Johnson's eyes and led to his departure from the government. Through the end of 1965, however, he was at the center of Vietnam policy making and national security management. [18]

Known around Washington as the "awesome foursome," Johnson, Bundy, McNamara, and Rusk worked effectively as a team and dominated policy making on national security matters through the fall of 1965. [19] Adapting to Johnson's administrative preferences and to a device he had employed in the Senate, they began to meet informally for lunch at the White House in 1964, usually on Tuesday, where they discussed with the utmost candor the pressing issues of the day. Originally instituted to give Johnson better access to his top advisers, the "Tuesday Lunch" later evolved into the primary instrument for management of the Vietnam War. Johnson was certain that the privacy of the luncheon, his intimate personal relationship with his top advisers, and the breadth of vision of Rusk and McNamara gave him access to the best advice. The secretary of defense, the president told a journalist, was keenly sensitive to the diplomatic dimensions of a military problem, and Rusk had been "only 20 minutes from being a professional military man, so they understood each other's job."[20] "When the 'awesome foursome' got together," Thomas Schoenbaum has written, "everything seemed so clear, so easy to understand. They were confident. It was impossible that all four of them could be wrong."[21]

In fact, there were problems from the start. Rusk did offer advice to McNamara on military issues, much of it derived from his World War II experience and much of it cautionary. He was deeply skeptical, for example, that air power could be decisive in Vietnam, and he worried that the army had no real strategy for dealing with the insurgency. When it came time for decision, however, Rusk normally deferred to McNamara and the Joint Chiefs. He did not think it his role to challenge the military in their own bailiwick, and he wanted no hint of disagreement within the administration. "In for a penny, in for a pound," an aide heard him tell McNamara in support of a Vietnam decision. In addition, the very format of the Tuesday Lunch was not one that encouraged intellectual exchange. At least through 1965, however, the machinery seemed to be working smoothly, and the "principals" saw no reason to fear that the closed system they had created would insulate them from real debate about the wisdom of their course.[22]

III

The Johnson administration did not modify its national security machinery after going to war in July 1965. In part, undoubtedly, this was because it felt no need to do so. The United States entered the war confident, if not absolutely certain, of success, and the war appeared manageable without making any changes. The policy of gradual escalation had the same effect. Expanding the war by stages eliminated any sense at any particular point that major changes were required. Not until very late did the problems appear sufficiently difficult to require exceptional measures. Limited war theory also mandated that wars be waged on a business-as-usual basis without disruption of ordinary processes. And in the existing system, control remained firmly in civilian hands, where limited war theory dictated that it must be. Thus the Johnson administration ran a steadily burgeoning war with essentially peacetime instruments.

At the top, the "awesome foursome" continued throughout 1965 to run the

war through the system that had existed prior to July 28. McNamara remained the key figure during most of this period, continuing, much as before,
to serve as the "desk officer" for Vietnam. The Tuesday Lunch continued to
be the primary means for making major wartime decisions. It stayed small,
although Press Secretary Bill Moyers and Director of Central Intelligence
Adm. William Raborn were added. It also met more regularly in the first
months of the war than before, seven of nine weeks in August and September,
although issues other than Vietnam were generally considered. Over lunch in
the White House the president and his top advisers approved bombing targets,
discussed force increases, and considered major initiatives such as the December 1965 bombing pause.[23]

As the war progressed, there were important personnel changes. McGeorge
Bundy left in early 1966, in part apparently as the result of a conflict over his
role. Johnson was increasingly annoyed with Bundy's public reputation as the
indispensable man and the preeminent figure in foreign policy, even more
important than the president himself. Perhaps to prove that Bundy had not
been indispensable, Johnson appointed no one to replace him. The director
of the State Department's Policy Planning Staff, economist Walt Whitman
Rostow, was appointed a special assistant to the president, and the duties
Bundy had performed were divided among Rostow, Moyers, and several
White House staffers. Part of the new arrangement was an agreement that
copies of all foreign policy proposals for the president emanating from Rostow's office be sent to Rusk.[24]

Under the new arrangement, Rostow and Moyers shared primary responsibility for coordinating Vietnam policy. Moyers's function, apparently as
conceived by the president, was to keep an independent eye on foreign policy
issues and to provide ideas and information that might not make it to the top
through the regular channels of the bureaucracy. To accomplish this, he developed an elaborate network of contacts with the federal departments and
agencies and the National Security Council staff providing him information
he was able to pass on to the president informally or at the Tuesday Lunch.
He became a sort of conduit through which second-level policymakers in the
government could get ideas to the top, and on Vietnam in 1966 he became a
vehicle through which dissent was increasingly expressed.[25]

Rostow's role involved a variety of tasks, and it steadily grew during his
years in the White House, especially after Moyers departed in December
1966. He assisted in the preparation of some presidential speeches, helped
arrange White House visits by foreign dignitaries, conducted regular briefings
of journalists, and drafted letters to congressmen. His most important function was to facilitate decision making by ensuring that the president had be-

fore him the widest possible range of options, generating the material needed for him to analyze those options, and making available the latest intelligence on the issue. He often represented the White House on interdepartmental coordinating committees dealing with Vietnam and other matters. He set the agenda for Tuesday Lunches, giving him direct liaison with the secretaries of state and defense. Through a staff member, Air Force Col. Robert Ginsburgh, he also maintained informal contact with the Joint Chiefs of Staff. Like Bundy, Rostow was responsible for seeing that once presidential decisions were made, the departments and agencies were informed of the decisions and followed through on tasks assigned them. He once described his office as a "channel of two-way communication between the President and the national security agencies." [26] As the years went on, he and Johnson became as close as the president and Rusk, LBJ praising his special assistant as a "hell of a good man" and "a man of conviction who doesn't try to play President" and Rostow describing Johnson as the most considerate person he ever worked for. [27]

In addition to major personnel changes, there were changes as the war progressed in the relative influence of the people who remained. McNamara's influence began to wane after the December 1965 bombing pause. The secretary of defense had pushed the pause and accompanying peace initiative and LBJ, grudgingly and against his better judgment, had endorsed it. When it failed, as Johnson predicted it would, McNamara's infallibility was challenged and the president held him responsible for a major policy failure. After December 1965, moreover, the once indomitable secretary of defense was increasingly skeptical that the war could be won militarily, and as his skepticism grew and more and more manifested itself in his policy recommendations, his influence declined still further. At some point late in his tenure, he was cut off from some information because of his growing opposition to the war and his suspected ties to dovish Senator Robert Kennedy (D-NY). [28]

As McNamara's position declined, that of the military and especially Joint Chiefs of Staff chairman Gen. Earle Wheeler increased. Wheeler never became a Johnson confidant, to be sure. The president retained to the end a southern populist's suspicion of the military, and especially on the bombing of North Vietnam he feared that acceptance of the Joint Chiefs' proposals might lead to World War III. Still, as a limited war grew into a full-scale war, however limited, the military inevitably moved closer to the center of the decision-making process. Ever the politician and ever fearful of the right wing in American politics, Johnson also had to take into account the military position and had to appear to consult closely with his military advisers.

Rusk's position is the most difficult to evaluate. Traditionally, it has been argued, because of his weakness on Vietnam, the State Department was "the dinghy dragged behind the Pentagon's yawl," and scholars have subsequently argued that Rusk's failure to balance military input with political and diplomatic advice undercut a competitive bureaucratic process and led to the militarization of the Vietnam issue.[29] In fact his role was more complex. As Rostow pointed out, McNamara and Rusk fully agreed that "military power was and should be the instrument of political policy," and the differences between them could easily be exaggerated.[30] One of the president's most trusted advisers from the outset, he found himself from 1966 on taking a middle position between McNamara on the one hand and Rostow and the military on the other. He continued to advocate caution in terms of escalating the war, especially the air war. But he did not share McNamara's impatience and pessimism. On the contrary, he felt that the United States had established a militarily impregnable position and negotiations would come about if it remained patient. Rusk's views probably accorded most closely with those of the president. As the most visible and dogged public defender of the war, he also became most closely identified with it. The war became by 1967 his "personal agony," and increasingly he became a scapegoat for what was called "Dean Rusk's War."[31]

Although the president refused to establish any special instruments to manage the war, he did create mechanisms to better coordinate the varied activities of the government in prosecuting it. A Vietnam Public Affairs Policy Committee, chaired by Bundy, met throughout the fall of 1965 to coordinate public information and public relations activities. For a time in early 1966, a top-level committee called the President's Vietnam Group met regularly on Saturday mornings, sometimes with Johnson in attendance. These meetings were designed to provide briefings for top officials and permit review of major issues. They also provided a place, White House official Robert Komer noted, where the president "could keep the needle in on various matters under way."[32] The group discussed issues ranging from inflation in Vietnam to the possible appointment of a "czar" to run the civil side of the war in Washington.[33] Later in 1966, Komer met regularly with Undersecretary of State Nicholas deB. Katzenbach, Deputy Secretary of Defense Cyrus Vance, and Rostow to discuss Vietnam issues.[34]

Under the direction of former army general and ambassador to South Vietnam Maxwell Taylor, a more serious effort was made in 1966 to better coordinate the implementation of foreign policy generally. From his experience in Saigon, Taylor concluded that America's overseas programs had become so large and complex that better management tools were needed in Washington. As a result, he secured from Johnson a mandate to reorganize the government to provide for better interdepartmental coordination.

Taylor and his deputy U. Alexis Johnson subsequently worked out what became National Security Action Memorandum (NSAM) 341. Based on the Mission Council or Country Team concept that operated in embassies abroad, NSAM 341 gave the State Department the role of executive agent in implementing overseas programs. To assist the secretary in the performance of this function, a Senior Interdepartmental Group (SIG) was established including the deputy secretary of defense, the Agency for International Development administrator, the directors of the Central Intelligence Agency and the U.S. Information Agency, the chairman of the Joint Chiefs of Staff, and the national security adviser. The undersecretary of state served as executive officer of the group and had the power to decide an issue subject to the right of any member to appeal to the secretary of state or the president. NSAM 341 also created Interdepartmental Regional Groups (IRGs) at the assistant secretary level to monitor U.S. policies and projects in various regions and countries and to anticipate crises.[35]

Like most grand administrative designs, Taylor's scheme never quite worked out as intended. Undersecretary of State George Ball, the first executive secretary of the SIG, did not use it extensively, and McNamara did not hesitate to go directly to the president when decisions were made that he did not like. Johnson nominally approved the system, but people were more important to him than committees, and he preferred to operate as he had before. Some of the IRGs worked well, especially in areas outside the mainstream such as Africa and Latin America, but on matters where top officials were deeply interested and involved—such as Vietnam—the assistant secretaries could not function effectively. When he replaced Ball as undersecretary, Katzenbach revived the SIG and found it an effective means of getting the regional groups to work and minimizing disputes at the senior level. Still, the groups established by NSAM 341 never achieved the centrality that Taylor had anticipated, and on Vietnam the new machinery played an insignificant role.[36]

Johnson used National Security Council meetings only sparingly and under tightly controlled circumstances. The membership of the NSC remained much the same in his administration as in Kennedy's.[37] At first, even fewer meetings were held, and those meetings, to the consternation of some members, were used largely to rubber stamp decisions already made by Johnson, McNamara, Rusk, and Bundy. Later, the president agreed to hold more NSC meetings and to regularize them, in part to counter former President Eisenhower's charges that the NSC machinery was not being properly used, in part to head off growing media criticism of a closed decision-making process. Still, the NSC did not become central to Johnson administration policy making.

The president did not like large meetings with freewheeling discussion, and the agenda was thus tightly controlled and the meetings short. Normally, NSC meetings were used to brief members on decisions the president had already made or was on the verge of making. Sometimes they were used to extract information that might be useful for designing long-range policies on secondary issues. Almost never were top-level, urgent matters discussed.[38]

Although it became in time a subject of much controversy inside and outside the government, the Tuesday Lunch remained to the end of the Johnson administration the primary instrument for making policy on Vietnam and other major issues. As David Humphrey has pointed out, from 1964 to 1966 the Tuesday Lunch followed an erratic pattern—there were only six meetings in the first twenty weeks of 1966, for example. Once Rostow got established in his new post, however, the luncheon gradually took on greater regularity, and starting in January 1967 it met four out of every five weeks until the end of the Johnson administration and became the central policy-making device. Rostow, Rusk, McNamara, and Moyers (later George Christian) were the regular attendees, although the vice-president sometimes attended, as did Gen. William C. Westmoreland. The membership was broadened in late 1967 when CIA director Richard Helms and Joint Chiefs chairman Wheeler were added on a regular basis. The lunches sometimes went on for two to three hours. They generally grappled with front-burner issues that required presidential attention and action.[39]

Opinions on their value differed sharply at the time. Rostow thought the Tuesday Lunch a "powerful instrument," an "admirable device" which brought together the president and the principals on a regular basis after staff work and with a formal agenda. The style was relaxed and informal, except, of course, in times of crisis, and the setting was congenial. It was possible, Rostow later recalled, to "get through a lot of business in an orderly way with men who knew each other well."[40] The lunch provided a regular forum where cabinet heads could bring up major issues and be assured of access to the president. Because the meetings were small, it was possible to have informal, candid discussion and disagreements. Even the taciturn Rusk, it was said, spoke out. The lunch also made certain that the president went over Vietnam each week with the people in charge of implementing his major policies and programs. It ensured that on major problems there was "informal, intimate, off-the-record, non-reportable conversation and give-and-take exchange." Johnson especially liked the fact that there were no leaks. NSC meetings were like "sieves," he later complained, but the Tuesday Lunch group "never leaked a single note. Those men were loyal to me."[41]

The very secrecy that so appealed to Johnson greatly annoyed and sometimes frustrated lower-level officials. Assistant Secretary of State William Bundy labeled the Tuesday Lunch an "abomination," and NSC staffer Chester Cooper said it had "much the character of a cabal." Because the results of the luncheons were conveyed orally and informally instead of through formal notes and memos, the word got down to the next level imperfectly if it got there at all, and in the minds of some second-level officials this caused serious problems. Even those who favored the Tuesday meetings agreed that "readout" might have been handled better if more formal and in writing.[42]

By mid-1967, criticism of the Tuesday Lunches had spilled over to the public forum. In a full study of decision making in the Johnson administration, the *Washington Post* observed that "Rusk and McNamara are tired men; there is too much secrecy; there is an inadequate upflow of ideas and an inadequate downflow of results; it is more crisis management than forward-looking decisionmaking."[43]

In part perhaps because of the problems the Tuesday Lunch caused at the second tier of the bureaucracy, yet another committee was created. This so-called Non-Group or No Committee was established in May 1967 at Johnson's instance and was comprised of officials at the assistant secretary level. Katzenbach set it up and chaired it, and assistant defense secretaries Paul Warnke and Paul Nitze and Assistant Secretary of State William Bundy, along with Rostow and Wheeler, met weekly for an hour or so to discuss informally over drinks the past week's developments in Vietnam. The ground rules provided that members could only send superiors as alternates. The committee did not as a rule discuss "action items" or make decisions. It could not even take a position. Ideas that emerged from it had to be initiated by a member of the committee through regular departmental channels. It was even less formal than the Tuesday Lunch. There was no agenda, and no notes were taken or records kept. It was designed as a place where officials at the working level could compare notes and discuss mutual problems openly and candidly. Those who participated cannot recall any specific things done. Indeed, that was not its purpose. Its main function was to look at the big picture and improve communications among the various departments involved in Vietnam.[44]

On major issues, Vietnam included, Johnson often sought advice outside regular bureaucratic channels. He especially relied on a sort of "kitchen cabinet" comprised of old friends and Washington lawyers Clark Clifford and Abe Fortas, who had counseled him long before he became president and continued to do so after he entered the White House. Often he would invite the two for dinner and ask their views on a particular issue. If they agreed, he was comforted. If they disagreed, he enjoyed and learned from watching these giants of the legal profession spar back and forth. He especially valued their advice, Clifford later noted, because he felt it was "unencumbered by the pressures that bureaucracies exert on cabinet members." He felt secure with them because he was certain they would not leak their intimate conversations to the media.[45]

IV

Ultimately, regardless of organizational scheme or formal machinery, the personality, leadership style, and administrative methods of the chief executive determine the way things are done, and Johnson's own highly personalized style indelibly marked the conduct of the war in Vietnam.

Most of his associates would agree with Clark Clifford that LBJ "was the most complex man I ever met." He was prodigiously energetic, obsessively ambitious, proud, outwardly vain. He was a driven man, single-minded, manipulative, overbearing, and capable of great meanness to those closest to him. Despite his huge achievements, he remained profoundly insecure, and he was sensitive to the smallest slight, real or imagined. At the same time, he could be compassionate and warm toward other people, and he was capable of great generosity and magnanimity. He was fiercely loyal to those who stood by him. He was committed with every fiber of his being to large causes. He had as "many sides to him as a kaleidoscope," Dean Acheson once observed, and presented an "unbelievable combination of sensitivity and coarseness, of understanding and obtuseness." "He could be altruistic and petty, caring and crude, generous and petulant, bluntly honest and calculatingly devious—all within the same few minutes," Joseph Califano later recalled.[46]

The role of commander in chief in limited war is an especially difficult one. In total war, the president can wrap himself in the flag, employ the trappings of his office to boost his own image and leadership position, even subdue the criticism that in peacetime normally goes with the office. A fundamental principle of limited war, on the other hand, is that it should be waged without too much intrusion into the life of the nation. The commander in chief must set the tone. He cannot appear preoccupied with the war to the exclusion of other things. But with men and women dying in the field, he cannot appear indifferent either. He must walk a very high and very thin tightrope.

LBJ was in many ways miscast in the role of commander in chief in the war he chose so reluctantly to fight. He did share to some degree the yearning for military glory common to his generation. He took great pride in the Silver Star he won in World War II. Later, in the White House, draping the Medal of Honor around the neck of a chaplain who had distinguished himself in battle, he was overheard to exclaim: "Son, I'd rather have one of these babies than be President."[47] On the other hand, he had little of the boyish fascination with war of his mentor and idol, Franklin Roosevelt. He had no lust for combat, and his one day under fire in World War II was deliberately contrived as a military means to a political end.[48] He was innately suspicious of military men. More important, most of his political career had been devoted to the cause of domestic reform. Inexperienced in foreign policy, he would have preferred not to have been distracted by it. He especially resented the Vietnam War as an intrusion and an obstacle to his ambition to go down in history as the greatest American reform president.[49]

In terms of personality, he was particularly ill-suited to be commander in chief in a limited war and especially the confusing and intractable war in Vietnam. He was a flamboyant and impulsive man in a situation that demanded restraint. He was an emotional man given to wild mood swings in a situation that required calmness and steadiness, perhaps even a degree of detachment. He was a man with a passion for success and a yearning for greatness, whose whole life had been a single-minded quest for measurable achievement in the form of bills passed, wells dug, and schools built, fighting a war in which it was difficult to establish criteria for progress much less apply them. He was a restless and impatient man waging war against an enemy who thought in terms of years, not days, centuries, not decades. He was a man for whom defeat was intolerable, even unthinkable, fighting a war that may not have been winnable.

From the outset, Johnson dutifully grappled with the challenge. His credo from his youth had been that "if you do *everything*, you'll win," and in every crisis he had faced he had pushed himself beyond his limits.[50] He thus brought to his war the same enormous energy and compulsive attention to detail that had characterized his approach to politics, the presidency, and life in general. From the outset, he demanded the final word on the tonnage, timing, and targets of air strikes against North Vietnam. He insisted on being informed of every troop movement. "He sleeps fitfully at night when he knows that U.S. pilots are on their way against the enemy," a journalist observed.[51] Often in the early morning hours, wearing a dressing gown and carrying a flashlight, he would descend into the Situation Room to examine casualty reports from Saigon. He would doze by his bedside telephone waiting to hear the outcome of attempts to rescue pilots shot down over North Vietnam.[52] "We could never break him of the habit," Rusk later recalled, and each casualty "took a little piece out of him."[53] He stopped drinking in 1966 the Scotch he so loved for fear that he might not be at full capacity at some point when he had to make a decision affecting American troops.

Whatever public image he sought to convey, during most working days he could not escape the burdens of war leadership. His mornings usually began with edited summaries from a National Security Council staffer of cables reporting the latest developments in Vietnam.[54] It was not unusual, however, for him to call the Situation Room at midnight, 4:30 A.M., and 6:30 A.M. and ask in a concerned voice, "What's going on?"[55] During rare minutes of free time in his daily schedule, he might scan summaries of damage done by the bombing of North Vietnam, examine a report from Westmoreland, or fret over rising domestic opposition to the war.[56]

The same standards applied at the end of his tenure in office. In the early days of the 1968 Tet offensive, *Time* wrote, he was on constant alert, "pouncing on more than 25 reports rushed to him through the evening and night."[57] He was up at 5:00 A.M. for a Situation Room briefing and talked to McNamara twice before a breakfast meeting with congressional leaders. "He's working like a dog," Press Secretary George Christian observed, "keeping tabs on everything." "Not a sparrow falls," a former aide noted, "that he doesn't know about it."[58] In October 1968, he called Gen. Creighton Abrams home from Vietnam to consult on a total bombing halt and convened a meeting of his top advisers upon Abrams's arrival—at 2:30 A.M.—"bizarre behavior," his wife admitted, "even for him."[59]

His passion for information was legendary. In the morning, he would devour several major newspapers and the *Congressional Record* while watching three television networks simultaneously. He bombarded his advisers with requests for information about such things as relations between North Vietnam and the People's Republic of China, conditions in the port of Saigon, politics in South Vietnam, and aircraft losses.[60] NSC staffers were "amazed" to see him tear pieces out of his "Earlybird" morning briefing and send them back to the Situation Room with the instruction to fill in a reporter about them. During his Asian trip in late 1966 he called back to the White House from each time zone at all hours to check on the situation. During the siege of Khe Sanh, he called directly to the fortress to talk to the commander on the scene.[61]

He faithfully and at times even eloquently executed his public, ceremonial role as commander in chief. He regularly visited wounded war veterans, his voice sometimes sinking "to a barely audible whisper as he murmured over and over: 'Your country is grateful to you.'"[62] He presented Medals of Honor to war heroes, on one occasion quoting an eve of battle prayer attributed to George Washington: "Good God, what brave men must I lose today?"[63]

And of course in late October 1966 he made the famous visit to Camranh Bay, a trip that became the subject of ridicule at home after his notorious injunction to the troops to "nail that coonskin to the wall," but that had a significant impact on Johnson himself. It was the first visit by a president to a war zone since Franklin Roosevelt's journey to Casablanca in 1943. Clark Clifford called it one of the "emotional high points" of Johnson's presidency, further surmising that because he had seen the war firsthand with "his" troops, the commander in chief's personal and emotional commitment to it increased "exponentially." "I have never been more moved by any group I have ever talked to," Johnson observed upon his return, "never in my life." [64]

Despite conscious efforts to do so, he was not able to balance the war with other concerns, and his absorption in it became near total. He insisted through much of his presidency that Vietnam was not diverting him from other foreign and domestic issues. It was his critics, he often complained, not he, who were preoccupied with the war. He had accomplished great things at home, but the press could only whine "Veetnam, Veetnam, Veetnam, Veetnam." To emphasize the point, he would savagely mimick a baby crying. [65] Yet those close to him knew better. As early as August 1965, *Time* noted, Vietnam was "devouring" the great majority of his hours and disrupting his regular routine. [66] With Johnson, Adm. Thomas Moorer later recalled, "you always discussed Vietnam, no matter where you were." [67]

From early on, it is equally clear, Vietnam was a source of great frustration for the commander in chief. "He stalks the White House corridor," a journalist observed, "longingly paraphrasing to aides the World War II order that Franklin Roosevelt gave to General Eisenhower: 'Seek out the German army and destroy it,'" wistfully implying that if only Vietnam were that simple. [68] When Senate dove George McGovern presented him a memorandum explaining why the United States had erred in intervening in Vietnam, he exploded, "Don't give me another goddamn history lesson. . . . I don't need a lecture on where we went wrong. I've got to deal with where we are now." [69] As the war dragged on, opposition mounted, and that elusive light failed to appear at the end of the tunnel, his frustration grew. "I can't get out," he complained. "I can't finish it with what I've got. So what the hell do I do." [70]

For the emotional Johnson the war became a source of great personal grief. "There is no American killed or wounded in battle for whom I do not feel a sense of personal responsibility," he wrote the parents of a GI killed in battle. [71] "No man felt more deeply and more heavily the burdens and responsibilities of the decisions he was called on to make," a sympathetic Secretary of the Treasury Henry Fowler later remarked. "And if the American public could have seen the Lyndon Johnson that I saw in those private sessions with this deep and overpowering concern for the lives of . . . the men, women, and children in the war zone . . . people would be ashamed of the things they've said." [72]

Johnson in fact believed that his position required him to keep to himself the grief that he felt lest it show weakness to his own people and his foes in Hanoi. But it is poignantly captured in a photo, "an image of pure tragedy," not released until twenty years later, of a president, bent over in distress, head in his hands, after listening to a tape sent to his daughter from Vietnam by her husband, Charles Robb.[73] Fowler compared Johnson to Lincoln, a comparison the president himself found solace in, adding that "if the mothers of the men who went to Viet Nam could have seen him on occasion as I saw him reading their letters with the deepest emotion they would have felt as sorry for him as I did, for the grief he had to suppress publicly, but gave way to privately, of carrying on this dreadful conflict."[74]

Grief could give way to melancholy and self-pity, feelings the president sometimes sought to inflict on others. Throughout his life, when faced with pain or defeat, he had attempted to evoke sympathy from others and get them to share his suffering or sense of failure. He told a group of labor leaders in August 1967 that the first thing he reviewed each morning was a list of the men who had died in Vietnam the day before, and he added: "Remember that every time you criticize me it is just another rock of cement that I must carry."[75] The president's old mentor and confidant, Senator Richard Russell, stopped going to the White House alone because, he explained, when he did Johnson would start crying uncontrollably and he could not stand to be subjected to that kind of emotionalism.[76] Another close friend, journalist William S. White, confirmed that more than once he saw Johnson "weep surreptitiously" when reports of the day's casualties were placed before him.[77]

Although he took on the job of commander in chief with the greatest reluctance, Johnson gave it his full attention, applying himself with characteristic single-mindedness. For the most part, he carried out the ceremonial aspects of the position with restraint and quiet dignity. He worked hard at managing the war, seeking to oversee each detail, agonizing over it, eventually suffering from it. His failure was not from want of trying. He can be more readily faulted for getting too involved in the day-to-day detail of the war, for letting the trees obscure his view of the forest.

V

Within months after Johnson's July 28 press conference, the United States' commitment in Vietnam began to outgrow the presumed dimensions of limited war. As each escalation failed to produce the desired results, the administration moved to the next level. The result was what William Bundy later called, with no apparent sense of paradox, an "all-out limited war," a huge, sprawling, many-faceted, military-civilian effort, generally uncoordinated, in which, all too frequently, the various components worked against rather than in support of each other.[78]

A small-scale counterinsurgency effort quickly mushroomed into a vast military engagement contained within a relatively small area. The U.S. Navy and Air Force waged a full-scale air war against North Vietnam, flying 108,000 sorties in 1967 and dropping 226,000 tons of bombs. By this same time, the United States had in South Vietnam close to half a million ground troops and a gigantic supporting apparatus executing a variety of different types of operations in a frustrating and ultimately futile effort to root out and destroy North Vietnamese and NLF main forces.

The civilian side of the war expanded to even more elephantine proportions. For fiscal year 1967, U.S. assistance to South Vietnam equaled $625 million, 25 percent of the American foreign aid program for the entire world. In Washington, 300 people worked on the Vietnam program; in South Vietnam more than 6,500.

Those Washington officials who visited Vietnam for the first time were stunned by the sheer enormity of the U.S. effort. White House aide John Roche, sent there as a "presidential spy" in 1966, delivered to LBJ a "caustic commentary" on the size of the American presence, describing it as "just unbelievable," "the Holy Roman Empire going to war." Cutting its size by two-thirds, Roche sarcastically added, might increase its efficiency by 50 percent. Speaking of the "colossal size of our effort," speechwriter Harry McPherson added in 1967 that the big issue on U.S. campuses, whether or not the United States should be in Vietnam, was "almost beside the point. We *are* there in such enormous force, in such totality, that the fact of our presence is where you start from."[79]

Despite the size and complexity of U.S. efforts, the Johnson administration continued to run the war on a peacetime basis. There was no Vietnam "high command," no central mechanism to coordinate the various facets of a huge war carried out by bloated bureaucracies in Washington and Saigon. Below the presidential level, as Komer has noted, everybody and nobody was responsible. "I don't think we had an effective war governing mechanism in Washington at any time," William Bundy later recalled.[80]

Within the various departments and agencies, the same thing applied. There was no single focal point for Vietnam operations in the Pentagon. Until very late in the war, the enormous foreign assistance program for Vietnam was the responsibility of a relatively low-level official in the Agency for International Development. In the State Department, day-to-day responsibility was in the hands of a deputy assistant secretary responsible to an assistant secretary who, by one estimate, was able to spend no more than 50 percent of his time on Vietnam. In the White House, Vietnam was only one of several matters dealt with by a single member of Bundy's and later Rostow's staff.[81]

From time to time, top officials urged Johnson to address what they considered an obvious and pressing problem. Bill Moyers advised the president in 1966 that the administration was fighting the war on a "part-time basis." No one spent full time on Vietnam, he observed, and as a consequence the government was simply not getting the sort of results required for eventual success. "We're just not orchestrating the handling of the most critical problem we face," Moyers concluded. Late in 1966, Komer proposed the creation of a "war cabinet" to monitor a coordinated strategic plan, and Rostow urged that Katzenbach's No Committee be given responsibility to put "centralized drive and direction" into all elements of the Vietnam program.[82]

Despite such concerns, nothing was done. In part, perhaps, the administration's resistance to change reflected limited war theory. Such wars were supposed to be fought under peacetime conditions and without special bureaucratic arrangements. Partly also, as Komer has noted, it reflected the gradualist approach that derived from limited war theory. Not until fairly late did the problems of managing the war appear sufficiently difficult to require exceptional measures. By that time, as Komer further observed, it was hard to effect changes. Once large organizations became committed to a particular course of action, "the ponderous wheels set in motion, vast sums allocated, and personnel selected and trained," programs acquired a momentum of their own. When obstacles were encountered, the natural bureaucratic tendency was to try more of the same rather than rethink or adapt.[83] Even small efforts at coordination met stubborn resistance. In late 1966, Komer's quite modest attempt to better integrate the various elements of U.S. strategy through a National Security Action Memorandum (NSAM) died at the hands of agency opposition.[84]

No doubt also, the reluctance to effect needed bureaucratic change reflected Johnson's management style, an approach, Chester Cooper noted, that mixed "tight personal control and loosely structured organization."[85] Unwilling to share the overall direction of the war with any person or agency, determined, as always, to keep control tightly in his own hands, the president resisted all proposals to appoint a Vietnam high command or even establish a coordinating agency modeled on the Office of War Mobilization of World War II. "The President took it *all* in his own hands," according to William Bundy. "All the threads ran only to him and not sideways to others."[86]

At the same time, according to Cooper, he permitted, even encouraged, a "fluid, in-and-out, bird-of-passage style of operation among a wide sector of policy makers and policy kibitzers." It was difficult even for those close to him to know the key players at any point in the game.[87] His style "carried lack of system and structure way too far," William Bundy later noted. It was hard to see what was being done, hard to "take a real bite at a problem."[88] In addition, his obsessive secrecy and his inability to trust people made it difficult for him to share responsibility and communicate decisions to lower levels.

To be sure, limited war posed enormously complex problems of manage-ment blithely ignored by its theorists. The use of military power to convey clear, understandable signals; the coordination of force and diplomacy; the management of domestic opinion in a war fought in cold blood all required delicate handling and the most precise coordination of many diverse and often conflicting elements in a huge, unwieldy bureaucracy. Yet without mobiliza-tion, there was no instrument at hand to do this. And limited war was even less predictable than total war, as Fowler later observed, because everything depended on the response of the enemy.[89]

These problems conceded, it must still be concluded that the Johnson ad-ministration did not establish effective mechanisms to manage its "different kind of war." Among the departments and agencies parochialism was the or-der of the day, each doing its own thing without sufficient regard for the other and each proliferated to the point where they competed for increasingly scarce resources and got in each other's way. There was a notable lack of creativity and even less adaptability. The result was a vast war effort, notably unorga-nized, in which the various components were often at odds with one another.

VI

For Lyndon Johnson, it proved much easier to take the nation into a limited war than to wage that war. In what can only be described as a textbook opera-tion, he employed all his legendary political skills to forge a solid consensus behind his policies and take the nation to war "in cold blood" in July 1965. The North Vietnamese did not respond as limited war theory said they should, however, refusing to bend to American pressure and matching U.S. escalation by escalating themselves.

Johnson's limited war therefore quickly outgrew its anticipated propor-tions, presenting enormous management problems for the man who had launched it. It was extremely difficult to formulate and implement an effective military strategy within the existing command system, and Johnson was un-willing to change that system. It proved even more difficult to find means to "pacify" the Vietnamese countryside and to coordinate pacification with mili-tary operations. For Johnson and his advisers, waging peace turned out to be every bit as complicated as making war, and the administration learned only through hard experience the importance of responding to peace feelers and coordinating peace moves with military initiatives. In view of America's frustration on the battlefield, it became increasingly difficult to sustain the public support Johnson had so carefully nurtured in 1965 without violating the basic precepts of limited war, and to violate those precepts posed unacceptable risks. The "different kind of war" Johnson had spoken of in his July 28, 1965, press conference, with "no marching armies or solemn declarations," thus posed challenges of which he could not have been aware and with which he could not cope, ultimately crippling his presidency and driving him from the White House.

No More MacArthurs

TWO   *Johnson, McNamara, the Military,
                                     and the Command System in
                                     Vietnam*

At a meeting in Honolulu in February 1966, Gen. William C. Westmoreland found his commander in chief "intense, perturbed, uncertain how to proceed with the Vietnam problem, torn by the apparent magnitude of it." At one point, Lyndon Johnson confided to Westmoreland, "General, I have a lot riding on you." At another, he blurted out, "I hope you don't pull a MacArthur on me."[1]

Although deeply dissatisfied with the way the war was being fought, Westmoreland did not "pull a MacArthur" on Johnson, and yet, despite surface harmony in civil-military relations, the command system functioned as badly in Vietnam as in any American war. Johnson did not provide clear strategic direction to his military leaders. On the other hand, they did not (or could not) make clear to him the full depth of their own objections to the way the war was being fought. No one was really satisfied with the strategy, but there was little discussion of the major issues, no airing of the differences. The result by 1967 was a makeshift strategy that was doomed to failure and enormous frustration on all sides. The imposition of a false consensus on the command system may therefore have been far more damaging to the national interest than MacArthur's challenge to presidential authority in the Korean War.

I

Devising a workable system of military command within the American form of government has posed difficult problems from the beginning of the republic. The nation was born into a hostile world and its survival depended on adequate military power properly employed. It also originated in a revolt against European monarchy and the standing military establishments that were one of its major underpinnings. American republican institutions therefore sought to balance the need for civilian control against the need for military expertise. The constitution did that by affirming the president's preeminence as commander in chief of the armed forces. It did not precisely define the duties and powers of the office, however, and the exercise of this role has varied considerably among America's wartime chief executives. There has been a great deal of ambiguity in the lines of authority between the president and his civilian and military advisers. The constitution also left unclear the division of authority between the president and Congress, inviting executive-legislative conflict and giving disgruntled military officers an outlet for their grievances. In actual operation, the system has functioned differently from era to era and war to war, the result, according to T. Harry Williams, of "extemporized arrangements reflecting the national genius for improvisation."[2] It worked best under the sort of strong presidential direction provided by James K. Polk, Abraham Lincoln, and Franklin Roosevelt.

The pace of events and the magnitude of the threat in the nuclear age seemed to leave too little time for extemporizing, and after World War II the command system was institutionalized to a degree unknown before. But the result was a series of compromises that sacrificed rationality for political expediency. Rejecting unification of the armed forces, the Congress superimposed a Department of Defense over the respective military services, reducing the power of the civilian service secretaries in favor of a single secretary of defense. First created on an ad hoc basis to advise President Roosevelt in World War II, the Joint Chiefs of Staff were given formal status within the military bureaucracy, but their role was notably anomalous. Members had no position outside their own services. They had only a small staff over which they had no real professional control. They had no forces under their command and were in fact excluded from the chain of command, the line proceeding from the president through the secretary of defense to the field commander. They were nominally the primary military advisers to the president and the secretary of defense, but the civilian leaders were not legally obligated to consult with them or even keep them informed.[3]

The new system worked imperfectly at best. The military services openly warred with each other and the White House and lobbied with Congress for the procurement of expensive weapons systems. The first civilian secretaries of defense to try to control the sprawling postwar military bureaucracy met dire fates. A deeply depressed James Forrestal jumped to his death from a hospital window. His successor Louis Johnson was fired.

The command system functioned adequately in the first, desperate stages of the Korean War but broke down completely after the smashing U.S. victory at Inchon. A complete lack of communication between Washington and Gen. Douglas MacArthur was the source of most of the problems. Intimidated by the victorious MacArthur after Inchon, the Joint Chiefs of Staff gave him free rein in Korea while they focused on larger, global issues. The now overconfident MacArthur, in turn, bungled into disaster while the Pentagon was developing plans to dismantle and relocate his forces after the war had been won. The president and the JCS repeatedly deferred to MacArthur on tactical questions as he drove pell-mell toward the debacle at the Yalu. Finally, when MacArthur sought to rectify his own errors by expanding the war and played politics to get his way, the president had no choice but to relieve him. Although often seen as a victory for civilian control of the military, the Truman-MacArthur confrontation gave the military increased domestic political influence. In reality, as Ernest May has observed, "Congress and the public had followed one set of military leaders instead of another."[4]

During his eight years in the White House former general Dwight D. Eisenhower engaged in a running battle with his Joint Chiefs of Staff over the size and shape of the defense budget. Certain that the national security hinged on a sound fiscal system, Eisenhower repeatedly slashed military requests for more of everything. In response, the Joint Chiefs regularly took their case to the Democratic-controlled Congress. Accusing his military advisers of "legalized insubordination," Eisenhower ordered them to get on the team and keep their disagreements inside the executive branch. When the chiefs continued to defy him, he privately spoke of relieving them all. The battle reached a crisis point in 1960, when the president's near cancellation of the B-70 bomber provoked yet another military revolt. "I hate to use the word," he fumed, "but this business is damn near treason."[5]

The system broke down completely in the Kennedy years. As early as 1950, the *Washington Post* had warned of the emergence of a "garrison state," a situation in which "the military is under constant temptation to take advantage of its power."[6] Antimilitarism was on the rise in the United States by the early 1960s, clearly manifested in such popular films as *Seven Days in May* and *Dr. Strangelove*, which warned, respectively, of a military takeover and the possibility of nuclear war through military recklessness. This spirit carried over to the Kennedy White House. Youthful and insecure civilian leaders feared the power of the military, its ties with the right wing in American politics, and its clout in Congress. They deplored the lack of sophistication of military leaders, especially their inability to conceive of the use of force for anything but fighting a large-scale war and their perceived recklessness, which, if unchecked, might provoke nuclear war. Some military officers, on the other hand, were contemptuous of the inexperienced civilians in the White House, especially the liberals and Ivy League intellectuals, the "computer types," Gen. Thomas Powers complained, who "don't know their ass from a hole in the ground."[7] They deplored the civilians' perceived political naiveté and softness on communism and feared that their weakness would lead to war.

From the Bay of Pigs through the Nuclear Test Ban Treaty, civil-military conflict steadily grew. Blaming the Cuban debacle at least in part on the Joint Chiefs, the president and his civilian advisers instinctively distrusted military recommendations, excluded the military from decision making, and involved themselves in military affairs, even down to the level of operational details. On the other side, Kennedy's unwillingness to "go all the way" in Cuba infuriated many military leaders. The military also felt they got the blame for the Bay of Pigs while, in fact, according to Air Force Chief of Staff Gen. Curtis LeMay, "we didn't have a God damned thing to do with it."[8]

The gap widened in the Cuban missile crisis of 1962. As at the Bay of Pigs, the military felt the civilians had not acted decisively. On the other hand, military advocacy of air strikes and an invasion in this hour of supreme nuclear crisis frightened the civilian leadership. "The military are mad," Kennedy is said to have remarked, and Secretary of Defense Robert S. McNamara developed an abiding fear of blundering into a nuclear disaster. McNamara haunted the military command center throughout the crisis, even invading the navy's Flag Plot and issuing orders directly to ships at sea, but he was still unable to maintain complete operational control over the nation's military forces. The administration emerged from the Cuban affair convinced that crisis management was the key to maintaining world peace. It was more certain than ever that the military could not be trusted and that effective crisis management required their close supervision. Military officers' worst fears of civilian weakness were confirmed, and they resented their growing isolation. "Right from the start we got the back of the hand," LeMay later snarled.[9]

McNamara's efforts to bring order and businesslike efficiency to the Defense Department provoked further conflict. A confirmed rationalist, intolerant of history, experience, and tradition, the secretary of defense substituted scientific method for military professionalism. He revolutionized the Pentagon budget process, instituting a Planning, Programming, Budgeting System (PPBS) to bring the operations of the Pentagon into a coherent whole and centralize his own authority. His "Whiz Kids" applied business techniques of systems analysis and cost effectiveness to the complex problem of weapons procurement. To the dismay of his military colleagues, he even sought to standardize weapons systems.[10]

Military leaders deeply resented McNamara's intrusion into their domain. They spoke of a "McNamara Monarchy" at the Pentagon—a "civilian on horseback"—and warned of the dangers of substituting social science for military expertise. The national security was too important, they insisted, to be an area for "experimentation by sophisticates sublimely ignorant of both the knowledge and history of war." By forcing the services to speak with one voice, critics claimed, the secretary of defense had eliminated a natural system of checks and balances within the military. His muzzling of senior officers enforced a uniformity of view that posed a greater danger to the nation than the fictional threat of a military coup in *Seven Days in May*. It could well produce a generation of "yes men" and the eventual sapping of the American fighting spirit. Determined to resist the "McNamara Monarchy," General LeMay and Chief of Naval Operations Adm. George Anderson fought openly with the secretary of defense.[11]

By 1964, McNamara appeared to have wrought miracles at the Pentagon. Using the age-old technique of divide and conquer, he took advantage of differences among the Joint Chiefs of Staff to dominate them. He contained them politically by restricting their ability to testify before Congress and speak with the press. When they were able to secure congressional funding for items he opposed, he refused to spend the money. Eventually, he got rid of the recalcitrants. Admiral Anderson was kicked downstairs to the ambassadorship in Portugal and in 1965 LeMay retired.

Gradually, he replaced the chiefs he had inherited with a "new breed" of military leader. White House favorite Gen. Maxwell Taylor was installed as chairman of the Joint Chiefs, after serving for a time as Kennedy's personal military adviser. McNamara handpicked Gen. Earle Wheeler as army chief of staff, Gen. John P. McConnell as air force chief of staff, and Adm. David McDonald as chief of naval operations. These "new breed" military leaders lacked the prestige and combat record of a LeMay or Arleigh Burke. They were, *Time* said, "planners and thinkers, not heroes," "team men, not gladiators."[12] They were men allegedly as much at home behind a desk as in the field, men whose military expertise was complemented by knowledge of politics, economics, science, and diplomacy. They were not "yes men," as "Thirty-One Knot" Burke and *New York Times* military analyst Hanson Baldwin charged, but they were men who seemed to understand the full complexity of national security problems in the nuclear age. Above all, they were men who accepted and deferred to civilian authority. The appointment of McConnell, a soft-spoken Arkansan, as replacement for the gruff, cigar-chomping Lemay was seen as symptomatic of the changing of the military guard, a new trend, the *New York Times* observed, toward a "military man whose excellence is demonstrated in fields as much intellectual as purely military."[13] Thus by the time the Johnson administration confronted the emerging crisis in Vietnam, McNamara had revolutionized the defense establishment, formulated new techniques of crisis management, and appointed a new military leadership to implement them. After nearly twenty years of civil-military struggle, he seemed to have established firm civilian control over a workable command system.

II

From McNamara's perspective, Vietnam was to be a test case for the new style of crisis management and the new command system, but the result was much different from what he imagined. As a consequence of the escalation of the war in Vietnam in 1964 and 1965, the military began to regain some of the influence lost during the Kennedy years. By July 1965, moreover, civil-military tension had resumed and the foundation for a new period of conflict had been established. Most important, during this critical period, the new system did not facilitate or even encourage a full discussion of the issues and an airing of the emerging differences among the policymakers.

The Kennedy administration had all but excluded the military from its major decisions on Vietnam. Rejecting in his first months their recommendations for intervention in Laos, the president had increasingly pushed the military aside, relying on his personal adviser, General Taylor, McNamara, and a small group of civilians. "We in the military felt we were not in the decision-making process at all," LeMay later complained.[14] Kennedy's distrust of the military apparently deepened as a result of the overoptimistic reporting from Saigon of Gen. Paul D. Harkins in 1962 and 1963. The president informed an aide he could not believe a word the military command in South Vietnam told him and had to read the newspapers to learn what was actually going on.[15]

Deterioration of the situation in South Vietnam following the overthrow of Ngo Dinh Diem and the assassination of Kennedy produced major changes. The steady growth of the NLF insurgency and political chaos in South Vietnam led to consideration of more direct U.S. intervention. Perhaps sensing an opportunity to regain some of the influence they had lost, the Joint Chiefs took the lead in recommending U.S. military actions against North Vietnam, thus increasingly setting the agenda for internal policy discussions.

In late 1964, moreover, under the skillful leadership of their new chairman, General Wheeler, the Joint Chiefs rendered themselves less vulnerable to McNamara's manipulation by developing unified positions. In fact, they differed sharply on the proper response to the impending crisis in Vietnam. The air force and marines were most "hawkish," advocating the provocation of new incidents to justify a full-scale bombing campaign. The army and navy at this point were more cautious.[16] At Wheeler's direction, the JCS put aside their differences and presented the administration with consensus recommendations, thus strengthening their position within the bureaucracy.

Despite their reluctance to get involved militarily in Vietnam, McNamara and Johnson increasingly listened to the military. Unwilling to consider withdrawal and aware that limited measures had failed, they saw no choice but greater U.S. military involvement. McNamara was at the height of his influence, directing policy on Vietnam almost like a desk officer. But neither he nor Johnson was experienced in or had confidence in their ability in military matters, and they deferred to the Joint Chiefs. Ever the political animal, with a full legislative agenda, and all too aware of the military's ties with conservative congressmen, Johnson, as early as November 1964, made clear that no Vietnam decisions would be made without "signing on" the Joint Chiefs, giving them a chance to be heard and making them part of the consensus.[17]

Johnson's early 1965 decisions to bomb North Vietnam and commit the first combat forces to South Vietnam marked a major turning point in his war policies and in the civil-military balance. After this point, the military became more aggressive, bombarding the civilians with requests for additional troops and an expanded mission. With U.S. forces now in action in Vietnam, the political risks for the president increased, and he was keenly aware of the dangers. The illusion of civilian dominance persisted, and each step along the way Johnson and McNamara sharply pared down the military proposals. But the frame of reference of the discussions was set by the military, and as each step failed to produce the desired result, the administration moved to the next step.[18]

Thus by the time the United States made what amounted to a decision for war in Vietnam in July 1965, patterns of decision making had been established, producing great frustration on both sides. The Joint Chiefs were increasingly impatient with the restraints on military action and the limits they felt mitigated the U.S. response. For his part, Johnson was undoubtedly alarmed with the step-by-step movement toward war, and he was increasingly frustrated with recommendations that appeared to leave him no choice but to move in that direction. "Bomb, bomb, bomb. That's all you know," he is said to have burst out to Army Chief of Staff Gen. Harold Johnson in the spring of 1965. "You generals have all been educated at the taxpayer's expense, and you're not giving me any ideas and any solutions for this damn little pissant country. Now I don't need ten generals to come in here ten times to tell me to bomb. I want some solutions. I want some answers."[19]

The critical decision of February 1965 to initiate regular bombing raids against North Vietnam had an "air of unreality" about it, Clark Clifford later recalled. The Joint Chiefs did not reveal to Johnson what they must have known themselves, that the bombing of North Vietnam would inevitably lead to requests for ground troops. The president and his civilian advisers, on the other hand, did not question the military persistently enough to get answers they perhaps did not want to hear.[20]

Johnson's July 1965 decisions for war in Vietnam illustrate quite clearly the flaws in the command system. Determined to avoid the sort of public debate that might threaten his cherished domestic programs, the president rigged the decision-making process to produce consensus rather than controversy. As a result, some major questions were raised but not answered; others were not even raised. Profound divisions within the administration over the way the war should be fought were glossed over in the interest of maintaining surface harmony. Gen. Bruce Palmer is correct in claiming that these deliberations comprised the only full-scale, top-level examination of U.S. strategy until after Tet, 1968.[21] But Johnson ensured that the sort of debate that might have led to a reconsideration of the U.S. commitment or to a more precise formulation of U.S. strategy did not take place. And the tensions and divisions that were left unresolved would provide the basis for bitter conflict when the steps taken in July did not produce the desired results.

The story of Johnson's decisions for war has been told elsewhere and need not be repeated in detail here.[22] The military and political situation in South Vietnam deteriorated drastically in the spring and summer of 1965, and on June 7, Gen. William Westmoreland requested an additional forty-four battalions, roughly 150,000 men, and the authority to take the war to the enemy through an aggressive search and destroy strategy. The request set off an intensive period of deliberation among Johnson's top advisers. The Joint Chiefs supported Westmoreland's recommendations and proposed in addition a major escalation of the bombing of North Vietnam. McNamara subsequently endorsed the military's proposals and recommended a partial mobilization of the reserves to meet the manpower requirements.

The president's other civilian advisers were more cautious. In-house "dove," Undersecretary of State George W. Ball, warned of the grave dangers of massive intervention and urged the president to find a way to cut the nation's losses and extricate it from a hopeless entanglement. Assistant Secretary of State William Bundy sought a middle way, a more modest increase in the force level and no escalation of the bombing. After two weeks of intensive discussion and endless rounds of meetings, Johnson in late July quietly authorized the increase to forty-four battalions and the shift to search and destroy, but he rejected expansion of the bombing and mobilization of the reserves.

During the July discussions, the civilians dominated the decision-making process. To be sure, Westmoreland and the JCS framed the agenda, but having done that they had only very limited influence. During the entire period of deliberation, the Joint Chiefs met with the president only once, and most observers agree that this meeting was pro forma, carefully staged to create the appearance of discussion and debate while building a consensus for what the president wished to do.[23] Fearful of the implications of the military's proposals, wary of their possible influence in Congress, Johnson kept the Joint Chiefs at arm's length, ensuring that they were "on board" but conceding them little actual influence. At the same time, the civilians did not provide the military strategic direction, set precise limits, or even define with clarity what they wanted done. National Security Adviser McGeorge Bundy later conceded that a "premium [was] put on imprecision."[24]

The discussions of June and July 1965 skirted many of the major issues. The debate centered on whether and how the troops would be provided, not how and for what purpose they would be employed. Yet even here there were omissions. On perhaps the fundamental issue, Johnson rejected mobilization of the reserves as proposed by the Joint Chiefs and supported by McNamara without permitting any discussion or debate. Every contingency plan for fighting a war of the size proposed called for mobilizing the reserves. The Joint Chiefs were therefore alarmed and deeply concerned by Johnson's decision, but they quietly acquiesced.

Sharp divisions on strategy were subordinated to the tactical necessity of maintaining the facade of unity. The Joint Chiefs themselves remained sharply divided on how the war should be fought. The marines strongly objected to the army and especially Westmoreland's determination to fight guerrillas by staging large-scale conventional battles.[25] Air Force Chief of Staff McConnell wanted a short and intensive bombing campaign, beginning in the south of North Vietnam and moving steadily northward, in which the United States applied all available assets and hit all designated targets. The other chiefs preferred concentrating on North Vietnamese lines of communication (LOC) to cut them off from external sources of supply. Apparently at Wheeler's insistence, the JCS in the summer of 1965, as before and indeed after, compromised their differences and developed unified positions to prevent the civilians from exploiting their divisions. The marines acquiesced in Westmoreland's design while fighting their own war in I Corps. McConnell abandoned his program, and the Joint Chiefs incorporated some of his targets into their LOC plan.[26]

There were even deeper divisions between the military and the civilians. The military seem to have perceived—perhaps much more accurately than the civilians, as it turned out—the scale of the conflict and the difficulty of the task in Vietnam. They had bitter memories of the frustrations of Korea, of limited objectives and crippling restrictions on the use of force. The Joint Chiefs correctly saw that involvement in Vietnam would require a full-scale war. They wanted to mobilize the reserves and declare a limited national emergency to make clear that the nation was not embarking on some "two-penny military adventure."[27] They felt, as Gen. Harold Johnson put it, that if the United States was not willing to go all the way it should not go in at all and that if military forces were committed, they should be committed at the "most rapid rate possible and not . . . at the rate of . . . an eye dropper."[28]

The civilians continued to regard Vietnam more as an exercise in crisis management than the war it had become. They persisted in believing that slow and carefully measured increases in military pressure would locate that point where the North Vietnamese were convinced that the cost of war would be greater than the potential gain. Once the North Vietnamese had been persuaded to stop infiltration of men and supplies, the southern insurgency could be contained.

These differences never surfaced in the June and July discussions. On those few occasions when they spoke to each other, the civilian and military leaders did not speak frankly and directly. Perhaps each preferred it that way. If they had confronted each other, David Halberstam has observed, the "vast and perhaps unbridgeable differences" between them would have been exposed.[29]

Even on those issues that were discussed, including the crucial and fundamental question of what would be required to achieve U.S. objectives, clarity and candor were not always the order of the day. The Joint Chiefs later claimed that they presented the harsh realities to the president—it would take 500,000 to 1 million men and five years simply to prevent North Vietnam from taking over the south. Perhaps they did. An article planted in the *New York Times Magazine* in February 1965 by the Joint Chiefs warned that a war in Vietnam would be "long, nasty and wearing" and might require from 200,000 to 1 million Americans. [30]

If the military accurately foresaw what the United States was getting into, however, it pulled its punches when the issue came up in July. At President Johnson's request, an ad hoc study group of the Joint Chiefs of Staff, chaired by Gen. Andrew Goodpaster, analyzed early in the month the fundamental—and notably ambiguous—question of whether the United States could "win" if it did everything it could. The conclusions were closely qualified and carefully phrased but generally positive and optimistic. Goodpaster's group operated on the assumption that the Soviet Union and China would not intervene. It made clear that success would require additional forces, an offensive ground strategy, a "full scale air campaign," and the "removal of restrictions, restraints and sources of delay and planning uncertainty." Badly miscalculating or erring on the side of optimism, the report grossly underestimated the North Vietnamese ability to match U.S. escalation. It therefore concluded optimistically that the United States might have to add only seven to thirty-five infantry battalions beyond the forty-four requested by Westmoreland to achieve its goals. "Within the bounds of reasonable assumptions . . . ," it concluded, "there appears to be no reason we cannot win if such is our will—and if that will is manifested in strategy and tactical operations."[31]

The president's top military advisers were anything but starry-eyed optimists in the brief, tightly controlled discussions of late July. Marine Corps Comm. Gen. Wallace Greene called for 72,000 marines in addition to the men requested by Westmoreland and warned that it would take five years and 500,000 men to prevail. General McConnell would go no further than predict that with the forces requested by Westmoreland "we can at least turn the tide to where we are not losing anymore." Wheeler admonished that it would be unreasonable to expect to win in a year. The United States might do no better than reverse the trend, and it could take as long as three years to register real progress.[32]

Still, in responding to Johnson's questions, the JCS evinced a firm, can-do spirit, and, like the ad hoc study group, they either grossly underestimated the North Vietnamese reaction or minimized the difficulties. Wheeler confidently affirmed that the mobility provided by airpower and particularly by the helicopter drastically reduced the ten to one "textbook" ratio for fighting guerrillas. When LBJ asked what North Vietnam would do if the United States escalated, Greene flatly retorted, "Nothing," and Admiral McDonald indicated that they could do nothing if the United States increased the bombing. Wheeler conceded that the North Vietnamese might themselves escalate, but he insisted that they would put in no more than 25 percent of their 250,000-man army and affirmed that they "can't match us on a buildup." He went on to suggest that large-scale North Vietnamese intervention would be a good thing because it would "allow us to cream them."[33]

The Joint Chiefs were deeply disappointed with Johnson's July decisions. Hanson Baldwin, a mouthpiece for the Pentagon, reported in the *New York Times* on July 29 that the military viewed the president's decisions as no more than a "stop-gap" measure. The buildup might not be fast enough to match the rate of deterioration in South Vietnam, and the refusal to mobilize the reserves left American manpower inadequate to meet its global commitments.[34] Yet while they vented their frustration to Baldwin, the military did not protest to Johnson, and when the president inquired at an NSC meeting on July 27 whether they were on board, Wheeler nodded in the affirmative.

The July discussions thus comprised an elaborate cat-and-mouse game, with the nation the ultimate loser. Johnson was keenly aware of the JCS view that the United States was "only pin pricking" the North Vietnamese, "just goosing them."[35] Yet he chose not to confront them directly. Eager to get them on board, he gave them enough to suggest that they might get more later, and he did not set limits or dictate strategy to them. At the same time, without permitting any real debate, he denied them several of the items they deemed crucial to their own strategy. The Joint Chiefs did not deliberately deceive the president, and on the crucial issue of North Vietnam's ability to match U.S. escalation they may have miscalculated as badly as the civilians. Perhaps to prevent Johnson from moving to George Ball's position, however, they tended to minimize the difficulties the United States might face, and they quietly acquiesced when Johnson rejected mobilization of the reserves and the type of air war they considered indispensable to their overall concept of operations.

It has been argued that they should have resigned at this point, forcing the debate that Johnson did not want and sparing them from being accomplices to the president's deviousness. In fact, a deeply frustrated Army Chief of Staff Harold Johnson did contemplate resignation, removing his stars and driving to the White House gates before deciding that he could accomplish more by working within the system.[36] There is no evidence to suggest that the other chiefs, individually or as a group, ever considered resigning, however. Unlike such predecessors as LeMay, Burke, or Anderson, McNamara's political generals and admirals appear to have learned how to play the game, soft-pedaling their disappointment with the president's decisions, perhaps assuming that once the United States was committed they could maneuver him into doing what they wanted. Civilian and military leaders thus went to war in Vietnam in July 1965 without clear channels of communication and operating under vastly different—and largely unspoken—expectations about each other and the war they were entering.

III

Warfare is an "art," Earl Tilford has written, and its conduct "requires intellectual sophistication, mental dexterity, and the ability to think abstractly."[37] Limited war, in particular, demands the most sophisticated strategy, precisely formulated in terms of ends and means, with special attention to keeping costs at acceptable levels. What stands out about the Johnson administration's management of Vietnam is that in what may have been the most complex war ever fought by the United States there was never any systematic discussion at the highest levels of government of the fundamental issue of how the war was to be fought. The crucial discussions of June and July 1965 had at best skirted that issue, at worst avoided it altogether, and this was the only such discussion until the Tet offensive of early 1968. Strategy, such as it was, emerged from the field, with little or no input from the people at the top.

Simple overconfidence may be the most obvious explanation for this phenomenon. From the commander in chief to the GIs in the field, Americans could not conceive that they would be unable to impose their will on what Lyndon Johnson once dismissed as that "raggedy-ass little fourth-rate country." The tremendous advantages the United States appeared to have in resources, technology, and equipment contributed further to self-delusion. With every conceivable advantage on its side, there seemed no need for America to think in terms of strategy.

But the explanation goes much deeper than that. Although he took quite seriously his role as commander in chief, personally picking bombing targets, agonizing over the fate of U.S. airmen, and building a scale model of the Khe Sanh battlefield in the White House Situation Room, Lyndon Johnson, unlike Polk, Lincoln, or his hero Franklin Roosevelt, never took control of his war. In many ways a great president, Johnson was badly miscast as a war leader. He preferred to deal with other matters, the Great Society and the legislative process he understood best and so loved. In contrast to Lincoln, Roosevelt, and even Harry Truman, he had little interest in military affairs and no illusion of military expertise. He had read virtually nothing of such things and had done only brief and token service in World War II. He thus deferred to the military as the experts. He was fond of quoting his political mentor, Sam Rayburn, to the effect that "if we start making the military decisions, I wonder why we paid to send them to West Point," probably a rationalization for his own ignorance and insecurity in the military realm.[38] Johnson thus "failed to do the one thing that the central leadership must do," Stephen Peter Rosen has noted. He did not "define a clear military mission for the military" and did not "establish a clear limit to the resources to be allocated for that mission."[39]

Indeed, at crucial points in the war, the commander in chief gave little hint of his thinking. McGeorge Bundy literally pleaded with him in November 1965 to make clear his positions on the big issues so that McNamara could be certain he was running the war "the right way for the right reasons, in your view." By late 1967, private citizen Bundy's pleading had taken on a tone of urgency, warning Johnson that he must "take command of a contest that is more political in character than any in our history except the Civil War."[40]

McNamara himself might have filled the strategic void left by the president, but he was no more eager—and probably no better qualified—to intrude in this area. In many ways a superb secretary of defense, he was not an effective minister of war. His revolution at the Pentagon was a managerial revolution that in no way challenged prevailing military doctrine, and he was out of his element when compelled to go beyond the managerial aspects of military policy. Conceding his ignorance, he refused to direct the formulation of strategy. When asked on one occasion why he did not tell his officers what to do and reminded that Churchill had not hesitated to do so, he shot back that he was no Churchill and would not dabble in areas where he had no competence.[41] At times, he talked boldly about imposing his views on the Joint Chiefs, but in fact he challenged them only on the bombing. When Dean Rusk urged him to insist on better use of South Vietnamese forces and to institute a unified military command system in Vietnam, he responded that he already had enough problems with the JCS and did not want more.[42] Moreover, as his successor Clark Clifford has noted, inasmuch as McNamara sought to manage the war, he did so as he approached everything else, employing "pure intellect and his towering analytical skills," failing to appreciate until too late that war contains great uncertainties and many irrationalities and that Vietnam in particular defied normal logical analysis.[43]

Johnson and McNamara saw their principal task in war management as maintaining tight operational control over the military. On Johnson's part, of course, a compulsive determination to micromanage was an essential part of his makeup. Even as a young congressman, he had insisted on overseeing the most minute detail, never sure "that things would go right," an aide later commented, "unless he was in control of everything."[44]

The tendency to micromanage must also be understood in the context of the strains in civil-military relations during the Vietnam era. A powerful peacetime military establishment was something new in post–World War II American life, and civilian leaders were uncertain how to handle it. They recognized the necessity of military power in an age of global conflict, but they also feared the possibility of rising military influence in government. If it confirmed the tradition of civilian preeminence, MacArthur's defiance of presidential authority during the Korean War seemed also to dramatize the dangers.

Suspicious of the military and operating in an age of profound international tension with weaponry of enormous destructive potential, civilians felt compelled to keep the generals and admirals in check. Modern communications technology gave them the means to involve themselves in day-to-day events in a way not feasible in early wars.[45] Most important, perhaps, the missile crisis had induced among them a form of "nuclear neurosis," a pervasive fear that an impulsive military commander might take rash action that could lead to nuclear war.

Johnson brought to the White House the southern populist's suspicion of the military. "This goddam military," he once snorted to USIA director Carl Rowan, "I just don't know when I can trust 'em and when I can't." In his heart a private who hated colonels, he kept his distance from and was very circumspect with his senior officers. He deferred to the military on occasion to prove to them he was as tough as they were. Suspecting at the same time that they needed war to boost their reputations, he, like McNamara, was determined to keep a close rein on them.[46] The consequence in Vietnam was a day-to-day intrusion into the tactical conduct of the war on a scale quite unprecedented. The larger result, Rosen observes, was an unhappy combination of "high-level indecision and micromanagement."[47]

Inasmuch as McNamara and Johnson's civilian advisers thought strategically, they did so in terms of the limited war theories in vogue at the time. Strategy was primarily a matter of sending signals to foes, of communicating resolve, of using military force in carefully measured increments to deter enemies or bargain toward a settlement. This approach must have appeared expedient to Johnson and his advisers because it seemed to offer a cheap, low-risk answer to a difficult problem. It also appeared to be controllable, thereby reducing the risk of all-out war. The Kennedy administration's successful handling of the Cuban Missile Crisis seems to have reinforced in the minds of U.S. officials the value of such an approach. "There is no longer any such thing as strategy," McNamara exclaimed in the aftermath of the Soviet backdown, "only crisis management."[48]

He could not have been more wrong, of course, and the reliance on limited war theory had unfortunate consequences. It encouraged avoidance of costly and risky decisions. It diverted attention from real strategy and caused the military problem of how to win the war in South Vietnam to be neglected. It led the decision makers into steps they must have sensed the American people would eventually reject. And when North Vietnam refused to respond as bargaining theory said it should, the United States was left with no strategy at all.

In theory, the Joint Chiefs of Staff might have filled the strategic vacuum and to some extent they did, but the result was far from satisfactory. The advent of global responsibilities and complex weapons systems after World War II had brought civilians into a once exclusive preserve, and the military had increasingly been displaced in the realm of strategic thought and planning. Post–World War II military officers had also been "civilianized" through indoctrination in management techniques and limited war theory at the expense of their more traditional folkways. The new breed of "military managers," the Joint Chiefs handpicked by McNamara, had achieved their prominence largely as staff officers, and they were in many ways ill-equipped to devise sophisticated strategies for a complex war.[49]

In addition, the JCS system was not well designed to produce intelligent, forceful, and independent military advice. The JCS had no position within the chain of command. They were merely advisers, and there was no requirement that they be consulted. Each had his own service as his major concern, and the time he could devote to matters of mutual interest was limited. The chairman had a joint staff to assist with planning, but its members also were representatives of their own services rather than independent actors. Throughout the process, the system tended to produce the least common denominator, what the individual services could agree upon, rather than independent counsel.[50]

McNamara's Joint Chiefs were also increasingly politicized. The secretary of defense made clear in the aftermath of LeMay and Anderson that he wanted "planners and thinkers, not heroes . . . , team men rather than gladiators." His new breed of "military sophisticates" were no doubt more sensitive to the political and diplomatic implications of military decisions, and, as *Time* put it, they could "cooperate in the overlapping area between military and political policy without breaking a lot of crockery."[51] They were also less inclined to go against the grain. To some extent, they were coopted. They had seen the damage caused by LeMay's outspoken opposition, and they were therefore more inclined to go along or to oppose by subtle and indirect means.[52]

The ambiguity that had characterized the decision-making process grew worse under conditions of war. Following Kennedy's practice, Johnson kept the military at arm's length, usually excluding them from the most important deliberations on major decisions until it was time to secure their acquiescence.[53] Not until October 1967 did General Wheeler regularly attend the Tuesday Lunches, where the most important military decisions were made. In theory, Wheeler had direct access to the president, but most JCS recommendations were actually presented through McNamara, who often filtered them through his own views. Determined that the military would not become a rallying point for opposition to his policies, Johnson made enough concessions to their point of view to keep them on board, and he left the impression that more might be obtained later.

The military was no more able to level with Johnson than he with them. Westmoreland, commander in chief, Pacific, Adm. U. S. Grant Sharp, and the Joint Chiefs increasingly chafed under the restraints imposed by Washington. Sensitive to MacArthur's fate in Korea, they would not challenge the president directly or air their case in public. Nor would they develop a strategy that accommodated to the restrictions imposed by the White House. Rather, under Wheeler's leadership, they attempted to chip away at the restrictions through a "foot in the door" approach until they got the strategic freedom they wanted.[54] The result was considerable ambiguity in purpose and method, growing civil-military tension, and a steady escalation that brought increasing costs and uncertain gains.

Two examples early in the war illustrate the bureaucratic fog in which the command system operated. The Joint Chiefs presented to McNamara on August 27, 1965, a "Concept for Vietnam" to guide the military effort. The objectives of U.S. military action, as outlined in the document, were to compel North Vietnam to stop supporting the southern insurgency, to defeat the NLF, and to deter China from intervention or defeat it if it intervened. These "aims" were to be accomplished by intensifying U.S. air and naval actions against North Vietnam, including the mining of Haiphong harbor, by hitting North Vietnamese infiltration routes in Laos and Cambodia, by search and destroy operations against the southern insurgents, and by a military buildup in Thailand to deter the Chinese. The JCS called for "aggressive and sustained exploitation of superior military force" by the United States and explicitly warned against the sort of slow, gradual escalation that would allow the Communists to keep pace, limit U.S. choices, and even perhaps lead to a general war. They asked that the commander in chief, Pacific, be given "as wide latitude as possible" to execute the plan.[55]

The civilian leadership ignored the JCS proposal. To be sure, the concept represented a strategy only in the most narrow sense of the word. It merely formalized and called for expansion of the means already in use. It was vague and general on both means and ends. More important—and typical of the way the system would work—it was never even discussed with the civilian leadership, much less approved or disapproved. Assistant Secretary of Defense John McNaughton conceded to McNamara that many of the JCS recommendations caused no problems. He went on to warn, however, that others were highly controversial, especially the intensified bombing campaign, the buildup in Thailand, and the mining of North Vietnamese ports. He therefore proposed that since an "overall approval" was not required the concept not be "specifically approved," and McNamara readily concurred.[56] The document was quietly shelved.

The bombing pause of December 1965 further illustrates the way in which Johnson and McNamara handled the military. The president's civilian advisers persuaded themselves by late 1965 that a temporary cessation of the bombing might lead to serious negotiations. Even if it failed, they reasoned, it would help prepare the public for the escalation that would soon be necessary. Johnson was keenly aware that the JCS would oppose such a move—"the Chiefs go through the roof when we mention this pause," he said. McNamara firmly reminded the president that "we decide what we want and impose it on them."[57]

In fact, the civilians went around the military rather than dealing with them directly. The JCS were not invited to meetings at which the pause was considered. Johnson did discuss the matter with Wheeler the day before the decision was made and shortly before the chairman was to depart for East Asia. By the time Wheeler communicated further doubts to Washington, however, a cable announcing the pause had gone out under the name of the JCS. The cable was drafted in the office of the secretary of defense. Air Force Chief of Staff McConnell was asked to sign it and refused. When McConnell and Chief of Naval Operations McDonald protested that the JCS had not been consulted, McNamara and Deputy Secretary of Defense Cyrus Vance retorted that the president was aware of their views, and they refused McConnell's request to see him. Having bypassed them at this stage, McNamara appears later to have feared a possible military reaction. On December 29, he called in the chiefs, carefully explained the reasons for the pause, and, apparently to appease them, promised a major escalation early in the new year.[58]

December 1965 and January 1966 represented what William Bundy later called a major "break point" in U.S. Vietnam policy.[59] The bloody battle of the Ia Drang valley in November made clear that the United States had underestimated its North Vietnamese enemy and that a major escalation of the war would be required. There was growing pressure from the military for a "jugular from the air." "No one ever won anything by remaining on the defensive," Wheeler warned.[60] In the minds of some civilians, including McNamara, the Ia Drang raised gnawing doubts that the war could be won militarily and sparked a frantic search for alternatives like the bombing pause. During the frequently heated discussions on the pause, the civilian leadership manifested grave concern. McGeorge Bundy ruminated about the complexity of waging limited war with "limited means and limited objectives," while Clark Clifford wondered "where the hell we are going—further and further in with no prospect of a return." The president continued to fret about the possible consequences of escalation on the one hand and a bombing pause on the other. He still sought to apply "the maximum amount of pressure with [the] minimum amount of danger." "I don't want to take off till I know I can get back," he observed.[61]

Yet the administration was as unwilling as in July 1965 to confront the fundamental issues of the war. While warning frankly that a military victory might not be possible, McNamara continued to recommend more of the same. No one pursued Clifford's question to its logical conclusion or pressed the military as to what might be required. There was no change of approach or reevaluation of strategy, and neither the president nor McNamara was any more inclined than before to take control of what was now obviously a complicated and possibly very long and costly war. Indeed, when the bombing pause failed to produce peace negotiations, McNamara, who had pressed it so vigorously, lost favor with the White House, and a frustrated and angry Johnson was even less inclined to take on the Joint Chiefs.

In the absence of direction from the top, American "strategy" emerged from below, to a large extent from practices already in operation. The ground strategy—search and destroy, as it came to be called—derived from the field commander. Westmoreland had pushed for aggressive, offensive operations against enemy main force units from early in the year. Such an approach fitted the army's traditional doctrine, and the JCS probably supported it in the early stages as a way of getting U.S. forces into the war. Once the United States was at war, no one was inclined to challenge Westmoreland. Neither Johnson nor McNamara saw reason to take on the general, and those military officials who were skeptical of his strategy, were inclined to defer to him. The strategy, later widely regarded as ill-advised, emerged almost by default and was not seriously challenged for nearly two years.

The air "strategy" developed through a much more complex process. For the air force, as Earl Tilford has noted, strategy was target selection and the generation of sorties. The air war thus evolved out of air force doctrine and from the adjustment of conflicting bureaucratic pressures.[62] The military in general pressed for a quick, hard-hitting bombing campaign against major North Vietnamese targets, although the navy and air force differed sharply on the focus and major objectives of the bombing. The civilians and especially President Johnson sought to keep the bombing under tight restriction. Johnson was near paranoid in his fear that reckless bombing might provoke a larger war with the Soviet Union or China.[63] In addition, at the outset, at least, the president's civilian advisers saw slow and steady escalation of the air war as a way of persuading North Vietnam of America's power and determination and therefore convincing it to abandon the southern insurgency. Administration officials also sought to minimize civilian casualties to appease rising criticism of the bombing at home and abroad.

The complex process of target selection reflected the way in which the air strategy was made. Air force and navy targeteers sent weekly proposals to the air commanders in the Pacific and on to the commander in chief, Pacific, in

Honolulu. A specially created Rolling Thunder team in Washington then evaluated the proposals for General Wheeler. If time permitted—not always the case—Wheeler consulted with the other Joint Chiefs on the proposals. He then made recommendations to McNamara, who presented them to the Tuesday Lunch, where the president and his top civilian advisers approved or disapproved them. Until late 1967, General Wheeler did not regularly attend the Tuesday Lunches, and in this first phase of the war, McNamara dominated the targeting process. Sometimes he proposed targets that did not come from JCS recommendations and on other occasions, when the Tuesday Lunch did not meet on a regular basis or Johnson felt that targets did not need his personal approval, the secretary of defense approved targets on his own.[64]

From the outset, conflict developed over strategy, and it intensified as gradual escalation did not produce the expected results. Far more than has been recognized and than was revealed in the *Pentagon Papers*, no one in the Johnson administration really liked the way the war was being fought or the results that were being obtained. What is even more striking, however, is that despite the rampant dissatisfaction, there was no change in strategy or even systematic discussion at the highest level of the possibility of a change in strategy. As in June and July 1965, the entire system seems to have been rigged to prevent debate and adaptation.

Westmoreland's search and destroy strategy evoked increasingly strong opposition within the military itself. Air power advocates like Adm. Thomas Moorer thought it foolish to use American high school graduates in a war of attrition against Vietnamese "coolies."[65] Perhaps more significant, within the army there was growing concern about Westmoreland's approach. A small group of officers, some former advisers in Vietnam, others specialists in counterinsurgency warfare, maintained a steady and generally ineffectual opposition to Westmoreland's big-unit war and pushed for greater emphasis on pacification.[66] More important, as early as November 1965, after the Ia Drang, Army Chief of Staff Harold Johnson had grown skeptical of Westmoreland's attrition strategy, and increasingly thereafter he questioned the wastefulness and apparent fruitlessness of search and destroy operations. Vice Chief of Staff Creighton Abrams seems to have shared at least some of Johnson's skepticism, as did some top officers in the field in Vietnam.[67]

The most heated opposition came from the marines. From the outset, marine leaders had strongly objected to the army's determination to fight guerrillas by staging decisive battles "along the Tannenberg design."[68] Perceiving the guerrillas as the main threat and the South Vietnamese people as the key to the war, they ignored North Vietnamese/NLF main units in favor of the more classical counterinsurgency strategy of building ties with the local population.

Westmoreland opposed this ink-blot approach, insisting that the marines should get out of their "beachheads" and go after enemy main units, and in the summer of 1966 he imposed search and destroy on the marines, provoking a rearguard action by Marine Gen. Victor Krulak to force an overall change in strategy. But the marines were unable to secure more than minor concessions from Westmoreland. "The Chiefs were interested," Marine Comm. Wallace Greene later recalled, "but Westmoreland wasn't and being CGMACV his views of the 'big picture' . . . prevailed." [69]

The divisions within the military paled compared to the civil-military tensions that mushroomed after August 1965. Civil-military conflict was already well advanced when the United States went to war in Vietnam, and it grew steadily amidst the tensions of fighting a limited war. Military leaders increasingly resented the administration's refusal to mobilize, Westmoreland, in particular, expressing frustration at being "restricted to peace-time procedures which are not compatible with the requirements of the situation." [70] McNamara became the central figure in the controversy and the focal point and lightning rod of military hostility. Trying to apply in a limited war situation the standards of cost effectiveness he had used in the automobile industry and in managing the peacetime Pentagon, the secretary sought to fight on existing inventories of supplies and avoid the surpluses and waste that characterized most wars. As a result, there were shortages of key items, including ammunition, and bitter complaints from a military forced to fight on short rations in an age of abundance. Jokes about McNamara's efforts to standardize weaponry revealed growing military anger with his supply policies. The secretary of defense, it was said, was going to put a twelve-round clip in the F-lll aircraft and issue it as the standard infantry weapon. [71]

Military leaders also bitterly protested Washington's oppressive oversight of the war. "The daily micro-management by Johnson and McNamara . . . was for me *unbelievable*," Marine Commandant Greene later observed, "and usually resulted in actions contrary to the views of the JCS and made with grossly bumbling ignorance of proper, common sense application of military weapons, strategy, and tactics." [72] Chief of Naval Operations McDonald expressed deep resentment at the Whiz Kids, "these smart analysts with no experience." [73] Westmoreland, similarly, complained of the "naive, gratuitous advice provided by 'lesser' civilians" in the Defense Department and by the "self-appointed field Marshals" in the State Department. [74] "The appetite of Washington for details is insatiable," Krulak protested in 1967. "The idea . . . is to take more and more items of less and less significance to higher and higher levels so that more and more decisions on smaller and smaller matters may be made by fewer and fewer people." [75]

The major source of conflict was the conduct of the war. It quickly became apparent that the escalation of July 1965 would not be enough, and from that point on Westmoreland regularly sought major increases in the ground forces at his disposal. Faced with an increasingly serious strain on America's global manpower resources, the JCS repeatedly proposed mobilization. Johnson just as adamantly resisted their proposals, and McNamara regularly reduced the number of troops given Westmoreland. Westmoreland increasingly complained that he could not do the task assigned with the troops given him, and civilian critics increasingly questioned the search and destroy strategy.[76]

The military and civilians also disagreed over expanding the war. The JCS August plan had called for operations in Laos, Cambodia, and North Vietnam, and from that point on Westmoreland regularly pushed for operations outside South Vietnam, warning that he could not accomplish his goals as long as the enemy had privileged sanctuary. The civilian leadership made some concessions, but it did not permit the sort of operations Westmoreland wanted, and he and the officers and men under him were increasingly frustrated by the restrictions they felt prevented them from winning the war.[77]

The hottest issue was the bombing. At least through the first year of the war, many civilian leaders were still beguiled by the notion that a slow and steady escalation of the bombing would bring the North Vietnamese to their senses, and McNamara continued to insist on "carefully measured attacks on clearly defined military targets." Rusk vigorously opposed any bombing near the Chinese border. Johnson, in particular, was "haunted by the ceaseless fear" of Soviet and Chinese intervention. Once when he asked Wheeler how the Russians and Chinese might respond to a particular move and the general said they would do nothing, he sharply retorted: "Are you more sure than MacArthur was?"[78] Hence, the White House parceled out targets grudgingly, kept a tight rein on the bombing, and in particular kept the bombers away from Hanoi and Haiphong and the Chinese border. On several occasions, targets were disapproved or the bombing cut back or stopped for essentially political reasons.[79]

The military chafed under the restrictions. In keeping with traditional airpower doctrine, they pressed for destruction of major industrial targets and closing the ports to destroy North Vietnam's war-making capacity. They protested that gradualism made it impossible to achieve their goals and complained about what seemed to them ridiculous ground rules that severely limited the effectiveness of the bombing. They objected that many important targets were off limits, that the sequence of attacks was random and militarily illogical, especially when the bombing was delayed for "political" reasons. They did not share the administration's squeamishness about civilian casualties. "This war is a dirty business, like all wars," Admiral Sharp complained. "We need to get hard-headed about it. That is the only kind of action these tough-minded Communists will respect. . . . When Hanoi screams, hit them again."[80]

During 1966, divisions on the bombing got more complicated and more intense. Through the first year of the war, McNamara had supported escalation of the bombing, sometimes reluctantly. After a major campaign against North Vietnam's petroleum supplies failed to reduce infiltration or affect the enemy's will, he became increasingly disillusioned. In the late summer of 1966, he commissioned an independent group of scientists to evaluate the effectiveness of the air war. Their negative report confirmed his suspicions, and on October 14, 1966, he advised the president that "at the proper time we should consider terminating all bombing in North Vietnam."[81] To the consternation of the military, the secretary of defense also began to push for the construction of an elaborate barrier across the demilitarized zone as a substitute for the bombing. The lines were tightly drawn, and conflict between the secretary of defense and his military advisers would escalate over the next year.

Still, despite widespread dissatisfaction with the way the war was being fought and the results that were being obtained, there was no change of strategy or even open and general discussion of the possibility of a change in strategy. There are several major reasons for the persistence of this bureaucratic and strategic gridlock. Certainly the military tradition of autonomy of the field commander inhibited debate on and possible alteration of the ground strategy. Although greatly concerned with the cost and consequences of Westmoreland's excessive use of firepower, Army Chief of Staff Johnson deferred to the field commander. "I would deplore and oppose any intervention from the Washington level to impose limitations on further firepower application," he reassured Westmoreland. He would go no further than suggest that it might be "prudent" to "undertake a very careful examination of the problem."[82]

More important was the leadership style of the commander in chief. To some degree, the overpowering personality of the president by itself inhibited questions being asked unless he himself raised them or events compelled it. In addition, as a means of maintaining control, Johnson discouraged discussion among his advisers. He encouraged them to write him memos but not to show them to each other. "Don't you gang up on me," McGeorge Bundy recalled him saying.[83]

Most important, Lyndon Johnson's entirely political manner of running the war, his consensus-oriented modus operandi, had the effect of stifling debate. Throughout his political career, on the most controversial of issues he had always positioned himself comfortably in the middle, and on Vietnam he did the same. On such issues as bombing targets and bombing pauses, troop levels and troop use, by making concessions to each side without giving any what it wanted, he managed to keep dissent and controversy under control. From the beginning of the war to the end, as Clark Clifford has observed, Johnson acted more like a legislative leader maintaining consensus among his divided colleagues than a commander in chief running a war.[84]

The president and his top advisers also imposed rigid standards of loyalty on a bitterly divided administration. Unlike Franklin Roosevelt, Johnson had no tolerance for controversy, and he established for his advisers the "Macy's window at high noon" brand of loyalty made legendary by David Halberstam.[85] In the aftermath of the July 1965 decisions, he even directed McGeorge Bundy, Clifford, and kitchen cabinet adviser Abe Fortas to develop methods to keep silent those who left government.[86]

Unfortunately, the two men who might have influenced him, McNamara and Secretary of State Rusk, shared his perverted notions of team play. "I don't believe the government of a complicated state can operate effectively," McNamara once said, "if those in charge of the departments of the government express disagreement with decisions of the established head of that government." Whenever someone dissented, it made more difficult the attainment of the larger group goals.[87] In-house devil's advocate George Ball later recalled that McNamara treated his dissenting memos rather like "poisonous snakes." He was "absolutely horrified by them," considered them "next to treason." Throughout much of 1966, McNamara and Ambassador-at-Large W. Averell Harriman joined in a conspiracy of silence, privately sharing their distaste for the bombing and their conviction that it would not work but refusing to challenge it before the president or resign. It is obvious now that when McNamara himself became a "dissenter" in 1967 it was an excruciating experience for him.[88]

Rusk's position is even more curious. In general, to be sure, he supported the existing strategy, and he was therefore not inclined to discuss alternatives. In addition, as he put it years later, he was "not willing to yield to pessimism in Vietnam just because the outlook was bleak," and he feared that a policy reappraisal, if leaked to the press, would encourage further pessimism, thus constituting a self-fulfilling prophecy. Even if he had been skeptical, however, he would probably not have pressed for change because of his decidedly restrictive view of his own role as a presidential adviser. "There is a delicate line between raising questions about policy and failing to support the policy," he wrote later. "When the president has decided what the policy shall be, an officer should either support that policy or resign." "Guerrilla warfare among those at the top of the government is simply too dangerous in the kind of world in which we live." [89]

Finally, and perhaps most important, is what might be called the MacArthur syndrome, the pervasive fear among civilians and military of a repetition of the illustrious general's challenge to civilian authority. Westmoreland kept on his desk in Saigon a quotation from Napoleon affirming that a commander must resign rather than carry out a plan he considers defective. Despite his growing frustration with the restrictions on his conduct of the war, the general appears never to have contemplated resignation. Indeed, he seems to have gone out of his way to avoid putting undue pressure on the president. He made clear to McNamara in October 1966 that he was "very sensitive" to Johnson's position and had refrained from putting him on the spot by making "exorbitant demands." [90]

Johnson, as noted, lived in terror of a military revolt and did everything in his power to avert it. In their February 1966 meeting in Honolulu, Westmoreland later recalled, the president carefully sized him up, eventually satisfying himself that *his* general was "sufficiently understanding" of the constraints imposed on him and was a "reliable" and "straightforward soldier who would not get involved in the politics of war." [91]

An encounter in July 1967 is even more revealing of the delicate game being played between the general and his commander in chief. An increasingly frustrated and restive Westmoreland reminded the president that he had made every effort to "ease his burden by my conduct and demands." But he added an only slightly veiled warning that he must think of his own requirements first. Johnson flattered Westmoreland by expressing great admiration for the way he had handled himself. He cleverly sought to disarm the general by hinting that he did not always favor his civilian advisers over his military. [92]

Themselves learning from Korea, Wheeler and the Joint Chiefs carefully refrained from anything smacking of a direct challenge to civilian authority. Although they remained deeply divided on the conduct of the war, they continued to present unified proposals to the civilians, thus stifling debate within their own ranks. A sophisticated politician skilled in bureaucratic maneuver, Wheeler reserved for himself and jealously guarded the role of mediator not only among the Joint Chiefs but also between the military and civilian authorities. His approach was political rather than confrontational and emphasized short-term acquiescence and silence. Hoping eventually to get strategic license by gradually breaking down the restrictions imposed by the White House, he encouraged Westmoreland to continue to push for escalation of the war and to accept less than he wanted in order to get a "foot in the door." He also implored the field commander to keep his subordinates quiet. If escalation were to occur following reports of military dissatisfaction, he warned, critics would conclude that the military was "riding roughshod" over civilians. Officers must understand the "absolute necessity for every military man to keep his mouth shut and get on with the war." [93] Thus rather than confront their differences directly, the president and his top military leadership continued to deal with each other by indirection.

In various ways, between July 1965 and August 1967, debate was stifled and dissent squelched. When Army Chief of Staff Johnson warned in a speech that the war might last ten years, Barry Zorthian later recalled, "he got his ass chewed out. That was denied awfully fast." [94] On what he later called a direct "order" from Ambassador to South Vietnam Henry Cabot Lodge, Jr., Gen. Greene in a "deep backgrounder" in Saigon in August 1966 affirmed his belief, based on formal military analysis, that it would take 750,000 men and five years to win the war, requiring at least partial mobilization and a reserve call-up. The reaction, Greene later recalled, "was immediate, explosive, and remarkable." An "agitated" and "as usual, profane" Lyndon Johnson, over long-distance telephone, demanded to know "what in the God-damned hell" Greene meant by making such a statement. [95] The commandant was forced to issue denials, and the White House denied the existence of studies leading to such conclusions. [96]

Deeply alarmed with the ground strategy, marine general Krulak sought to change it. Certain that the strategy of attrition played to North Vietnamese strengths, he proposed an alternative strategy that would have combined protection of the South Vietnamese population with the slow liberation of NLF-controlled villages. [97] In addition, an intensive air campaign would be launched to disrupt supply in North Vietnamese ports. Krulak was well connected in Washington, and with the blessings of Gen. Greene and Adm. Sharp he took his proposal to McNamara, presidential assistant Averell Harriman, and eventually the president himself. As Krulak later recalled it, McNamara made "only brief comment." Harriman evinced interest in Krulak's proposals for pacification but expressed fear that in a more aggressive bombing campaign U.S. planes might hit a Russian ship and "Communist pride would cause them to react." Krulak got nowhere with Johnson. When he mentioned attacks on North Vietnamese ports, the president "got to his feet, put his arm around my shoulder, and propelled me firmly toward the door." [98]

Even modest efforts to better integrate the disparate and unconnected elements of existing strategy got nowhere. In early 1967, Krulak pressed McNamara to generate a "comprehensive plan of campaign" that would "integrate" the various kinds of military operations and other military activities with the multifarious civilian programs, South Vietnamese and American, weighing the possible results of each against the risks and costs.[99] He got nowhere. At about the same time, Walt Rostow and Robert Komer of the president's NSC staff pushed for a National Security Action Memorandum (NSAM) that would formalize the administration's "strategy" and establish machinery to better coordinate its various elements "as a means of getting a clear focus on the all-out effort needed next year." The NSAM was never approved or even formally discussed.[100]

IV

Civil-military conflict deepened and sharpened in 1967. As the war dragged on inconclusively, the Joint Chiefs on the one hand and McNamara on the other pressed for major changes in strategy either to end the conflict through military force or to extricate the United States from what seemed increasingly a quagmire. Largely because of the president, the debate, if indeed it can be called that, produced no change. Determinedly plowing down the middle in an administration now bitterly divided against itself, Johnson deflected discussion of strategy without resolving or even addressing the fundamental issues. And by continuing to make concessions to each side without giving in to either, he perpetuated the process of gradual escalation—and indecision.

A major military request to expand the war touched off the 1967 conflict on strategy. Wheeler appears to have concluded early in the year that his foot-in-the-door approach was working. There was a "new sense of urgency" at the top levels of government, he excitedly informed Westmoreland and Sharp. He had just secured authority to strike new bombing targets and conduct new ground operations, and he hoped to receive "even broader authority" in the future. The president seemed to have recognized, Wheeler advised his colleagues, that the sound advice given him by the military in the past had been responsible for the success thus far obtained, and he appeared increasingly inclined to dismiss conflicting advice. Taking the line he had taken throughout the war, the chairman again stressed that the military must continue to be patient and discreet and use good judgment in dealing with civilian authorities.[101]

In mid-March, the military submitted new proposals to expand the war. Westmoreland requested an additional 200,000 troops. Certain that at last they had the president's ear, the Joint Chiefs used Westmoreland's request to address the whole range of problems that had vexed them since 1965. Once again, they sought authority to go after the enemy's sanctuaries in Laos and Cambodia and across the demilitarized zone. Increasingly troubled by the deterioration of America's global military strength, they warned that the

United States could not respond to Vietnam and other crises without additional forces and again pressed for mobilization of the reserves. They advocated expansion of the bombing and mining of North Vietnam's major ports. In effect, they called for mobilizing the nation to win the war. On April 27, Wheeler and Westmoreland met alone with the president and, in words chosen to appeal to the political animal that was Lyndon Johnson, warned that unless drastic measures were taken to break the will of the enemy, the war might go on for five years.[102]

Alarmed by the JCS proposals, civilians in the Defense and State departments mobilized as they had not before to head off expansion of the war. Undersecretary of State Nicholas Katzenbach, Assistant Secretary of State William Bundy, and Assistant Secretary of Defense John McNaughton all agreed that invasion of North Vietnam and mining of the ports ran grave dangers of Chinese and Soviet intervention and that mobilization of the reserves risked a major debate in Congress when opposition to the war was already on the rise. The civilians disagreed among themselves on what should be done about the bombing, but they generally agreed that henceforth the major effort should be in the area south of the twentieth parallel, and there was some feeling that it might be stopped altogether.

By this time, even the ground strategy had come under fire. Like McNamara despondent about the course of the war, McNaughton warned of the "fatal flaw" of continuing to approve incremental increases in troops, falling into the "trap that has ensnared us for the past three years. It actually *gives* the troops while only *praying* for their proper use." At the very minimum, he insisted, an upper limit should be imposed on American forces. But he urged McNamara to go further. The "philosophy of the war should be fought out now," he said, "so everyone will not be proceeding on their own major premises, and getting us in deeper and deeper."[103]

McNamara took the lead in the battle against expansion of the war. He had grown increasingly disenchanted with Vietnam since late 1965 and increasingly troubled as a consequence. David Lilienthal observed in March 1967 a "harassed and puzzled look on the no longer sprightly" secretary of defense, and McNamara virtually conceded to Lilienthal that his exercise in crisis management had failed. "We have poured more bombs onto North Vietnam than in the whole of World War II," he said, "and yet we have no sign that it has shaken their will to resist."[104] In a draft presidential memorandum (DPM) first shown to Johnson on May 19, the secretary went further than the Pentagon and State Department civilians, advancing positions the authors of the *Pentagon Papers* later accurately described as "radical."[105] The war was acquiring a momentum of its own, he urgently warned, and this must be stopped. He expressed grave doubt that the JCS proposals would produce victory, and by provoking conflict with the Soviet Union or China they could lead to a "national disaster." Giving Westmoreland 200,000 additional troops would create "irresistible pressures" to expand the war. Mobilization of the reserves would spark a "bitter debate" in Congress.

As an alternative to the JCS proposals, McNamara sketched out a complex politico-military "strategy" that raised the possibility of compromise and even hinted at extrication. The bombing of North Vietnam should be cut back to the area around the twentieth parallel. Additional troop deployments should be limited to 30,000 men, after which a firm ceiling should be imposed. While keeping military pressure on the enemy, the United States should more actively seek a political settlement. McNamara insisted that Vietnam must be considered in its larger Asian context. Pointing to the defeat of the communists in Indonesia and the current turmoil stemming from the Cultural Revolution in China, he advised Johnson that events in Asia were running in favor of the United States, thus reducing the importance of South Vietnam. He proposed a scaling down of objectives, indicating that the United States should not be obligated to guarantee an independent, noncommunist South Vietnam. He spoke of a compromise, even "involving, inter alia, a role in the South for members of the VC." He called for an NSAM "nailing down" the new policy and without naming names proposed "major personnel changes within the government."[106]

The Joint Chiefs responded immediately. Unaware that McNamara had shown the DPM to Johnson on May 19, they urged the secretary not to forward it to the president. Privately denouncing his proposals to cut back the bombing as an "aerial Dienbienphu," they advised him that such steps would only encourage Hanoi to resist. The American public would support the war, they said, if properly informed of the issues, while the "drastic changes" proposed in the DPM would "undermine and no longer provide a complete rationale for our presence in Vietnam or much of our efforts over the past two years."[107] A no longer optimistic Wheeler now warned Sharp in Honolulu to "batten down for rough weather ahead." A comprehensive review of strategy seemed in the offing, and the secretary of defense's views were "at considerable variance with our own thinking and proposals."[108]

The review never occurred. The intrusion of the Arab-Israeli crisis and the Six-Day War deflected attention at a crucial point from Southeast Asia to the Middle East, and the untimely death of McNaughton in a plane crash on July 19, 1967, removed one of those officials most committed to reevaluating policy. But the major obstruction continued to be the president himself. By this time, Johnson was also deeply troubled by the war. Lilienthal described him as an "agonized man"; former president Dwight D. Eisenhower called him a "man at war with himself." "We have got to get this thing [Vietnam] straightened out," he told Lilienthal on March 2. "It is ruining everything."[109] The president looked "stunned" at the Guam Conference in March when Westmoreland warned that the war might last ten years.[110] At a meeting with Wheeler and Westmoreland in April, he revealed his growing frustration. "When we add divisions can't the enemy add divisions," he pointedly asked. "If so, where does it all end?"[111]

Despite his frustration, Johnson was no more willing to confront the issues in the spring of 1967 than before. He continued to fear that adoption of the JCS program would provoke a larger war. On the other hand, like Rostow, he seems to have felt that McNamara's proposals went "a bit too far" to the other extreme. He was undoubtedly concerned at what Rostow, with some under-statement, described as "the dangerously strong feelings" within the admin-istration. He was therefore all the more fearful of a policy review involving numerous people and departments that might expose to public scrutiny the divisions in his government. He sought, like his national security adviser, a "scenario" that could "hold our official family together in ways that look after the nation's interest and make military sense."[112]

Characteristically, he avoided a direct and open confrontation between the views expressed by the Joint Chiefs and McNamara. He delayed a decision for weeks, and when he decided he did so on a piecemeal basis, carefully avoiding the larger issues. Thus, according to the authors of the *Pentagon Papers*, the spring and summer 1967 discussions of strategy "floundered toward a compromise on the issue of tactics, without any shift in war aims."[113] The president approved a modest expansion of the bombing but stopped well short of mining North Vietnamese ports. He refused to extend the ground war into Laos, Cambodia, and North Vietnam. He agreed to deploy only 55,000 ad-ditional ground troops, but he would not set a ceiling and he scrupulously avoided discussion of how and for what purpose the troops would be used.

The president's nondecisions provoked a near revolt within the military. Throughout the military establishment, there was growing frustration with the restrictions on the war, and relations with McNamara, strained since 1961, approached the breaking point. Anger with the secretary of defense carried over in some cases to the Joint Chiefs he had appointed. As early as 1966, Hanson Baldwin had detected among army officers growing criticism of the military leadership in Washington. By 1967, some dissidents within the mili-tary contemptuously referred to the Joint Chiefs as the "five silent men" and ridiculed their "Charlie McCarthy answers" to LBJ's questions.[114]

The closest thing to a real debate on strategy and to a MacArthurlike military challenge to civilian authority occurred almost inadvertently in the late summer of 1967. Since the beginning of the war, hawkish Mississippi senator John Stennis's Preparedness Subcommittee had kept up a drumfire of criticism of administration policy and especially of McNamara. The committee maintained close ties with the military and frequently voiced positions the JCS were not willing to state publicly. Alarmed by reports of McNamara's May recommendations, it announced in late June its intention to conduct hearings on the air war. Stennis's aim was to "get McNamara," administration officials speculated, and, more important, to pressure the White House to do what was necessary to win the war.[115]

Ironically, McNamara saw hearings designed to "get" him as a chance to combat pressures for expanding the war without violating his own rigid standards of loyalty to the president. By the late summer of 1967, the secretary was a man "visibly in torment."[116] Although keenly aware of the growing gap between his own views and those of the White House and increasingly fearful that further expansion of the war would result in a "national catastrophe," he retained a powerful sense of loyalty to the president. To convince the executive branch, the Congress, and the public that further escalation would be ruinous, he determined to analyze the air war publicly as he had not before. The Stennis hearings would give him a chance to build a foundation for partial or total cessation in the future and head off pressures for expansion while defending the president's basic policy.[117]

In a strange, almost surreal way, the Stennis committee hearings of August 1967 became the forum for a debate that could not take place within the inner councils of the executive branch. The military dominated the first phase of the hearings. They prepared their case with the utmost care, and for two weeks, top brass paraded before a sympathetic committee.[118] They insisted that the air war against North Vietnam was an indispensable element of the overall military effort, inflicting heavy damage on the enemy and significantly restricting its capacity to fight in the South. A partial or total bombing halt, they warned, would be a "disaster." The military muted their arguments considerably, refraining from openly advocating expansion of the air war. Still playing by the rules, Wheeler, especially, went out of his way to minimize civilian-military conflict over the air war, vigorously defending the decisions that had been made. But the military did make clear that the effectiveness of the bombing had been limited by the gradualism under which it had been conducted, "severe handicaps which were contrary to military principles." The slow pace of escalation had given the enemy time to adapt and adjust and develop a highly effective air defense system. Important targets remained unstruck.

McNamara spent all of August 25 before the committee, and according to friendly accounts gave a "masterful performance," perhaps the performance of his career. As usual, his testimony was "carefully prepared and exquisitely balanced." He bombarded the committee with statistics, hard facts, and logic and made and remade his essential points in numerous different ways. He seemed to concur with the JCS that the bombing campaign had been effective, and to a point he minimized the differences between himself and the military. Privately, he admitted to former Secretary of State Dean Acheson that he was not telling the whole story. Still, in a move that for him approached heresy, he tried to destroy the case for expanding the air war, thus highlighting the fundamental differences between himself and the JCS. He vigorously defended the restrictions that had been imposed on the bombing. Most important, he warned that no amount of bombing could totally interdict the flow of men and supplies to the south or break the will of the north. The air war against the north could not be a substitute for the ground war in the south. "You cannot win the war on the cheap by bombing," he affirmed. It was a do-or-die performance on McNamara's part with the president and the nation as much his intended audience as the committee.[119]

According to one account, McNamara's testimony provoked a near-revolt on the part of the Joint Chiefs. Wheeler appears to have felt that while he had played by the rules, McNamara had not, and, as journalist Mark Perry tells it, after the secretary's August 25 attack on the bombing, the chairman called a special emergency meeting of the chiefs at which it was decided to resign en masse. That decision allegedly was reversed the next morning after Wheeler had second thoughts. "It's mutiny," Perry quotes him telling his colleagues. "In any event," he is said to have added, "if we resign they'll just get someone else. And we'll be forgotten." Perry's story has sparked considerable controversy and has been emphatically denied by the two living members of Johnson's Joint Chiefs of Staff.[120]

Whatever the case, the Stennis hearings represented what Johnson had most feared since the start of the war, division within his own administration and the threat of a military revolt backed by hawks in Congress.[121] Remarkably, he was able to contain it. Publicly, he dealt with the problem by vehemently denying its existence. There were "no quarrels, no antagonisms within the administration," he said. "I have never known a period when I thought there was more harmony, more general agreement, and a more cooperative attitude." He went on to say that 300 of 350 significant targets had been hit and there had been full military and civilian agreement on them. He would concede only "some little difference of opinion" on some of the remaining targets.[122]

Administration officials followed to the letter the script written by their president. Years later, McNamara admitted that he "went through hell" on the Stennis hearings. Yet at a White House meeting, he praised his adversary General Wheeler for a "helluva good job" before the committee and observed that the small differences between himself and the JCS were "largely worked out."[123] Wheeler publicly dismissed rumors that the JCS had contemplated resignation with a terse "Bullshit!"[124]

Johnson "resolved" the strategic debate among his subordinates as he had resolved it before—without addressing the fundamental issues. He did not give the military the war it wanted or even adopt all of its proposals for the air war, and to that extent McNamara achieved his major goal. On the other hand, he categorically rejected McNamara's own position on the air war and during and after the Stennis hearings made major concessions to the military. On August 9, the day the hearings began, Johnson approved sixteen new targets and expanded armed reconnaisance. Six of the targets were in the Hanoi area, and they included bridges, rail yards, and power plants. On September 5, over the opposition of McNamara and Rusk, he approved military recommendations to hit the ports of Campha and Hongay.[125] Less than two weeks later, to appease the military and the right wing in Congress, he literally ordered a reluctant McNamara to initiate an antiballistic missile system.

In other ways, in the immediate aftermath of the Stennis hearings, the president tilted in the direction of the military. Recognizing that McNamara's dissent threatened his cherished consensus and was becoming a political liability, perhaps also to spare his loyal lieutenant further torment, Johnson began to make plans to relieve him. In October, for the first time, General Wheeler was formally brought into the Tuesday Lunch discussions as a regular member. In meetings with his military and civilian advisers, the president's tone was distinctively more hawkish. He invited the Joint Chiefs to "slip in the side door" if they had a complaint. "There is nobody that stands between you and me if the issue is serious enough to bring it up," he insisted. The *New York Times* exaggerated on September 1 when it warned that the generals were out of control, but for the moment at least they seemed to have the upper hand.[126]

V

The battle over strategy simmered on as inconclusively as the war for the remainder of the year. The focal point continued to be the struggle between McNamara and the Joint Chiefs over the air war. By late 1967, however, there were also growing pressures from inside the administration for changes in the ground strategy. As before, Johnson skillfully parried the conflicting pressures and clung stubbornly to his middle course, all the while publicly denying the divisions within his administration.

Frustrated by the lack of results, battered from left and right, and increasingly fearful of losing control, an agitated president at the September 12 Tuesday Lunch asked the acting chairman of the JCS to "search for imaginative ideas" to "bring this war to a conclusion." Making clear his dissatisfaction with the military advice he had received thus far, he affirmed that he did not want recommendations simply to add more men or to use nuclear weapons. He could "think of these ideas."[127]

Ignoring the president's call for new ideas, the JCS, in a way that had become almost ritualistic, responded in mid-October with the same recommendations they had offered repeatedly since July 1965. The rate of progress had been slow, they observed, because U.S. military power had been restricted in ways that crippled its effectiveness, and the war could not be won as long as these limits were in place. Conceding the risks of a major escalation, they continued to insist that the chances of Soviet or Chinese intervention were "remote." Asking McNamara to submit their memo to the president, they called for an expansion of the bombing, especially around Hanoi and Haiphong, for mining of the deep water ports and inland waterways, for naval operations against North Vietnam, for expanded operations in Laos and Cambodia, and for increased covert operations in North Vietnam. In the meantime, Wheeler and Air Force Chief of Staff John P. McConnell pressed for new Rolling Thunder targets.[128]

A now blatantly dissident McNamara counterattacked. At the Tuesday Lunch on October 31, he warned that stubborn persistence in the present course "would be dangerous, costly in lives, and unsatisfactory to the American people." The following day, he handed the president a long memorandum he had not cleared with Rostow, Rusk, or Wheeler. As so often in the past when he had the president's ear, he urged Johnson to authorize him to discuss the memo with other senior advisers and submit formal proposals. He warned again that continuation along the same lines would not end the war and added that a further erosion of public support would generate dangerous new pressures for withdrawal or drastic expansion of the conflict. Going beyond his proposals of May 19, he advocated an indefinite bombing halt and the stabilization of ground operations by publicly fixing a ceiling on force levels and by a searching review of ground operations with the object of reducing U.S. casualties and turning over more responsibility to the South Vietnamese.[129]

Johnson was deeply troubled by his advisers' proposals. He continued to fear the risks of an expanded war, and he remained wary of the JCS approach.

But he also doubted that McNamara's recommendations would bring the desired results. "How do we get this conclusion?" he scrawled on the memo where the secretary predicted that a bombing halt would lead to peace talks. "Why believe this?" he noted where McNamara had indicated a "strong possibility" that North Vietnam would stop military activities across the demilitarized zone after a bombing halt. [130]

Adamantly opposed to drastic changes in policy but increasingly concerned with the divisions in his administration, he sought validation for the course he was following. He recalled General Westmoreland and Ambassador Ellsworth Bunker to Washington for consultation. He submitted the McNamara memo to old friends and trusted advisers, people like Taylor, Fortas, and Clifford. By chance, the "Wise Men," a group of establishment figures occasionally called upon for advice, assembled in Washington the very day McNamara presented his "bombshell" memorandum, and he sought from them additional backing for his policies.

To some extent, the president got what he wanted. After lengthy briefings by Wheeler and CIA Vietnam expert George Carver, the Wise Men clearly favored the president's policies over the recommendations of the Joint Chiefs and McNamara. When Johnson asked if the United States should get out of Vietnam, the group's response, as summarized by McGeorge Bundy, was a "strong and unanimous negative." Even George Ball made only minor suggestions for tactical changes in policy such as restricting the bombing to the area around the demilitarized zone. Similarly, Clifford, Fortas, Rusk, Rostow, and Bundy rejected McNamara's major proposals. "This first meeting with the Wise Men strengthened President Johnson's resolve at a critical moment," Clifford later concluded. [131]

Ironically, however, while Johnson found the validation he sought, the discussion of the McNamara memorandum also initiated an unintended, impromptu, and informal policy review of the sort he had taken great pains to avoid, and it generated unexpected and unwanted pressure for a change in the ground strategy—and more.

While rejecting McNamara's more extreme proposals, numerous civilians from inside and outside the government joined the secretary of defense in urging Johnson to check the rising dissent at home by changing the ground strategy. Katzenbach, McGeorge Bundy, McNamara's top civilian advisers in the Pentagon, a group of establishment figures meeting under the auspices of the Carnegie Endowment, and the Wise Men all agreed that Westmoreland's search and destroy strategy should be scrapped. Warning, as the Wise Men put it, that "endless, inconclusive fighting" was the "most serious single cause of domestic disquiet," they proposed instead a "clear and hold" strategy that

would be less expensive in blood and treasure. Such a strategy they reasoned might stabilize the war "at a politically tolerable level" and save South
Vietnam "without surrender and without risking a wider war." They also
suggested an incipient form of what would later be called "Vietnamization,"
urging that a greater military burden be gradually shifted to the South
Vietnamese.[132]

Speechwriter Harry McPherson and presidential adviser McGeorge Bundy
went still further, getting closer to the heart of the flaws in Johnson's exercise
of presidential powers in time of war. McPherson chided his boss for expanding the bombing to head off military criticism. "You are the Commander in
Chief," he affirmed. "If you think a policy is wrong, you should not follow
it just to quiet the generals and admirals. Generals and admirals like to
bomb."[133]

Called back to the White House during the Six-Day War, Bundy continued
thereafter to offer informal advice, and in November 1967 he urged Johnson
to take control of the war. The president should arrange a "solid internal understanding" between Rusk, McNamara, and the Joint Chiefs on the bombing, a "basic command decision" to settle the issue once and for all. He should
initiate a careful review of the ground strategy at the "highest military and
civilian levels." Conceding that it was a "highly sensitive matter" to question
the commander in the field, Bundy went on to say that if the strategy was not
wise, "the plans of the field commander must be questioned." Now that the
principal battleground was domestic opinion, Bundy observed, the "commander-in-chief has both the right and duty . . . to visibly take command of a
contest that is more political in character than any in our history except the
Civil War (where Lincoln interfered *much* more than you have)." It was essential, the former national security adviser concluded, to end the confusion and
conflict in government and steady the home front.[134]

Johnson remained unmoved. He refused to make the hard decisions and to
take control of the war. Unwilling to admit that the policy he had pursued
was bankrupt, he continued to delude himself that he could find a solution
along the middle route. He continued to take recommendations from each side
without giving in to either. He rejected the JCS proposals, agreeing only to
follow through with bombing targets already approved and then stabilize the
air war at that level. He urged Westmoreland to use airpower to maximum
advantage against enemy forces in the south as a way of limiting the need to
strike the more politically sensitive north.[135] At the same time, he flatly rejected McNamara's most radical proposal, a bombing halt, and in dealing with
ground operations he would go no further than privately commit himself to
review the search and destroy strategy at some undetermined point in the

future.[136] Recognizing that McNamara's usefulness had ended and that, as Clifford has written, he would have to change his policy or his secretary of defense, perhaps fearing for the survival of his emotionally exhausted aide, he named McNamara to head the World Bank, a job he knew he wanted. The president handled the change with such consummate skill (deviously, according to critics, with great compassion, according to friends) that McNamara was still unsure years later whether or not he had been fired.[137]

McNamara's move to the World Bank naturally provoked a flurry of rumors in the press. There were reports of deep divisions within the Johnson administration—especially between McNamara and the Joint Chiefs of Staff. It was even rumored that the Chiefs had threatened to resign if McNamara remained in office or if the president endorsed his views on the air war.[138]

The reports of divisions were, of course, quite correct and even understated. Conflict on the war in Vietnam was deeply rooted in the larger civil-military strife of the 1960s. It was exacerbated by the military's ongoing conflict with McNamara, and it intensified as the war dragged on. Because of the way Johnson ran his administration and the system itself was structured, moreover, the conflict could not be addressed in any substantive way, much less resolved.

The resulting frustration took a heavy toll on those involved. McNamara left office a depleted and dispirited man. When the president praised him at his retirement ceremony as "just about the textbook example of the modern public servant," the normally composed secretary of defense wept uncontrollaby. With several minor exceptions he has refused to speak publicly about Vietnam to this day.[139] The Joint Chiefs of Staff departed the government exhausted and embittered. Admiral McDonald admitted to Hanson Baldwin that in his last months in office he found it hard to control himself. He later expressed shame for going along with policies he disapproved and wished he had simply walked out.[140] "I'm sick of it. . . . I have never been so goddamn frustrated by it all," General McConnell privately complained in 1967.[141] The normally calm Wheeler privately vented his rage in 1968 against those journalistic "bastards who seemed determined to prove that the military are irresponsible, bloodthirsty fools, whose only pastime is war."[142] Wheeler left the chairmanship of the JCS in 1969 an ill and broken man. He had gambled on a foot-in-the-door approach with Johnson and for a time thought it was working, only to find himself defeated "piecemeal" by a politically minded president. When Adm. Thomas Moorer came to replace him, a "very distraught" Wheeler, face in hands, warned his successor, "You'll never survive."[143]

Yet in their public demeanor, to the end the president's men loyally maintained the facade of unity. In their dealings with journalists, administration officials went to great lengths to minimize or obscure internal divisions.[144] In the immediate aftermath of the Stennis hearings, when divisions were at their height, General McConnell spoke publicly in terms completely in contrast to his private lament, dismissing as an "erroneous conception" the notion that there were "fundamental disagreements" between the president and the Joint Chiefs.[145] McNamara through his wife expressed to the Joint Chiefs great pride at the "amazing display of restraint and mutual respect" and the "dignity" with which they had worked together despite their differences.[146] When their terms expired, the individual members of the Joint Chiefs quietly left office, burying their frustrations and resentments.

And of course the White House, to the end of the Johnson presidency, continued to deny that significant differences had existed. No one wrote a better epitaph for a badly flawed command system than its architect, the man who had imposed his own brand of unity on a bitterly divided administration. At a time when the newspapers were full of reports of disagreements between the Joint Chiefs and McNamara, Lyndon Johnson proudly proclaimed to his National Security Council, "There have been no divisions in this government. We may have been wrong but we have not been divided."[147] It was a strange observation, reflecting a curiously distorted sense of priorities. And of course it was not true. The administration was both wrong *and* divided, and the fact that the divisions could not be worked out or even addressed may have contributed to the wrong policies, at huge cost to the men themselves—and especially to the nation.

The "Other War"

THREE   *Management of Pacification,*
1965–1967

As no other area of the war, "pacification" exposed the acute management problems that afflicted the American effort in Vietnam as a whole. From the outset, U.S. officials perceived the urgency of winning the support of the rural population of South Vietnam and mounted a variety of programs to that end. From the outset, the programs were plagued by vexing organizational problems. In a war fought in "cold blood" there seemed no reason to create special machinery, and the numerous U.S. agencies, in the parlance of the day, individually "did their thing." Through most of the period from 1965 to 1967, Americans working on pacification in Washington and Saigon were not under any effective form of centralized control, and there was a similar absence of coordination between American programs and those of the South Vietnamese. Perhaps more important, the very term "other war" that was applied to the pacification programs in 1965 and 1966 starkly reflected the lack of coordination between civilian programs and military operations, the absence of an overarching, integrated strategic plan, and the sense that there were two different wars, separate and unequal.

Eventually, in pacification, as in no other area, serious and partially successful measures were taken to resolve the management problems. In part, this resulted from Lyndon Johnson's special and highly personal commitment to the "other war." In part, it developed from a recognition by late 1966 that the magnitude and importance of the problem demanded exceptional measures and that progress in this crucial area would be impossible without better integration of the various programs and operations. Thus, after several false starts, the administration created in the spring of 1967 what has been hailed as a unique experiment in civil-military operations. The agency with the awkward name—Civil Operations, Revolutionary Development Support—and the simple acronym—CORDS—placed pacification under military command but provided for civilian influence at the highest levels. Through a single-manager organizational model, CORDS integrated U.S. pacification programs more effectively with each other, with South Vietnamese programs, and with military operations, and it remained in existence until the U.S. withdrawal in 1973. Its work had only begun at Tet, and scholars still debate whether it succeeded or failed. But it was far superior to anything that came before and in a managerial sense represents the one significant innovation of the Vietnam War.

I

The Vietnam War involved far more than air and ground operations against an elusive enemy. From the origins of the insurgency in the late 1950s, the National Liberation Front had launched a systematic, tightly integrated, and highly effective political-military campaign to undermine Government of Vietnam (GVN) institutions at the village level, mobilize the rural population of South Vietnam, and create an alternative governmental apparatus of its own. Thus from the outset, U.S. advisers and their South Vietnamese counterparts faced the daunting task of eliminating the enemy's presence in the villages, establishing or reestablishing a presence for the GVN, involving the people in the operation of local government, and creating institutions capable of providing basic services and amenities to meet their needs, and, in the popular phrase of the time, win their hearts and minds. These challenging and diverse tasks came under the general rubric of "pacification."

The United States was not without experience in this type of warfare. The army had pursued a strategy of annihilation against the Plains Indians after the Civil War, but at times its campaign had called for pacification measures, and some officers applied them effectively. In a turn-of-the-century war against local insurgents in the Philippines, the army showed considerable skill in pacification, improvising diverse strategies to combat the very different threats in the different regions of the islands and combining brute force with reforms and knowledge of local conditions to defeat the guerrillas. While the marines chased rebel leader Augusto Sandino in Nicaragua in the 1920s, army officers drew up electoral codes and supervised elections. After World War II, American advisers assisted in the suppression of uprisings in Greece and the Philippines.[1]

Such experience provided at best limited preparation for waging the "other war" in Vietnam. Fighting guerrillas comprised but a small and relatively insignificant part of the broader American military tradition, and in the twentieth century such operations were vastly overshadowed by the success of big-unit operations in World Wars I and II and Korea. John F. Kennedy's remarkable and quite unprecedented effort to redirect military *and* civilian thinking toward counterinsurgency enjoyed no more than limited results and met passive and active resistance on the part of the U.S. Army. America's success at warfare generally blinded it to the peculiar complexity of guerrilla warfare and to the differences among its types, especially, as Larry Cable has pointed out, between partisan and insurgent wars. America's general success also obscured the unique reasons for success in each individual case. Officials drew the wrong lessons if they drew any lessons at all, thus facing the "future with a confidence born of false promises." Civilians had only hazy and sometimes naive notions about guerrilla warfare and how to fight it. In the military and especially the army, doctrine developed more from capabilities than the reverse.[2]

In any event, by the time Johnson took the United States to war in 1965, the challenge in Vietnam in terms of magnitude and complexity was quite unlike anything the United States had faced before. The National Liberation Front insurgency within South Vietnam had developed to formidable proportions, the guerrillas controlling much of the territory and population of the country. By this time, moreover, the NLF was supported by North Vietnamese regular units that had infiltrated into South Vietnam. The South Vietnamese Army crumbled in the face of these external and internal pressures. And after the overthrow and assassination of Ngo Dinh Diem, the government for all practical purposes ceased to function. At the local level, the GVN simply did not exist. In Saigon, those who took power spent most of their energy trying to retain it, and governments changed so rapidly in 1964 and 1965 that it was nearly impossible to keep up with the changes on a day-to-day basis.

By July 1965, U.S. and South Vietnamese efforts at pacification had gone through a decade of trial and error with generally frustrating results. Under intense U.S. pressure, Diem had belatedly launched in 1958 the so-called Agroville Program and had followed it in the Kennedy era with the much-ballyhooed Strategic Hamlet Program. The former had been too small to have much effect and had been implemented in a manner that turned out to be counterproductive. The latter had a vast American commitment behind it but was at best a qualified failure. The Malayan model on which it was based was inapplicable to Vietnam. Diem and his sinister brother Ngo Dinh Nhu sought to use the program primarily to build their own power base, and in many areas their heavy-handed methods alienated rather than won over the peasantry. Diem and Nhu also exaggerated the gains that had been made under the program, and it was only after their assassination in November 1963 that Americans recognized how little had been accomplished.

After the overthrow of Diem, pacification went backwards. The National Liberation Front concentrated its forces against the highly vulnerable strategic hamlets and in a relatively short time undid most of the limited gains. In the year and a half after the coup, the Saigon government was too divided and embattled to pursue any program systematically and gave no more than lip service to pacification. The various U.S. agencies in Vietnam persisted, launching a variety of small-scale, village-level programs to promote security in the countryside, improve the standard of living of the villagers, and weaken NLF influence. As Douglas Blaufard has pointed out, however, these represented little more than a "scattered deployment of separate programs lacking an integrated strategy and low in priority."[3]

During the period of U.S. escalation, renewed attention was given pacification. In large measure to pacify the Americans, the South Vietnamese put together a Hop Tac (pacification or counterinsurgency) program focusing on the area around Saigon, but the plan was hastily concocted and achieved little. When the Saigon government finally gained a measure of stability under Nguyen Cao Ky and Nguyen Van Thieu after May 1965, it developed a more serious effort, the so-called Revolutionary Development Program, which sought to emulate NLF tactics by sending cadres into the villages to work with the people and build support for the government. Revolutionary Development benefited from the experience of earlier failures and provided a useful blueprint for future programs. But the absence of security in most villages made it difficult if not impossible to implement. It was not well integrated with other programs run by U.S. agencies. And at a time when U.S. attention was focused on military escalation—itself a substitute for the lack of effective action in the countryside—the program did not have a high enough priority to accomplish much.

II

Once the military buildup of 1965 had been completed, the United States gave pacification closer attention and began to experiment with organizational methods to manage it more effectively. American forces had blunted the North Vietnamese offensive by the end of the year and had established a measure of stability that had been lacking, providing an opportunity to develop programs that could not have been considered previously. The easing of the military crisis also brought home the realization of how little had been done. "I don't think we have done a thing we can point to that has been effective in five years," Secretary of Defense Robert S. McNamara complained to beleaguered officials in Saigon in November 1965. "I ask you to show me one area in this country . . . that we have pacified."⁴ A "tremendous US force on a bowl of jelly," was the way presidential adviser McGeorge Bundy described the pacification effort at about the same time.⁵

The return of Henry Cabot Lodge, Jr., as ambassador to South Vietnam gave a boost to pacification. During his first term in the embassy, Lodge had repeatedly labeled the war in the villages "the heart of the matter." On his arrival in August 1965, he committed the United States to the "true revolution" of the people of South Vietnam. He brought with him Edward Lansdale, the CIA operative who had masterminded the defeat of insurgency in the Philippines and Diem's early successes in Vietnam, and charged him "to get pacification going." The maverick who had accomplished miracles in 1955 quickly got bogged down in bureaucratic warfare and languished in the very different Saigon of 1965, but his mere appointment seemed to symbolize a growing American concern with the neglected but crucial war in the villages.⁶ Lodge opened the doors of the embassy to Americans and others who shared his vision of the war, and his cables repeatedly emphasized the importance of pacification.⁷

Lodge found a receptive audience in the White House. Lyndon Johnson was a reluctant warrior and Vietnam quickly became an affliction for him, but the one aspect of the war that excited him was the possibility of improving the lot of the South Vietnamese people. He was genuinely distressed by the short life expectancy of the villagers and by their desperate need for amenities of all sorts. He was deeply moved by the impact of the war on them. "Dammit," he exploded on one occasion, "we need to exhibit more compassion for these Vietnamese plain people." The possibility of helping these people touched his reformist instincts and helped him to rationalize a war he would have preferred not to fight. He could wax eloquent about the ways American technology and know-how might improve health care and education and enable the Vietnamese to raise larger hogs and more sweet potatoes. He dreamed aloud that every general could be a surgeon, every pilot a nurse, every helicopter an ambulance. "Exhaust every possibility, check out every idea, look at every possible move," he instructed an aide. "We've got to see that the South Vietnamese government wins the battle, not so much of arms, but of crops and heart and caring, so their people can have hope and belief in the word and deed of their government."⁸

The push from Lodge and the support of the president refocused attention on pacification in early 1966. AID director David Bell had gone to South Vietnam in late 1965 as LBJ's "eyes and ears" to review nonmilitary programs. He agreed with McNamara on the "melancholy fact" that "no significant progress has been made in pacification for the past several years despite a great deal of effort."[9] At a cabinet meeting on January 11, he labeled pacification the number one problem and called for a "new spirit" in addressing it.[10] Even as he spoke, senior U.S. officials from Washington and Saigon offices were meeting at Airlie House in Warrenton, Virginia, to review existing pacification programs and develop means to improve them.[11]

At the Honolulu Conference in February 1966, the president himself took the lead. The conference was hastily called and has often been dismissed as a public relations gimmick to divert attention from Senator J. William Fulbright's Foreign Relations Committee hearings on Vietnam. Whatever the purpose, the principal result was to give pacification a new priority. In the closed sessions, the president repeatedly pressed South Vietnamese and American officials to expedite and improve programs in such areas as health, education, and building democracy. He pronounced the Honolulu communiqué a "kind of bible" and demanded from Americans and South Vietnamese "not just high-sounding words" but results—"coonskins on the wall." "This week the word 'pacification' was on everyone's lips at the Honolulu Conference on Vietnam," Charles Mohr wrote in the *New York Times* on February 13, "and many important members of the Johnson administration embraced the idea with all the enthusiasm of a horse player with a new betting system."[12]

Most U.S. officials agreed that pacification needed better organization and management as urgently as it needed a higher priority. In Washington, no single person or office coordinated its work or acted as its spokesman in a fiercely competitive bureaucracy, and responsibility was diffused among numerous departments and agencies. A Vietnam Coordinating Committee had been established to oversee the proliferating U.S. programs, but it was staffed with lower-level officials and had little clout. Early in 1966, Maxwell Taylor secured from President Johnson NSAM 341, an ambitious attempt to streamline the administration of U.S. foreign policy in general. The scheme provided for a Senior Interdepartmental Group (SIG), headed by the undersecretary of state, to settle internal disputes and coordinate foreign policy initiatives, as well as regional groups to deal with specific areas and problems. The SIG was only put into operation about the time the pacification program began to attract attention, however, and, in any event, it quickly atrophied from lack of use.[13]

In Saigon, pacification was plagued by "staggering disorganization."[14] At the time of the Honolulu Conference, U.S. operations in Vietnam were being run by the Mission Council system established in the 1950s to oversee U.S. activities in other countries. Headed by the ambassador, the Mission Council brought together representatives of all agencies in weekly meetings with a prepared agenda and provision for follow-up. The system had worked adequately in South Vietnam under the firm hand of Taylor and when the U.S. effort was still relatively small. By the end of 1965, however, it had broken down completely. The huge proliferation of programs, personnel, and activities between 1963 and 1965 overloaded the circuits of a system created for normal peacetime conditions. Whatever his talents, Lodge was no manager, and, in the words of one of his colleagues, he "allowed almost total confusion to reign."[15] "Everyone is involved, and no one is in charge," Bell reported in early 1966.[16] In addition, there was so much turnover among top U.S. personnel, especially in AID, that the Vietnamese gossiped about the "coups" among the Americans.[17]

Each of the agencies operating in Vietnam ran separate programs at the village level. MACV had military-sponsored civil action programs that, among other things, provided medical aid, built schools, and drilled wells.[18] The CIA's Revolutionary Development Program also operated at the village level, furnishing medical services and building roads. The Joint U.S. Public Affairs Office (JUSPAO) combined the propaganda programs of the USIA and psychological warfare operations. AID exceeded all other agencies in the size and scope of its programs. Most of its resources went into the Commercial Import Program, which was designed to keep the South Vietnamese economy afloat and hold inflation in check, but it was also responsible for an array of nation-building projects, including agricultural development and refugee resettlement.

Lack of coordination existed at all levels. In the individual agencies themselves, the size of operations quickly exceeded the administrative capacity for handling them. In AID alone, a management survey team found in late 1965, objectives were "ill defined and subject to individual interpretations," and there was a singular lack of unity of purpose and central direction.[19] Each of the agencies had its own ideas on what needed to be done, its own personnel and administrative structure, its own field personnel operating separately in Saigon and in the provinces, and its own links to Washington, all of which it was prepared to defend to the death. When something went wrong, each agency was quick to blame the others. In theory, AID was responsible for coordinating the programs, but in fact no one did so, and each operated on its own in Saigon and in the provinces. In an ordinary morning, a confused and beleaguered Vietnamese province chief might have to deal with as many as five different U.S. officials from different agencies.[20]

There were even more serious problems coordinating American actions with those of the South Vietnamese. Overzealous U.S. officials created programs faster than the Vietnamese could absorb them. As early as 1964, Taylor counted sixty-eight separate programs the Vietnamese were supposed to be running. Chester Cooper compared the impact of the U.S. programs on the Vietnamese to that of a "fire hydrant attached to a garden hose." In a very real sense, pacification fell between two—or more—stools. It was everybody's business and nobody's.[21]

By the time of Honolulu, there was an acute awareness of the magnitude of the managerial problems and the urgent need for action. Westmoreland pressed for a "central coordinating mechanism" to pull together activities in Saigon. The Warrenton conferees reported the inadequacy of the machinery in Washington and Saigon to handle problems "quickly and decisively." Warning that mismanagement of U.S. programs in Vietnam was about to become a serious political problem, McGeorge Bundy advised Johnson in early February that the administration must "grab this issue before it grabs us."[22]

Despite the severity of the injury, the administration applied band-aids. Following recommendations offered by Westmoreland, Bell, and the Warrenton group, the president assigned to Lodge's deputy ambassador, William Porter, overall responsibility for coordinating civil operations in Vietnam. A senior Middle Eastern specialist with thirty years in the Foreign Service, Porter was experienced, competent, and a good manager, the sort of person who could be counted upon not to shake things up. His appointment was a relatively simple and unobtrusive step that did not threaten in any fundamental way the prerogatives of the individual agencies. Even then, it drew opposition from Lodge, who appears to have been offended by the implied affront to his managerial ability and was concerned about his deputy being given full responsibility for an important part of the war. The ambassador eventually and perhaps grudgingly acquiesced, but his persisting opposition sharply limited his deputy's role.[23]

In any event, Porter's authority was nominal. He remained Lodge's deputy ambassador, with many other duties to handle. With the assistance of a small staff, he was responsible for coordinating the civil side of pacification. His main role was to work out agreements among the various agencies whose methods of operation were not otherwise affected. Porter indeed made clear in his first statement to the Mission Council on February 28 that he did not intend to intrude in the work of the individual agencies and when he saw problems he would do no more than "call this to the attention of the agency for the purpose of emphasis."[24]

The president also dealt cautiously with the management problem in Washington. He rejected recommendations to appoint a "Mr. Vietnam" in the White House and confer on him broad authority to coordinate the many and varied military, economic, political, and diplomatic components of the war.[25] Instead, as in Saigon, he gave one man responsibility for coordinating what was coming to be called "the other war." He did put this person in a special office in the White House and authorized him through NSAM 343 to serve as a "focal point for the direction, co-ordination and supervision in Washington of U.S. non-military programs" and to see that "adequate plans" were prepared and "properly and effectively carried out."[26]

In appointing Robert Komer to this position, the president departed from the caution he had otherwise shown. A veteran of the Italian campaign of World War II, a Harvard MBA graduate, and a long-time CIA analyst who specialized in the Middle East, Komer had served on the NSC staff since 1961, where he was known for his boundless energy and brash self-confidence. Impatient, abrasive, and ruthless when necessary, he delighted in taking on the bureaucracy, and he could be so activist and so intrusive that a crisis between Egypt and North Yemen was labeled "Komer's War" by those officials subject to his pressure.[27] He was quickly named "Blowtorch" by Lodge for his volatile nature, and he delighted in the nickname, later explaining to a reporter that his job was "to hold a blowtorch to these agencies, to expedite. I figure out *how* to expedite as I go along."[28] He established himself as a "one-man, full-time, nonstop lobby for pacification" in Washington, and he prodded the Saigon bureaucracy relentlessly to get action.

Despite their limited roles as coordinators and expediters, Porter and Komer managed to edge pacification off dead center. In Saigon, with only limited authority, Porter brought at least a measure of coordination to CIA, AID, and JUSPAO programs and encouraged them to work together more effectively. He developed an effective public relations campaign that gave more attention to the "other war" and portrayed nonmilitary programs in a more positive light.

Not surprisingly, however, the real push came from Washington. More often than not, Johnson lost interest in programs once they were launched, but with pacification, after Honolulu, he continued to pay close attention and to prod his subordinates. He made clear to all concerned that Komer had direct access to him, and Komer took full advantage of the fact that, as he put it, "Washington does move when the President, the White House, speaks."[29] "The President wants action—not explanations—on the civil side," Komer warned Porter on May 11. "He has some idea, of course, of the bunch of mush we're trying to mold in the USG as well as the GVN. But he counts on thee and me to break the bottlenecks." Again on July 27, Komer admonished that "the President wants results" and to get them was relentlessly pushing his subordinates in Washington. Two months later, Komer explained to Porter that pressures from Washington were "not just because I enjoy prodding. It comes from the President himself, who is determined to see us step up 'the other war.'"[30]

Komer was a willing, indeed zealous, instrument of the president's wishes. He had no illusions about the enormity of the challenge of promoting "a socio-economic revolution in a non-country in wartime, working through a non-government which barely controls half the people and even less of the real estate." Characteristically, however, he maintained an "official posture" of "'can-do' optimism." He vowed to "give it the old college try," and he did so with customary energy.[31] He went to Vietnam seven times in the months he was in the White House. He bombarded Saigon with cables and messages and dispatched to Porter a series of "Literally Eyes Only" letters. When his prodding provoked anger from Saigon, he fell back on his boss. "It is the President himself who keeps bugging us about rice and pork prices," he assured Porter on August 10. Sensing at one point that officials in South Vietnam seemed to prefer that he expedite the approval of their requests in Washington and otherwise leave them alone, he responded quickly and firmly: "This is not the conception the President had in mind in setting up our operation, nor the way I intend to play the game."[32]

The "Blowtorch" produced some results. His relentless pressure helped to resolve immediate, urgent problems such as the spiraling inflation that accompanied the U.S. buildup and bottlenecks in the port of Saigon. He pushed for the revival of old programs that had languished, such as land reform, Revolutionary Development, and Chieu Hoi, a systematic effort to encourage NLF defections, and he urged the consideration of new ideas, even a food stamp program for employees of the South Vietnamese government. On one occasion he attacked the mushiness of an AID report that "came up with eight sickly and innocent wishes for the future, things with which no one is going to disagree but not specific targets to shoot at."[33] He prodded Porter to push the South Vietnamese and to use economic leverage if necessary to force them to act. He pressed the U.S. and South Vietnamese military to devote greater attention to pacification and to provide the security without which it could not succeed. Komer was the first senior U.S. official to put pacification at the top of the civil-military effort, and with Johnson's full support he was able to sustain the priority it had been given at Honolulu.

III

The Komer/Porter "solution" turned out to be a short-term expedient. Subtle changes in North Vietnamese strategy and growing skepticism among some U.S. officials about Westmoreland's search and destroy operations combined to draw more attention to pacification. The limited progress that was made in the summer of 1966 merely highlighted the enormity of the problems and the continuing deficiency of the means available to address them. Thus scarcely six months after the appointment of Komer and Porter, the United States sought to tighten the organization of pacification, veering sharply in the direction of military control.

Although his public statements tended to be optimistic, Komer privately conceded that the "civil side" was a "mess," even "farcical" compared to military operations.[34] Consolidation of old programs and launching of new ones was set back for weeks by the chaos in South Vietnam resulting from the Buddhist crisis of early 1966.[35] The erosion of GVN influence had been slowed a bit, but its control was not extended into new areas. Land reform, rice production, tax collection, and Chieu Hoi all lagged. Even after the end of the Buddhist crisis, the United States found it difficult to galvanize the South Vietnamese government and army into action.[36]

Admitting that the problems were difficult if not intractable, Komer and others still perceived that the administrative machinery was inadequate to the task. Even under Komer's firm hand, the Washington side of pacification was "mired in confusion" and bogged down in "wasteful duplication of effort."[37] Lodge remained indifferent to management problems and did not fully back Porter. Without the ambassador's support, Porter did not have the power to do what was asked of him, and the various agencies operating in Vietnam were reluctant to submit to the authority of the deputy ambassador, a mere Foreign Service officer.

The importance of pacification and the problems in its management were underscored in a number of reports submitted in the summer of 1966. An army study group appointed by Chief of Staff Harold K. Johnson and composed of field officers who had served in Vietnam submitted in March 1966 a "Program for the Pacification and Long-Term Development of South Vietnam" (PROVN). Implicitly critical of Westmoreland's approach to the war, the PROVN report proposed that the focus of the U.S. effort be shifted from anti–main force operations to territorial security and economic and political reform.[38] Highly critical of the management of U.S. operations in Vietnam, the PROVN officers also proposed that the ambassador be delegated "unequivocal authority as the sole manager of all U.S. activities, resources, and personnel in-country" and be directed to "develop a single integrated plan for achieving U.S. objectives."[39] A Priorities Task Force appointed by Porter in the spring of 1966 was far more cautious, but it also emphasized the "absence of agreed, definitely stated pacification roles and missions not only within the GVN and the U.S. Mission but also between the GVN and the U.S. Mission" and the "proliferation of various armed and unarmed elements not clearly related to each other."[40]

By the late summer of 1966, pacification had acquired an even higher priority. Komer and the president continued to push it relentlessly. More important, as North Vietnamese and NLF main forces increasingly avoided contact with American units, the military began to redirect its attention to the countryside, conceding to pacification a more important place in its overall plans. As the result of a major policy decision, the Army of the Republic of Vietnam (ARVN) was given direct responsibility for the support of pacification, and Westmoreland's annual campaign plan, submitted in August 1966, even indicated that some U.S. forces might be shifted to population security. Lodge overstated in exulting that pacification had attained its highest priority and was "in effect, the main purpose of all our activities," but its importance had increased beyond that of Honolulu.[41]

At the same time, there was growing recognition, anticipated in the PROVN report, that stronger direction was needed if pacification was to achieve the results its new priority demanded. Robert Nathan undertook yet another presidential mission to Saigon in the early fall of 1966 and reported the familiar refrain that "we are not organized, not mobilized, not staffed in Vietnam to do the job that must be done! We are functioning across the board on an ad hoc basis." Pacification programs were hampered by lack of planning and by competition for scarce supplies. No one seemed capable of setting sound priorities. Porter had too much to do and not enough staff to help him, and civilians from Lodge down seemed unwilling or unable to stand up to the military. According to Nathan, the United States desperately needed a "hardnosed, capably run system of planning and programming which can look ahead intelligently and produce a wherewithal for hard decisions in our joint total effort."[42]

In a long and thoughtful paper submitted at about the same time, Komer agreed that further strengthening of the management structure was essential and proposed three alternatives for doing so. Separate civilian and military organizations might be retained, but the capacity of the Mission Council and

MACV to manage each must be improved. Porter could be assigned operational control over all pacification activity. Or "the other war" could be placed under military control. Komer did not explicitly recommend any of the three, but he emphasized the necessity of a single-manager system and he highlighted the advantages of military control. He was increasingly persuaded that the only way to succeed in pacification was to flood the countryside with people and resources, and since the military had access to the requisite numbers of people and resources military control was the only workable answer. Komer was also convinced that the military alone had the capacity to manage the sprawling programs operating throughout South Vietnam under the chaotic conditions of war, and since military advisers outnumbered civilian by 8 to 1, it would be easier for the military to take over responsibility.[43]

McNamara was persuaded by Komer's arguments and took an even more forthright position in favor of military control. The secretary of defense frankly conceded to Westmoreland that State Department officials did not have the "executive and managerial abilities to handle a program of such magnitude and complexity."[44] In a draft presidential memorandum of mid-September, he stressed that pacification was essential to long-term success and that progress thus far had been "negligible." A major reason for the lack of progress, he argued, was the "split responsibility" between civilians and the military. What was desperately needed was a "reorganization of the military and civil resources in South Vietnam to produce concrete working plans, region by region." The principal requirement was for "clear-cut chains of command and assignments of responsibility on our side and the Vietnamese side." To accomplish all these things, McNamara proposed putting pacification under the direct command of MACV.[45]

McNamara's proposal set off a heated, month-long debate within the U.S. government. Komer and the Joint Chiefs of Staff firmly supported the secretary of defense and agreed that the need for change was urgent. Among the civilian agencies, in general, there was strong opposition. The CIA and USIA firmly resisted the proposed reorganization. AID agreed that the existing structure was not working but opposed a military solution, proposing instead a complicated system of committees. The State Department questioned whether the military had the know-how to do the job and proposed giving Porter more authority. Porter opposed military control with particular vigor, arguing that "militarization of our approach to this important civilian program runs counter to our aim of de-militarizing GVN through constitutional electoral process." The military already had enough to do, he added, and could not easily take on more responsibility. Military officers lacked the political understanding to handle pacification, and there was so much turnover among

them that it would be impossible to establish solid rapport with the Vietnamese. He also predicted that if the military were put in charge of pacification
there would be a "wholesale departure" of skilled and experienced civilians
from Vietnam.[46]

Eventually, a compromise was arranged. In mid-October, McNamara and
Undersecretary of State Katzenbach journeyed to Vietnam, and after discussing the dilemmas of pacification with civilian and military officials, proposed
alternatives to outright military control. To highlight the importance of the
military's role, a high-ranking army officer should be appointed Porter's
deputy. But Katzenbach agreed with Porter that civilian control was crucial
to the international image of the United States and civilian direction was
needed to ensure that military programs would "support rather than negate
efforts to win public support and participation." "In particular," he added, "it
is important not to block or reverse—by the way *we* organize our efforts—the
currently genuinely hopeful Vietnamese trend toward increased civilian influence and participation in government." He proposed therefore to increase
Porter's power by assigning him overall supervision of all pacification activities. Civilian lines of command within the agencies would be consolidated into
one. Civilian personnel would remain under the administrative control of their
agencies but would be placed under the operational control of Porter.

McNamara's report was notably gloomy and forms an important milepost
in his gradual disenchantment with the war. Conceding that the military situation had improved over the past year, he saw little hope for a dramatic change
in favor of the United States and "no reasonable way to bring the war to an
end soon." He thus advocated a shift in strategy that would make clear to
Hanoi that the United States was in the war for the long haul, thereby dis-
couraging its strategy of protracted conflict. His proposals included, among
other things, stabilizing U.S. force levels at around 470,000 men, holding the
bombing at its present level, building an electronic anti-infiltration barrier
near the DMZ, and launching new negotiating initiatives.

Pacification formed an important part of the McNamara strategy. Progress
in this crucial area, more than anything else, he argued, would persuade the
enemy to negotiate or withdraw. Yet in fact pacification was a "basic disappointment" and had "if anything, gone backward." The reasons were numerous: the pervasive absence of security in the countryside and a lack of commitment and competence on the part of the Vietnamese. In addition, he cited
the problem of "bad management" on both the American and Vietnamese
side. "Here split responsibility—or 'no responsibility'—has resulted in too
little hard pressure on the GVN to do its job and no really solid or realistic
planning with respect to the whole effort."

Calling for a "vigorous pacification program," McNamara insisted that "we must deal with this management problem now and deal with it effectively." Backing away from the position he had taken just a month earlier, he sided with Katzenbach, calling for an increase in Porter's power and the consolidation of U.S. civilian agencies under him. The addition of a top military officer would help to delineate responsibility between civilians and military. The first task of the new organization would be to produce within two months a "realistic and detailed plan for the coming year." McNamara's endorsement of continued civilian control was qualified, however. Conceding that the compromise was preferable from a political and public relations standpoint, he went on to insist that "we cannot tolerate continued failure." If, after a "fair trial," the plan did not work, it would be necessary to put pacification under Westmoreland.[47]

The president accepted the compromise proposal—with McNamara's qualification. At the Tuesday Lunch on October 15, he concurred with his secretary of defense that pacification was critical to U.S. success in South Vietnam and expressed his own dissatisfaction with the lack of progress. He deferred to civilian objections to placing the program under military control, but he made clear that he wanted action "soonest," and "soonest" was defined as a period of ninety days. The implication, Wheeler informed Westmoreland, was that at the end of that time if progress in pacification remained "unsatisfactory," he would transfer control to the military. Johnson shrewdly used the compromise to defuse civilian opposition to military control. He gave the civilians a chance—but not much of a chance—to get their house in order, with the clear understanding that military control would follow continued failure.[48]

The administration vigorously followed up the compromise decision. At a conference with allied leaders in Manila October 23–25, 1966, U.S. officials pressed the South Vietnamese, in Komer's words, to "get ARVN off its duff" and make a greater commitment to pacification.[49] Even earlier, the president had instructed Lodge to implement the proposed organizational changes, adding that careful "definition and delineation of responsibilities of the U.S. civilian and U.S. military sides" would be necessary "to ensure that nothing falls between the two stools and that the two efforts fully mesh." He also made clear that he was still inclined to put pacification under the military and that the compromise was on "trial" for 90 to 120 days, after which he would reconsider whether to assign all responsibility to MACV.[50]

Lodge protested. He agreed that civilian control should be retained, Porter's authority increased, and the civilian lines of command consolidated, but he raised strong objections to a possible transfer to military control, which, he said, would not solve old problems and would create new ones. He complained that the trial period was too short. Most of all, he objected that security, not defective organization, was the crux of the problem, and he called for the commitment of more U.S. troops to the support of pacification. "Clearly," he concluded, "there is very little that can be done economically, socially, psychologically, and politically for the 'hearts and minds' of men, if these men have knives sticking into their collective bellies. The knife must first be removed. It is not the case—as has so often been said—of which came first, the hen or the egg."

Nevertheless, the ambassador had no choice but to comply. After stalling for nearly a month, he announced in late November formation of the Office of Civil Operations, the second stage in the evolution of organizational machinery for pacification. OCO generally followed the outline proposed earlier by Katzenbach and McNamara. Westmoreland appointed a brigadier general to be his special assistant for pacification and to provide liaison between MACV and OCO. The field offices of the civilian agencies were removed from control of the agencies and transfered to OCO, whose head reported to Porter. Pay and other support for personnel continued to come from the individual agencies, but operations were to be executed under the direction of the new office. In addition, the civilian personnel and the activities of each agency in each province were unified under the direction of a single official who became the counterpart of the MACV province adviser and the Vietnamese province chief. A similar arrangement was set up for the four regional commands.[51]

OCO worked frantically to get organized. L. Wade Lathram, deputy director of USIA, was named director of civil operations, with responsibility for running the OCO staff under Porter's supervision. Regional directors were appointed to supervise the work of all American civilians in their respective regions. The appointment of the legendary and controversial John Paul Vann as regional director in III Corps seemed to symbolize the seriousness of the new organization's commitment to pacification. In Saigon itself, OCO officials had to relocate from their respective agencies into a central office, an important but very time-consuming step that temporarily brought work to a standstill.

Organizationally, at least, OCO registered important accomplishments during its brief existence. It established on the civilian side for the first time unified interagency direction with a chain of command and communication from Saigon to the regions and provinces. It centralized control of civil matters at each level in the hands of one official. The fact of physical relocation instilled a unity of purpose that had been missing before. Officials from different agencies working on similar problems were brought together and began working closely together. The physical, intellectual, and bureaucratic compart-mentalization that had characterized earlier efforts broke down at least a bit. Similarly, in the provinces, civilians spoke with a single voice and operated in unison. The establishment of OCO forced provincial officials to collaborate and consult with each other. Bringing together personnel from AID, CIA, and JUSPAO into a single section for planning also resulted in the first inte-grated plans for pacification on the American side. These plans required con-tributions from the military and therefore forced military officials for the first time to engage in intensive long-range planning.

Despite its accomplishments, OCO was doomed to failure. Porter had been given enormous responsibility, but he did not have commensurate power. He and Lodge had rebuffed Washington's recommendation to free him of other responsibilities by appointing another deputy ambassador to handle other em-bassy business. During much of the time OCO was getting organized, more-over, Lodge was away, leaving Porter as acting ambassador preoccupied with many matters other than pacification. Porter thus left the day-to-day decisions to Lathram, a cautious and methodical bureaucrat who lacked real power and was reluctant to impose coordination on the agencies from the top.

There were numerous other problems. Its first months were consumed simply getting organized, and OCO could do little in the way of developing and implementing programs. In addition, its limited efforts to coordinate ci-vilian operations provoked hostile reactions from the agencies involved. In Saigon, the directors of the agencies insisted that they must be involved in any decisions affecting the operations of their agencies, and there were cases where CIA and JUSPAO officers in the field refused to accept direction from OCO personnel. The CIA even initiated actions without direction from OCO. In Washington, the agencies were openly and justifiably skeptical of OCO from the outset and continued to deal directly with their own people in the field. OCO amounted to little more than a traditional country team, William Colby later recalled, providing "relatively passive" coordination of the work of civilian agencies and "no central strategic thrust."[52]

Conflict between civilians and the military continued unabated. In late De-cember, Westmoreland complained that civilians in Saigon, especially State Department officials, were blaming MACV for the "ills" of pacification, ar-guing that the basic mistake had been developing ARVN as a conventional force rather than preparing it for counterinsurgency.[53] Following the CEDAR FALLS search and destroy operation in early 1967, Gen. William Depuy blamed civilian officials for the disgraceful conditions in the refugee camps at Ben Suc, and the civilians angrily retorted that they were doing the best they could under impossible circumstances.[54]

OCO's existence was thus short-lived. Operating under an impossible deadline that virtually ensured its failure, it barely organized itself, much less got a handle on the seemingly insoluble problems of pacification. Almost as soon as it got started, it gave way to another and much more drastic organizational change.

IV

Sometime early in 1967, Johnson decided to do what he had probably intended to do from the outset, turn pacification over to the military. In doing so, he moved sharply beyond the OCO concept, placing pacification under Westmoreland's command and establishing in CORDS a unique experiment in civil-military cooperation in wartime.

It is not clear exactly when or why the president decided to act. It seems probable that the creation of OCO was simply a ploy to blunt criticism from those who feared giving too much authority to the military. Thus Johnson conceived a two-stage shift, giving the civilians a chance, but doing so with the near certainty that time and other constraints would make it unlikely that they succeed. He "stacked the deck," as Komer later put it.[55] As early as mid-February 1967, top U.S. officials were discussing the form that military control of pacification would take. LBJ appears to have made the decision by the Guam conference in March 1967, although it would not be formalized for another two months.

The administration acted with the realization that pacification was stalled and urgent action was required. In some quarters, indeed, there was a sense of impending disaster. OCO regional director Vann complained in early 1967 that the performance of South Vietnamese forces had deteriorated to such extent that "pacification in the real sense is doomed to failure."[56] A select group of officials experienced in pacification met in late March and agreed that success in the field was less even than official reports indicated.[57] U.S. officials continued to blame organizational weaknesses for the failure. The March conferees singled out for special criticism the persistent lack of overall direction to the U.S. effort. Lansdale warned that the organization of the South Vietnamese government and the U.S. mission did not provide the firm control needed to implement a sophisticated pacification strategy and singled out improvement as an "essential ingredient for success."[58]

In May 1967, Johnson instituted through new Ambassador Ellsworth Bunker what he described as an "unprecedented melding of civil and military responsibility to meet the overriding requirements of Viet Nam."[59] Devised by Komer and sold to the president and Westmoreland, the scheme was based on the rationale that since the civil and military dimensions of pacification were inextricably interrelated they must be coordinated. In particular, military security was the indispensable ingredient in the effective functioning of civilian programs, and since security was the responsibility of the military its efforts must be coordinated with civil operations.

The new arrangement combined civilian and military organizations dealing with pacification and established for them a single chain of command. In Saigon, OCO was integrated intact into MACV and combined with those sections of MACV responsible for pacification into an organization called Civil Operations and Revolutionary Development Support (CORDS). There was discussion of Westmoreland being named ambassador as well as commander of U.S. forces and possibly resigning from the military or heading a "MacArthur-type" operation.[60] As it turned out, he retained his existing position and was given overall command of CORDS and supported with a staff directorate. The directorate in turn reported to Westmoreland's deputy, a civilian assigned to supervise pacification and given the rank of ambassador with the "assimilated military rank of a four-star general."[61]

Unity of command was extended out from Saigon. At each level, personnel were detached from their agencies or services to work for CORDS, and at its peak strength, the organization had some 5,500 officials under its control. In each of the four regions, a civilian deputy was appointed to serve with the Field Force Headquarters and was given a mixed civilian-military pacification staff. In the 44 provinces and 234 districts, civilian and military operations were integrated and placed under a single individual, who might be civilian or military depending on local circumstances and needs and the qualifications and experience of the individuals. To ensure balance, a civilian chief would have a military deputy and vice versa. At the district level, possibly 20 percent of the senior advisers were civilians, but most district teams had at least one civilian in a major job.

What Komer called "a unique hybrid civil-military structure" had numerous advantages. It imposed the single-manager concept on the diffuse U.S. pacification support programs and "provided a single channel of advice at each level to Vietnamese counterparts." It pulled together all U.S. support for a great range of pacification programs: Revolutionary Development cadre, refugee resettlement, Chieu Hoi, police, local government, and rural economic and education programs. It created an institutional vested interest in pacification that could bid for personnel, materiel, and funds, a single organization to blame or credit. Integration of effort and streamlining of command and communications at the local level permitted U.S. officials to better deal with their Vietnamese counterparts in addressing local problems and strengthening local administration.[62]

Given the unprecedented nature of the operation, the transition was handled with remarkable smoothness, in part as the result of a strange but happy blend of personalities. Westmoreland cooperated splendidly, accepting with grace the odd concept of placing civilians under his command, supporting Komer in his dealings with MACV's military staff, and encouraging military cooperation with the civilians.

Lodge's replacement as ambassador, Ellsworth Bunker, provided, in William Colby's words, the "aura of authority" that held the new arrangement together. Seventy-two years young, a "tall, flinty Vermont patrician," Bunker had two decades of experience as a manager and diplomatic trouble-shooter. Most recently, in the Dominican Republic, he had worked twenty hours a day "without losing his starch," holding the fledgling Dominican government together "with his bare hands." He presided over the massive operation in Vietnam with firmness and equanimity, bringing far more unity to American activities than any of his predecessors.[63]

The appointment of Komer as the top civilian was as logical as it was inevitable. Neil Sheehan has labeled the CORDS administrator the "first civilian general," and indeed he comported himself as such. He was determined not to be submerged in the vast U.S. military machine in Saigon. He once half-jokingly referred to himself in military presence as "the high panjandrum of pacification," but he held out for military protocol, insisting to the startled MACV generals on the equivalent of four-star rank and on having four stars on his limousine, one of three black Chrysler Imperials in Saigon.[64] The appointment of this "self-described 'gadfly on the steed of state' " evoked cries of dismay from the Saigon bureaucracy. Other critics labeled Komer "Guildenstein at the court of Lyndon I," complaining that he had made a career of telling the president what he wanted to hear.[65] Still, the concept of CORDS was his. He was well equipped to put it into effect, and his drive, leadership, and close ties to Johnson were major factors in "launching CORDS with relative smoothness and speed."[66]

To a remarkable extent, the new team was able to overcome the suspicions that accompanied the formation of CORDS. Some military officials had strongly objected to having responsibility for pacification imposed on them, but Westmoreland's firm support helped to bring them around, and in time some officers concluded that support of CORDS might help deflect growing criticism of the army's search and destroy operations. Placing a civilian in charge of CORDS helped to calm civilian fears of being submerged in a huge

U.S. military machine, and Bunker went to great lengths to assure his civilian colleagues that they would not be buried in the reorganization.[67] The fact that OCO was already in operation and was integrated into MACV intact made the transition much less difficult than it might have been otherwise. In addition, the unity established through the creation of OCO placed the civilians in a better position to deal with the military on more equal terms, and in time, paradoxically, putting pacification under the military resulted in greater civilian influence and gave pacification a greater claim on resources.

The creation of CORDS thus represented a giant step forward. It brought together a disparate group of programs into a unified structure comprised of more than 6,500 civilian and military personnel, with a budget of about $500 million in U.S. funds and much more in U.S.-owned piasters and revenues appropriated by the South Vietnamese government. The organization extended from Saigon through the 4 regions and the 44 provinces to the 250 districts, where unified teams worked to carry out integrated programs and plans. "A single official presided over this entire advisory structure, supported by an adequate staff to give him control of his operations, to enable him to plan in detail and over a longer term than heretofore, and to support his field activities."[68] There was no real precedent for what one U.S. official called "this genuine innovation in government," an interweaving "of civilians and military in a single chain of command in an active theater of hostilities."[69] After months of trial and error, the United States finally had a workable organization in place.

CORDS faced a daunting challenge. At the time of its creation, pacification still languished. Conceding impressive results only in a handful of scattered hamlets, Leonhart warned the president on June 3 that status reports on pacification for the first quarter of 1967 made "unsatisfactory reading." The program in I Corps had been "hit hard"; those in III and IV Corps were "stalemated." Leonhart and Harry McPherson, who visited Vietnam for Johnson in June, agreed on the major problems: the persisting absence of security; lack of coordination between American and South Vietnamese military operations and civilian programs; lack of commitment and competence on the part of the South Vietnamese government and army. "This is nation building under the most difficult circumstances," McNamara told the cabinet on July 19.[70]

Komer eagerly took up the challenge. Soon after taking office he developed an ambitious eight-point program—Operation TAKEOFF—to give pacification "a new thrust during the last half of 1967 and sustain its momentum on into 1968."[71] Bunker called it the "most complete and comprehensive study" of rural development yet done. Komer was careful to focus on the most important and pressing programs so as not to dilute efforts or overtax the resources of South Vietnam.[72] Project TAKEOFF became the basis for a rein-vigorated pacification effort "on a greater scale than any other similiar program attempted by any government anywhere in the world."[73]

Much of Project TAKEOFF involved the expansion or acceleration of long-standing programs. Responding to pressures directly from the president, CORDS set out to double the rate of Chieu Hoi defections from the NLF to the Government of Vietnam, to double the number of Revolutionary Development teams operating in the hamlets, to provide for more and better handling of the ever increasing numbers of refugees, and to expand and accelerate land reform.[74]

Long persuaded that the major obstacle to pacification was the lack of security in the rural areas, Komer launched special programs to protect the villages. Under MACV, the Rural and Popular Forces, a sort of local militia, had been neglected. Perceiving the potential value of these forces in pacification, Komer secured a major policy decision, gaining for CORDS responsibility for their support and training. He used that authority to upgrade them through improved organization, training, and equipment, and he secured for them M-16 rifles and M-79 grenade launchers. He also created a People's Self-Defense Force some four million strong that was only partially armed but mobilized large numbers of civilians to help protect communities at night.[75] The CORDS arrangement was very useful in making these changes. Without CORDS in place, MACV would have been reluctant to turn over to civilians control of the local security program. Komer also secured Westmoreland's assent to remove MACV advisory teams from regular ARVN command channels, putting both chains of command in tandem.

The main problem in pacification continued to be working with the South Vietnamese, and here too the CORDS machinery worked far better than its predecessors. In launching Project TAKEOFF, Komer acknowledged that success in pacification ultimately depended on the Vietnamese. He also conceded that at present there was "no central GVN direction." Rather, there was a "vast melange of relatively low-grade GVN assets, reporting to all sorts of different Saigon ministries, largely independent of each other, with no sense of common purpose." He sought to combat this problem by improved management on the U.S. side and with intensive and systematic efforts to get the Saigon government to improve its own management techniques and to "jack up" local officials to implement U.S. programs. CORDS also established as a rule of policy that whatever leverage available should be used whenever possible, and to a much greater degree than before U.S. officials applied pressure at all levels to get action from GVN officials.[76]

We "are urging, encouraging, pushing, persuading, and suggesting to the

Government of Vietnam areas in which its performance should be improved," Bunker informed the president, and U.S. prodding secured some results. Previous planning had been at best sporadic, but in the fall of 1967, Komer worked out with GVN officials a Revolutionary Development program for 1968 calling for a major increase in the number of RD teams. He also secured from the Saigon government a commitment to increase the number of pacified hamlets to two thousand and the Revolutionary Development budget from three to five billion piasters. In what Bunker labeled a "minor breakthrough," the United States persuaded the South Vietnamese to develop a program for a systematic attack on the Vietcong infrastructure, what would later be called the Phoenix Program. Bunker thus concluded at the end of 1967 that one of the major payoffs of the establishment of CORDS was to produce increased Government of Vietnam attention to and planning for pacification.[77]

At the local levels, U.S. officials under CORDS also got tougher with their Vietnamese counterparts. Incompetent province chiefs were removed in Go Cong and Kien Giang provinces. CORDS officials systematically compiled dossiers on inept and corrupt province and district chiefs and pressed the Government of Vietnam, sometimes successfully, to remove them. At times, the threat or actual withdrawal of aid was employed to force change. The use of such leverage did not always work, Komer later conceded, but with the unified system provided by CORDS the "batting average" was "respectable."[78]

By January 1968, U.S. officials were generally pleased with the *organizational* progress in pacification. Westmoreland, Bunker, and Komer had established an effective working relationship, which in turn had vastly improved planning for pacification and had facilitated working with the Vietnamese. Even in Washington, the individual departments and agencies were much more sharply focused on pacification than before, and each had established special groups to promote planning and monitor progress.[79] Comprehensive plans for 1968 had been approved, an accomplishment in itself, and increased resources had been committed. "Single management has paid off," Bunker exulted on December 13, 1967, and the CORDS reorganization had been "even more successful than expected."[80]

Progress in organization and planning was not matched by progress in actual performance. Year-end surveys comprised the "usual combination of good news and bad news," in Bunker's words. Enthusiasts for the U.S. effort could hail the appearance of concrete sidewalks and community television sets, as well as schoolhouses and dispensaries in the Mekong Delta.[81] But top officials admitted to no more than a "modest" increase in the number of secure hamlets, and in some areas, notably embattled I Corps, veteran observers claimed that the situation had "never been worse."[82] The Chieu Hoi rate lagged, and such was the slow rate of progress generally that the priority areas of Project TAKEOFF were scaled back from eight to five. Even the ebullient, eternally optimistic Komer would concede no more than that "we're up from the crawl to a walk; next year perhaps a trot."[83]

More important, perhaps, as the United States got its act together, there was an increasingly painful recognition that success in pacification ultimately depended on the South Vietnamese, and in this area, especially, performance continued to leave much to be desired. The chronic problem of leadership—what Bunker labeled a "thin crust of managerial talent"—could not be easily solved.[84] And relations with the United States became increasingly difficult. The more leverage the United States sought to apply, the more it provoked criticism from Vietnamese officials and from the Vietnamese press. There was also a growing and increasingly painful recognition among U.S. officials by late 1967 of the impact of the pervasive Americanization of the war. There were too many Americans in Vietnam doing too much. The veritable bonanza of money and supplies produced war profiteering at American expense. There were so many Americans indeed that the administration of the U.S. organization consumed much of the effort. "AID is taking in its own laundry without much time for anything besides running the organization we have created," Bunker conceded.[85]

The achievements of CORDS in pacification for the rest of the war remain highly controversial. Some authorities contend that after a slow start it worked splendidly, bringing greater security to the countryside than at any point in U.S. involvement. Indeed, it has been suggested, the war might have been won if this sort of approach had been adopted earlier and had produced results before war weariness at home undercut the U.S. commitment to South Vietnam. CORDS was a "winning combination that came too late," according to William Colby, who succeeded Komer as its director.[86] Conceding that CORDS worked administratively, journalist Neil Sheehan argues that in the larger scheme of things it failed to achieve anything that mattered. "The unique civil-military pacification" organization Komer had created "was operating briskly in a void."[87]

It is very difficult to come up with satisfactory answers to these questions. Most authorities agree that from a managerial standpoint CORDS worked well. Indeed, under the firm guidance of Westmoreland, Bunker, and Komer programs ran so smoothly that Johnson never intervened again. Komer's "blowtorch" Washington office, filled by William Leonhart after his departure for Saigon, was abolished in late 1967. It also seems clear that however unreliable the measurements of success, post-1967 pacification programs brought results. By 1970, the NLF's hold on the countryside had been broken and rural South Vietnam was more secure than it had ever been. In part, to be sure, this resulted from the devastation of the NLF main forces at Tet, but it also derived from the improvement in U.S. and South Vietnamese pacification efforts.

Still, despite their success, these programs never really came to grips with the fundamental problems of rural life in South Vietnam. U.S.-run programs, no matter how efficient, could not compensate for the chronic deficiencies of South Vietnamese leadership. Nor could the United States, in the final analysis, force the Saigon regime to take the steps necessary to win the allegiance of the rural population. Organizational success aside, the United States never really faced, much less resolved, the basic dilemma of counterinsurgency in Vietnam. As Douglas Blaufard has put it, "Effective programs require governmental stability, but successful counterinsurgency requires granting the rural population a strong voice in its own affairs. Steps toward the latter appear to threaten the former and are usually pushed aside with ultimately disastrous effects on counterinsurgency." [88]

Even in an organizational sense, CORDS was no more than a partial success. Whatever its achievements, it did not and could not solve the major problem that afflicted the war effort as a whole—integration of its many diverse components, including pacification, into a comprehensive strategy. Classic counterinsurgency doctrine emphasized the essentiality of integration of effort. The new organization effectively coordinated civilian and military activities in the area of pacification, but it did not integrate pacification with military operations and other programs.

This was true at the top and at the local level. The civilian side under the ambassador remained separate from the military, and there was nothing to force them together. In Phuoc Tuy province, to cite but one example at a lower level, the Australian military forces had responsibility for military operations, but responsibility for civilian matters rested with the South Vietnamese province chief and his U.S. adviser. There was little coordination between them, and their activities were fragmented and disjointed. [89]

There are several reasons why this was the case. U.S. military history provided no precedent for placing the military in combat under local civilian control, and there would have been strong military and congressional opposition to such a step. Thus the civilian proconsul model used by the British in Malaya was not attempted or even considered. [90]

The army would clearly have opposed any such effort. As it was, even with CORDS, the army's acceptance of pacification was far less than complete. Harry McPherson warned Johnson in June 1967 that the military had "'accepted' revolutionary development as an assignment, but only in their heads; their hearts are committed to the shooting war against the VC main forces."[91] Throughout the war, Andrew Krepinevich has concluded, the army continued to practice "counterinsurgency American-style." Whenever choices were required in terms of priorities or resources, it came down on the side of big-unit operations, operations that in many ways were counterproductive in terms of the goals and methods of pacification.[92] Indeed, as it turned out, one of the principal tasks of pacification forces was to clean up the debris left from U.S. military operations.

Ultimately, the problem went back to Johnson's perception and execution of his role as commander in chief. He refused to institute unified management. In terms of pacification, as elsewhere, he responded to conflicting pressures by attempting to build up pacification activities and forces without choosing between the conflicting approaches or integrating them in any effective way. In a still larger sense, as Komer himself later concluded, the absence of unified management of the war meant that there was no institutional incentive to develop a comprehensive strategic plan and the machinery to implement it. CORDS functioned effectively and enjoyed some success, but only in its own limited area.[93]

FOUR

The Not-so-secret
Search for Peace

Even before committing U.S. ground forces to Vietnam, Lyndon Johnson discovered that the pursuit of peace could be as difficult, frustrating, and politically perilous as waging war. Limited war theory emphasized the importance of keeping open and regularly using diplomatic channels to send and receive signals and carry out the bargaining process that was central to that brand of conflict. In reality, the increasingly costly and unpopular limited war in Vietnam spurred numerous private and third-country peace efforts—Johnson counted more than seventy. The absence of a declaration of war left him without legal means of restraining domestic peacemakers, and in an open society the inevitability of press leaks caused further problems. Although skeptical of the value of most peace moves—he dismissed them as "Nobel Prize fever"—the president quickly learned the public relations perils of ignoring them. Responding to them or launching peace initiatives of his own, on the other hand, while necessary to test the diplomatic waters and appease critics at home and abroad, nevertheless risked raising false hopes, sending the wrong signals to Hanoi, or undermining the Saigon government.

Not surprisingly, the Johnson administration never quite mastered the difficult and delicate art of waging peace. When it ignored initiatives it considered unpromising, it paid a high price in terms of public relations. Yet responding to them brought nothing more than short-term political benefits, and on several occasions, when U.S. officials pursued seemingly promising initiatives, bureaucratic blunders undercut their work. Thus, as Stanley Karnow has written, the administration's handling of the various peace efforts seemed at times as "confused, disorganized, and aimless as the war itself."[1]

Still, given the complexity of the task, the administration did learn, and its last major peace move before the Tet Offensive, code-named PENNSYLVA-NIA, was handled with considerable skill, a model of this kind of operation. That it did not bring peace reflected the irreconcilable objectives of the combatants and the intractability of the issues, not the finesse with which it was handled.

I

There was no real precedent in U.S. military history for the problems Johnson faced. In America's twentieth-century wars, peace moves by private citizens and third countries had been limited and manageable, and in Korea, the war most like Vietnam, virtually nonexistent. In earlier wars with England and Mexico, James Madison and James K. Polk had faced stern domestic opposition but only sporadic and generally ineffectual challenges from would-be peacemakers, although Polk did have to grudgingly acquiesce in a settlement negotiated by Nicholas Trist, the "impudent scoundrel" he had appointed but subsequently repudiated.

The experiences of John Adams and Abraham Lincoln provided the closest parallels to Johnson's problems in Vietnam. Adams was bedeviled through much of the undeclared naval war with France by the unauthorized activities of George Logan, the Pennsylvania Quaker who went to France at his own expense in search of peace, and Elbridge Gerry, who ignored his president's instructions to return home after the failure of the XYZ mission. In 1799 the Federalist Congress passed the Logan Act to curb such activities, but Adams eventually silenced his critics by listening to them and negotiating with France.

Unwilling to give in to the Peace Democrats, who were prepared to save the Union at the cost of preserving slavery, Lincoln was forced to resort to other means. He ignored Copperhead leader Clement Vallandingham rather than martyr him with harsh punitive measures. At the same time, he sought to coopt and use the well-meaning but troublesome peace advocate Horace Greeley by authorizing him to present to southern agents terms he knew the Confederacy could not accept. The move backfired when the southerners released Lincoln's hard-line terms, almost costing him the election. The president recouped some of his losses by permitting self-appointed peace agents James Jaquess and James Gilmore to go to Richmond and expose Jefferson Davis's intransigence. Most important, the Union victory at Atlanta in September 1864 undercut the Peace Democrats and stifled further major peace moves by making clear to a troubled nation that victory was possible.

Without firm precedent to guide it, the Johnson administration quickly learned first-hand the high stakes of the peace game. Already under fire for the bombing of North Vietnam in early 1965, it brought additional criticism upon itself by mishandling several well-publicized initiatives. When it ignored an effort launched by UN Secretary General U Thant it rightly considered unpromising, it was accused of blocking an opportunity for peace. When it subsequently pursued with the utmost care another third-party peace move, it was undercut by a press leak that blew the initiative and provoked further attacks from its critics.

At the outset, the administration lacked sensitivity to and any special machinery for responding to peace initiatives. Most of the early efforts came from abroad and therefore were under the purview of the State Department. They were usually the responsibility of the Far Eastern Bureau. If they became serious or went public, they would naturally come to the attention of the secretary. Throughout the war, Dean Rusk was instinctively skeptical of such activities, and his skepticism was reinforced by early initiatives that had been generally ignored and produced nothing.[2]

The administration's almost casual mishandling of U Thant's 1964 to 1965 peace move quickly made clear the hazards of complacency. An old acquaintance of Ho Chi Minh, Thant had been alarmed by the American presence in Vietnam from the outset. As early as 1963, he had proposed a reconvening of the Geneva Conference of 1954, and after the overthrow of Ngo Dinh Diem in November he pushed for a coalition government in South Vietnam. U.S. escalation of the war during 1964 deeply concerned him, and after the Gulf of Tonkin incident he developed a more formal plan. Meeting with Johnson, Rusk, and U.S. ambassador to the United Nations Adlai E. Stevenson on August 6, he proposed in a very tentative way to arrange ambassadorial-level talks between U.S. and North Vietnamese diplomats on neutral territory. The proposal was not phrased in such a way as to require a formal American response, and when Johnson and Rusk made no attempt to block it, Thant felt encouraged to proceed.[3]

The secretary general's first effort met a roadblock in Washington. Deeply committed to his plan, Thant followed up the August meeting with specific measures. He claimed to have secured in late September through a Russian intermediary a commitment from Ho Chi Minh to participate in negotiations with the United States. Stevenson dutifully relayed to Washington word of Thant's initiative, but he was advised that the effort must be postponed because the president was preoccupied with the election.[4]

Undaunted, the secretary general in mid-January 1965 secured from Burmese president Ne Win an agreement to host direct talks between North Vietnam and the United States. Reporting this development to Stevenson, he continued to press the United States for an answer. Again, Washington deflected the proposal. Rusk trusted neither Thant nor Stevenson, and the Laos agreement of 1962 convinced him that negotiations were not the answer to America's problems in Southeast Asia.[5] The secretary remained deeply skeptical that the North Vietnamese were ready for serious negotiations, and Thant's report conflicted with simultaneous messages from Canadian diplomat Blair Seaborn just returned from Hanoi that North Vietnam was determined to prevail.[6] Rusk feared that the Thant peace proposal might drive a wedge between the United States and the Saigon government at a critical point, further undermining America's already shaky ally. On the verge of a major escalation of the war in early 1965, the United States also undoubtedly felt that it would be negotiating from a position of weakness. The secretary did not reject Thant's proposal out of hand. The response was simply, "There may be a time . . . but not now."[7] But he appears not to have taken it seriously. At Thant's insistence, the entire affair was handled by word of mouth and nothing was put in writing. At the start, at least, Stevenson apparently did not take it seriously either, and Rusk did not even bother to consult the president. Stevenson therefore told Thant on January 30 that he had received word from Washington that the United States would not participate in the discussions.

Stubbornly persisting, U Thant set forth yet another peace proposal. On February 7, the United States had initiated regular bombing raids against North Vietnam, escalating the war in the most dangerous way. Meeting with Stevenson on February 16, Thant proposed convening a seven-nation conference, again perhaps in Rangoon, to explore the possibilities of a negotiated settlement. Himself alarmed by this time at U.S. escalation of the war, Stevenson sent the proposal directly to Johnson and urged its acceptance. Praising the president's handling of Vietnam as "prudent and careful," the ambassador went on to warn of the dangers of expanding the war without at the same time making it "emphatically clear" that the United States was ready to negotiate. Stevenson thus urged Johnson to issue a statement warning that the United States was committed to stopping aggression by military means if necessary but adding that it was ready to explore a negotiated settlement. The secretary general would follow in a few days with an appeal to the seven nations to begin discussions to determine the possibility of a peaceful solution.[8]

Even before Johnson could consider the proposal, the U Thant initiative blew up in his face. On February 21, journalist Bill Frye published in the *Chicago Sun-Times* an account of Thant's initial peace move. Questioned about the report at a press conference three days later, an angry and increasingly impatient secretary general blasted the U.S. government for keeping its own people in the dark. While declining to discuss particulars, he admitted that he had been conducting discussions on Vietnam for some time. "I am sure that the great American people, if only they knew the true facts and the background to the developments in South Vietnam, will agree with me that further bloodshed is unnecessary," he added. "The political and diplomatic method of discussions and negotiations alone can create conditions which will enable the United States to withdraw gracefully from that part of the world. As you know, in times of war and hostilities, the first casualty is truth."[9]

The press conference caused consternation in Washington. Press Secretary George Reedy denied that the United States had turned down a U Thant peace initiative and that any "authorized negotiations" were going on. Johnson was reported to be "deeply disturbed." Rusk privately conceded to U Thant that he was aware of the secretary general's proposals. In a press conference, however, the secretary of state evaded questions of whether he knew about the initiative. He admitted that the United States had been talking with U Thant about Vietnam but insisted that all proposals had been "procedural" and that there was no indication that Hanoi was prepared to stop its aggression against South Vietnam.[10]

The administration paid a high price for mishandling the U Thant initiative. Whether North Vietnam was indeed interested in negotiations at this point remains unclear. But a pattern was set that was repeated over and over again. Ho Chi Minh's apparently forthcoming response gave Hanoi the propaganda advantage. In contrast, the caution, equivocation, and even obfuscation of the United States, although perhaps proper and appropriate from a diplomatic standpoint, cost it heavily from the standpoint of public relations. Washington seemed the major obstacle to peaceful settlement of the war.

Critics had a field day. Those congressmen who favored negotiations and those who opposed them demanded that Johnson explain U.S. policy. The president's brief and unrevealing "clarification," critics charged, raised more questions than it answered. The *New York Times* supported Thant's call for negotiations. Complaining that it could not determine whether an issue "so important to all mankind" had even been discussed in Washington, the *Times* denounced Johnson for not taking the American people into his confidence. "In a democracy like ours, this is an inexplicable procedure."[11]

The U Thant affair would not die, surfacing again in late 1965 with the United States—again probably unfairly—playing the role of villain. Adlai Stevenson had passed away in July 1965, deeply frustrated by Johnson's intervention in the Dominican Republic and by indications that the administration was on the verge of another major escalation of the war in Vietnam. Shortly before he died and, it was said, with a premonition of his death, Stevenson spilled his guts to journalist Eric Sevareid. Expressing great frustration with his distance from the centers of power and his inability to influence the government, he recounted the U Thant peace initiative, leaving the distinct impression that the Johnson administration had killed a promising opportunity for peace.

Publication of Sevareid's account in *Look* magazine in mid-November 1965, after the United States was involved in full-scale war in Vietnam, raised a furor. A State Department spokesman lamely defended his government, insisting that Secretary Rusk's "sensitive antenna" would enable him to pick up a real peace feeler when it came. Critics ridiculed the remark. The "outstanding—and many will think devastating—fact," the *New York Times* observed, "is that Hanoi offered to talk and Washington refused," a "heavy burden for the Johnson administration to justify." The *Times* compared Rusk's antenna to "the ancient Roman practice of drawing auspices from the flight or the entrails of birds." Political humorist Russell Baker sarcastically speculated that Rusk's antenna had been built to his specification at poolside at the LBJ Ranch and was able to pick up vibrations over water by "unpleasant aliens." [12]

The Sevareid article was a "very damaging episode," William Bundy later recalled. U.S. officials insisted that there was nothing to the U Thant initiative—the secretary general never had a real commitment from the North Vietnamese—and Rusk has claimed that Soviet diplomats later confirmed this. Still, it was impossible for them even to reconstruct precisely what had happened, and they spent much time unsuccessfully trying to fend off critics. [13]

Within a month, yet another contact came undone and again—this time unfairly—the United States appeared to be the heavy. At the direction of Italian foreign minister Amintore Fanfani, a Florentine law professor and peace activist, Giorgia La Pira, had undertaken in October a secret peace mission to Hanoi. There he met with President Ho Chi Minh, Prime Minister Pham Van Dong, and two representatives of the National Liberation Front. Ho expressed an earnest desire for peace and told La Pira that for negotiations to take place there would have to be a cease-fire in all of Vietnam, and the Geneva agreements and Hanoi's four points could serve as a basis for negotiations. La Pira got back to Rome in mid-November and eagerly reported his talks to Fanfani, who in turn conveyed the message in writing to President Johnson. [14]

The United States responded promptly. In fact, the State Department saw nothing new in Fanfani's report. A "bushy-tailed and eager" La Pira had got the "straight party line," William Bundy later recalled. "It was much more on sound and fury than substance." [15] After the Sevareid affair, however, the administration felt compelled to take the La Pira contact seriously, and on December 6 Rusk responded formally and in writing to Fanfani. The United

States was willing to negotiate with no preconditions and on the basis of the Geneva agreements, the secretary affirmed. A cease-fire was acceptable provided it was mutual. The administration did not see the four points as an authentic representation of Geneva and would therefore not accept them as preconditions, but it was prepared to discuss them.

Shortly after Rusk's response reached Hanoi, the La Pira contact became public. Fanfani had not kept his colleague informed of what he was doing, and an impatient La Pira had taken matters into his own hands, telling an American lawyer and fellow peace activist, Peter Weiss, what he had been told by Ho and asking him to spread the word in the United States. Weiss did so, passing a "confidential" memo to, among others, Arthur Goldberg, Robert Kennedy, Averell Harriman, and Harry McPherson.[16] As fate would have it, journalist Richard Dudman was at this time making separate inquiries about peace contacts and stumbled onto someone who had learned of the La Pira initiative from Weiss. Broaching the subject with a "responsible and informed" official, he was told that the administration did not "attach much importance to the overture" and he set out to report the incident. Administration officials and even Weiss tried to get him to kill his story, but they were too late. When it appeared in the *St. Louis Post-Dispatch* in mid-December on the heels of the Sevareid revelations, again suggesting that the United States had spurned a serious peace initiative, it caused an uproar. To protect itself, the administration saw no choice but to release the Fanfani-Rusk correspondence, in full knowledge that it was killing the contact. Hanoi quickly and vehemently denied that any probe had taken place and denounced reports of a contact as "sheer groundless fabrications."[17]

Again, the Johnson administration suffered grave public relations damage. Critics attacked the "grudging" tone of Rusk's letter to Fanfani and the fourteen days it took him to respond. Like the Sevareid affair, La Pira provided one more example of the administration's "failures of candor and communication."[18] Diplomats at the United Nations blamed U.S. escalation of the war for Hanoi's disavowal of what might have been a promising peace feeler. Senator J. William Fulbright (D-ARK), by this time a leading "dove" critic of the administration, affirmed that regardless of what had really happened, the United States for the second time in a year had given the impression it was not interested in negotiations. The *New York Times* conceded that Washington had not dismissed the La Pira initiative as it had U Thant's, even though it had been conducted by amateurs. The *Times* nevertheless complained that the positive effect of the response had been "diluted" by Rusk's argumentative tone and his "gratuitous expression of reserve about the good faith" of Ho Chi Minh and Pham Van Dong.[19]

Once more the loser in what the *Times* correctly labeled a "bizarre and

confusing diplomatic tale," administration officials were understandably annoyed and perplexed. In both the Sevareid and La Pira cases, the president
complained, the government's denials had never caught up with the accusations. In the Italian initiative, the intrusion of "amateurs" had been costly, and
having to reply to Dudman destroyed whatever value the contact might have
had. "Publicity seekers and amateurs cannot have a hand in our affairs with
other nations," the president solemnly affirmed. But he had no way to prevent
them from doing so, and La Pira would not be the last time he would be
victimized by their activities.[20]

II

The Johnson administration early recognized that it could not remain on the
defensive, constantly responding to initiatives launched by others, and in the
spring of 1965 and again late in the year it mounted major peace offensives of
its own. In large part its motivation was political, to defuse criticism at home
and abroad and to prove to skeptics that it was doing everything possible to
secure peace.

Whether the peace offensives were worth the effort that went into them
remains unclear. U.S. officials did not expect serious negotiations and at this
stage probably did not want them, and in this sense they lost nothing. In the
aftermath of each initiative, they carefully pursued faint and mysterious signals that led nowhere. The United States may have paid at least a small military cost since the North Vietnamese used each bombing pause to step up
infiltration into the south. Whether the offensives conveyed the wrong signal
to Hanoi is not clear and may never be known. Politically, they bought some
time and thus achieved their major purpose, although the administration
quickly found that the attitude of its critics was much like that of the party
boss toward the ward heeler: "What have you done for me lately?"

Apparently learning from the U Thant imbroglio, the United States in the
spring of 1965 took a more forthcoming approach toward peace. The initiation
of Rolling Thunder bombing raids over North Vietnam provoked widespread
domestic and international protest, and although deeply annoyed with what
he viewed as gratuitous criticism, Johnson recognized that he could not ignore
it. The administration had not at this point begun to formulate serious peace
proposals, but it felt compelled to do something, and most officials were convinced, in any event, that North Vietnam was not interested in negotiations.
Thus in a much publicized speech at Johns Hopkins University on April 7,
the president, while stressing America's determination to prevail in Vietnam,
added his willingness to engage in "unconditional discussions" and made pub-

lic an offer already secretly extended to Hanoi of a billion-dollar economic development program for Southeast Asia in which North Vietnam could participate once peace was restored.

A month later, the administration launched its first bombing pause, code-named MAYFLOWER. The Johns Hopkins speech had defused domestic and international criticism only temporarily, and Johnson's military intervention in the Dominican Republic in late April had caused further uproar. More important, the administration by early May was on the verge of another major escalation, and it concluded that a bombing pause, the step its critics had been demanding, would be a useful measure to take prior to expanding the war. Hanoi had responded to the Johns Hopkins speech by issuing four points that, it said, comprised the basis for an acceptable settlement. American officials took particular exception to point three, which seemed a thinly disguised cover for National Liberation Front domination of South Vietnam. Some of Johnson's advisers nevertheless felt that the United States should do something to regain the initiative and should at least explore with Hanoi the precise meaning of the four points to see if there was any room for compromise.

The administration launched the MAYFLOWER initiative on May 10. The bombing was suspended temporarily. The United States attempted to communicate to North Vietnam through the Soviet ambassador in Washington and through the North Vietnamese embassy in Moscow that a scaling down of North Vietnamese military activities in South Vietnam could bring an extension of the pause. Should no such deescalation occur, the messages warned, the United States would be compelled "to take such measures as it feels are necessary to deal with the situation in Vietnam." [21]

MAYFLOWER produced about what had been expected. The Soviet Union refused to serve as an intermediary for the United States. The North Vietnamese embassy in Moscow would not receive the U.S. ambassador and returned unopened messages delivered by third parties. Publicly, Hanoi denounced the bombing pause as a "worn-out trick of deceit and threat." Some administration officials felt that the MAYFLOWER initiative had been too hastily prepared and that the pause did not last long enough. But the president read the North Vietnamese response as a clear and unequivocal rebuff— Hanoi "spit in our face," McNamara said—and on May 18 the United States resumed the bombing. [22]

Despite the rebuff, the administration mounted a mini–peace offensive in conjunction with the July troop buildup. It was agreed that such a move might help to further pacify senatorial critics like Fulbright and Democratic Majority Leader Mike Mansfield, and emphasis was placed on bringing the United Nations into the peace process since that was one base not previously touched. Thus the president's July 28 news conference, while announcing the buildup, indicated that the United States would favor use of the UN if it could be brought into the act. It also endorsed free elections under international supervision, offered support for the purposes, if not the machinery, of the 1954 Geneva agreements, and made a concrete offer to discuss peace.[23]

Still learning its lessons from the U Thant affair, the administration during this period pursued diligently even the faintest leads. As so often during the war, North Vietnam, on the day the bombing was resumed, sent a mysterious signal through Mai Van Bo, its commercial representative in Paris and one of the key actors in Vietnam secret diplomacy. This "contact" led nowhere, but on July 29, the day after Johnson's press conference and follow-up signal, an equally mysterious American businessman informed the State Department of the possibility of establishing contact with Mai Van Bo. Johnson was anxious to pursue any lead to counter those critics like Mansfield and Fulbright who accused him of seeking military victory rather than a negotiated settlement. During the July discussions of the troop buildup, moreover, Secretary of Defense McNamara and Undersecretary of State George W. Ball, the latter the foremost opponent of escalation, had urged the president to explore whether North Vietnam might prefer a peaceful settlement to the prospect of a costly, drawn-out war.[24]

Thus the administration responded with the utmost care to what came to be code-named the XYZ Project. The president entrusted it to Ball, whose dovish instincts ensured that it would be treated seriously and pursued vigorously. Ball modeled his response on contacts that had preceded the opening of the 1954 Geneva Conference. He selected for the delicate mission Edmund Gullion, an experienced diplomat fluent in French who had served in Vietnam in the early 1950s. By using a private citizen he hoped to retain maximum flexibility, leaving the government free to disavow the contact if problems developed, while at the same time making clear to North Vietnam that Gullion had authority to speak for the United States. To ensure maximum secrecy, the contact was revealed only to a handful of top U.S. officials, the code letters X and R were used to designate Gullion and Bo, and communications were handled by "backchannel" and known only to the U.S. ambassador in Paris.

The principal purpose of the Gullion mission was to probe the meaning of Hanoi's private and public statements to determine if there was a chance for substantive negotiations. The United States was still determined to negotiate from a position of strength and was unwilling to concede anything on the fundamental issue—preservation of an independent, noncommunist South Vietnam. Ball's approach was nevertheless more conciliatory in tone and, on the surface at least, more flexible than that taken in earlier initiatives. Gullion was instructed to try to build a basis for negotiations around North Vietnam's four points without compromising the integrity of South Vietnam.[25]

During August and September 1965, Gullion and Bo engaged in the most serious and substantive discussions that would take place between 1964 and 1968.[26] They generally agreed that a reconvened Geneva Conference would be an appropriate forum for formal negotiations. There was no mention of a bombing halt as a precondition to negotiations, and Bo accepted the idea of mutual troop withdrawals. Whether American acceptance of the four points remained a precondition to negotiations or would provide the basis for a settlement remained unclear, but Bo at least held out the possibility of full South Vietnamese representation at the conference table, seemingly an important concession. U.S. officials were further encouraged by the arrival in Paris of a top-level North Vietnamese delegation, including Le Duc Tho, then virtually an unknown, later a key figure in the negotiations that ended the war.[27]

The contact aborted just as suddenly and mysteriously as it had begun. At a meeting on September 3, Bo pulled back from positions taken in earlier talks and even insisted that he had never taken them. He took an especially hard line on the troop withdrawal issue and insisted that the bombing must be ended "unconditionally, immediately, totally, and definitively." Gullion concluded that Bo "had been called up short" and even suspected that he was being watched by someone from behind a curtain, which, for the first time in their talks, had been drawn across a doorway in the room. Gullion's subsequent efforts to revive the talks were unavailing. U.S. officials speculated that Hanoi had determined that it could not get what it wanted and simply broke off the contact. Gullion came home.[28] Administration officials agreed that it was best not to appear too eager at this stage. They also agreed, as McGeorge Bundy put it, that "we now have a perfectly good public posture which does not need to be regilded every day."[29]

As in the spring of 1965, the United States in the aftermath of the Sevareid and La Pira debacles again took the initiative in the game of diplomatic one-upmanship. By the end of 1965, pressures had mounted to escalate the bombing and the ground war, and top administration officials debated the merits of preceding the anticipated escalation with some kind of peace initiative. McNamara had long advocated such an approach, arguing that it would be a good way to test whether American escalation had produced any tendency toward negotiations in Hanoi. It would also help defuse criticism at home and abroad, he continued, and would "lay a foundation in the minds of the American public and world opinion . . . for an enlarged phase of the war."[30] Rusk and McGeorge Bundy at first expressed strong skepticism, but by December they had been converted. The Sevareid and La Pira revelations had put the administration on the defensive. Rusk and Bundy appear also to have been influenced by hints that the Soviet Union might use its influence to encourage negotiations.[31]

Johnson reached the same conclusion more slowly and with considerable reluctance. He agreed to a brief holiday truce before going to his Texas ranch for Christmas, but only on December 27, possibly as the result of word passed by the Hungarian foreign minister that Hanoi would be receptive, did he commit himself to an extended pause. He later conceded that he had "grave doubts" about McNamara's proposal, but he went along because he "wanted to explore every possible avenue of settlement before we took additional military measures."[32]

On his own initiative and clearly reflecting his own personal style, Johnson combined the pause with a noisy "peace offensive." He dispatched such top officials as W. Averell Harriman, Vice-President Hubert H. Humphrey, and Assistant Secretary of State G. Mennen Williams to 34 capitals across the world to deliver the message to 115 governments that he was prepared to negotiate without condition. He sent personal messages to numerous heads of state and to U Thant underlining his desire for peace and indicating that he was looking for signs of restraint demonstrating that Hanoi too was ready to discuss peace terms. He used old and new private channels to inform North Vietnam of the bombing halt and to indicate that if it would reciprocate in some way the pause would be extended. It was a "flying fortnight the likes of which the world had never seen," *Time* noted, "mingling mystery and flamboyance, discretion and display in an unorthodox diplomatic maneuver unmistakably stamped LBJ."[33]

At the same time, Rusk released the first formal statement of American peace proposals, what came to be known as the fourteen points. They contained little that had not been said before, and on the salient issues conceded nothing. The United States would go no further than state that Hanoi's four points "could be discussed along with other points that others might wish to propose." While reiterating support for self-determination in South Vietnam in principle, the Fourteen Points conceded nothing regarding the status of the National Liberation Front beyond Johnson's earlier statement that they "would have no difficulty being represented and having their views represented if for a moment Hanoi decided she wanted to cease aggression."[34]

From the administration's standpoint, the peace offensive produced about what had been expected. A statement by the North Vietnamese Foreign Ministry on January 4 did not insist on U.S. recognition of the four points as a precondition to negotiations, a possible sign of interest in peace talks, and there were some indications of a decline in North Vietnamese military operations in January. The administration ignored the former and dismissed the latter as of less importance than the fact that North Vietnam had used the pause to rush large quantities of men and supplies southward. Private channels, including a Polish mission to Hanoi arranged by Harriman apparently in cooperation with the Soviets, turned up nothing. The North Vietnamese public response was harsh. The Foreign Ministry statement denounced the pause as a trick. A letter from Ho Chi Minh to various heads of state broadcast by Hanoi radio on January 28 accused the United States of deceit and hypocrisy, demanded the withdrawal of U.S. forces, and insisted that the NLF was the "sole representative of the people of South Vietnam." The "enormous effort" undertaken by the United States, Rusk said, produced "no runs, no hits, no errors." Ho's letter did not even contain the usual "confusion ploy." [35]

With virtually no debate, the administration resumed the bombing on January 31. William Bundy and others felt that the pause had been worthwhile in terms of mollifying domestic and world opinion and isolating Hanoi and Peking, but Johnson was not entirely persuaded. Never really convinced that it had been the right thing to do, he concluded that it had been a serious mistake, and from this point his views hardened. He was heard to ridicule those who pressed the pause on him, and his relations with McNamara began to cool. He summarily terminated the special peace assignment he had given Ball in the spring. He would not consider another extended halt to the bombing for more than two years—and then under very different conditions. [36]

Much as with the May bombing pause, the only positive signal from Hanoi came immediately after the bombing had been resumed, this time in Rangoon. Within hours after the pause ended, North Vietnamese consul general Vu Huu Binh invited U.S. ambassador Henry Byroade to meet with him. Binh offered nothing new, merely restating familiar positions in response to the message Byroade had delivered in connection with the pause. He did invite Byroade to respond, however, signaling that Hanoi at least was interested in keeping the channel open.

Much like XYZ, the contact code-named PINTA closed as abruptly and mysteriously as it had opened. By the time Byroade responded to Binh's overture on February 19, North Vietnam had apparently lost interest, and Binh simply said that the contact should be terminated. As with XYZ, it is impossible to determine why the channel was opened in the first place and then quickly closed. U.S. officials speculated that North Vietnam was engaging in a pattern of deliberately dangling tantalizing leads to keep them off balance. More may have been involved. It is possible that some Hanoi officials would have preferred at this time a compromise settlement to continuation of the war and would have accepted, at a minimum, a coalition government in South

Vietnam. Johnson's meeting with the South Vietnamese leadership in Honolulu in February, which seemed to preclude any such possibility, along with
the escalation of the war after the pause, may have played into the hands of
the hardliners in Hanoi and eliminated any reason to keep the channel open. [37]

III

On numerous occasions during the war, Johnson, with great emphasis, compared himself to a two-fisted prize fighter going against Jack Dempsey, with
Secretary of Defense Robert McNamara as his right hand responsible for
prosecuting the war and Secretary of State Dean Rusk as his left hand responsible for bringing peace. [38] Without intending to do so, the president thereby
suggested the compartmentalization of effort that afflicted his conduct of limited war in Vietnam generally and that especially bedeviled the coordination
of peace moves and military operations. In the year after the peace offensive
of early 1966, the administration bungled through a series of diplomatic mis-
adventures, possibly undermining a promising peace initiative, certainly damaging still further its already tattered credibility.

Peace, even in the form of harmless initiatives, took a back seat to war
during much of 1966. Political disarray in South Vietnam in the spring fore-
stalled any new U.S. initiatives, and when the situation had been stabilized
the Johnson administration sharply escalated the war, launching major ground
offensives and heavy bombing attacks on North Vietnam's petroleum resources. At the initiative of the Canadian government, retired diplomat and
Far Eastern hand Chester Ronning brought back from Hanoi during the
spring the message that if the United States would stop the bombing unconditionally North Vietnam would "talk." U.S. officials were not persuaded.
Distrustful of both Canada and Ronning, they saw in the offer a clever ruse
to secure their tacit acceptance of the four points. In any event, they were
committed to further escalation of the war. The United States thus responded
that North Vietnam must itself deescalate rather than promising merely to
talk, setting in concrete a deadlock on mutual deescalation that would persist
for nearly two more years. [39]

In large part for the public relations value, Johnson did create a new mechanism to promote negotiations, naming elder statesman W. Averell Harriman
"ambassador for peace" in August 1966. The president did not specify Harriman's mandate and put nothing in writing. The two men had never been
close, moreover, and by this time their relationship was based entirely on
mutual expediency. Harriman was no "dove" in the sense that he sought U.S.
withdrawal from Vietnam, but he increasingly disapproved the bombing of

North Vietnam and was certain that it would not work. Still, to retain influence within the administration, he refused to question existing policies and indeed in public he vigorously defended them. Hopeful that he might play a key role in negotiating an end to the war, he eagerly jumped at the new position. For his part, Johnson was wary of Harriman because of his known preference for negotiations and his closeness to the despised Robert Kennedy. At the same time, the president valued the elder statesman's ties to the liberal wing of the Democratic party.[40]

In addition, U.S. escalation of the war in the summer of 1966 had brought the usual appeals for peace from such world figures as Indian prime minister Indira Gandhi and French president Charles de Gaulle, and the president needed to prove to skeptics once again the sincerity of his peaceful intentions. There were at least faint hints from time to time that the new escalation might force North Vietnam to the conference table, and the United States needed to be ready.[41]

The vague and open-ended nature of the assignment neither troubled nor deterred Harriman, and he leaped into his new assignment with his customary vigor. He created and chaired an interdepartmental Negotiations Committee that met weekly to brainstorm ideas, develop and discuss options, produce policy papers, and closely monitor public and private statements by North Vietnamese and NLF officials. Once a week, he sent Rusk and the president a Secret-NODIS (no distribution beyond addressee) memorandum summing up the status of the negotiating track and proposing things that might be done. He also played a political role, putting the onus on critics like Fulbright to come up with ideas to promote negotiations.[42]

The principal assignment, as Johnson himself put it, was to follow leads "no matter how dubious or unpromising—in every corner of the world," and Harriman did this with great zeal.[43] In October 1966, for example, he journeyed 26,000 miles, explaining the U.S. position to world leaders and seeking new contacts. In one twenty-two-hour day, he had breakfast in New Delhi, lunch in Rawalpindi, tea in Teheran, and dinner over Greece, and he went to bed in Rome. On his seventy-fifth birthday, his staff gave their globe-trotting boss a table-size atlas.[44]

In retrospect Harriman's "peace-shop," as it was sometimes derisively called, appears more show than substance. Characteristically, Johnson claimed to have given him the broadest mandate he had received from any president, but in fact his charge went no further than searching out leads. Harriman was sharply circumscribed by the rigid negotiating position assumed by the United States. He had no power to launch peace initiatives or coordinate them with military moves and no ability to monitor contacts in progress. He was not given a seat at the Tuesday Lunches, where top-level decisions were made. Johnson and Rusk were undoubtedly serious in urging him to track down every possible lead—"the blind hog sometimes gets the acorn," the president would say. Beyond this, his appointment appears to have been primarily political, a means of appeasing doves and persuading critics at home and abroad that the administration was serious about peace. William Bundy thought Harriman's office essentially a "make-work" project, and even his top aide, Chester Cooper, was unsure whether Johnson was serious about it.[45]

Ironically, in the months after Harriman's appointment, the administration encountered its most damaging screwups. The first—and perhaps most serious—was a mysterious and possibly promising initiative code-named, with deceptive innocence, MARIGOLD. This initiative originated in South Vietnam. Its major instruments were the Italian ambassador, Giovanni D'Orlandi, an old hand at Vietnam peacemaking and dean of the Saigon diplomatic corps, Poland's representative to the International Control Commission, Januscz Lewandowski, and U.S. ambassador to South Vietnam, Henry Cabot Lodge, Jr. It was handled with the utmost care and secrecy, the long-legged Lodge frequently crouching in the back of a small, private automobile en route to the Italian embassy to avoid detection. Lewandowski was the prime mover, and his unorthodox methods leave continued uncertainty about what actually happened. Shuttling back and forth between Saigon and Hanoi, he attempted to formulate from oral discussions with Lodge and North Vietnamese officials terms that might provide a basis for negotiations. He also concentrated on the longer-range provisions of a settlement rather than the immediate and seemingly insoluble question of deescalation that had snarled earlier peace efforts. In part because of Lewandowski's modus operandi, it was not clear at the time and it remains uncertain today exactly what may have been accomplished.[46]

MARIGOLD began to bloom in November 1966. While Harriman and Cooper were in Rome on a globe-trotting peace mission, D'Orlandi brought Lewandowski's work to their attention and asked for a concrete proposal that the Pole could take to Hanoi. Excited that something might finally be happening, the two Americans returned to Washington and pressed their superiors in the State Department to give Lodge a formal peace proposal. The department subsequently sent to the ambassador a full statement of American ideas for a settlement. Most of the items had been stated before, but there was a "new and shiny" proposal—later to achieve a certain notoriety—designed to help bridge the gap on deescalation. According to this so-called Phase A–Phase B plan, the United States would stop the bombing unconditionally but on the basis of a previously arranged understanding that the two sides would then take mutual steps of deescalation. This would permit Hanoi to say that the United States had agreed to an unconditional bombing halt and would give Washington the mutual deescalation it had sought from the beginning.[47]

Lewandowski claimed to secure from North Vietnam an agreement to begin negotiations. He reduced the American proposals to ten points, then took them to Hanoi. Returning to Saigon, he reported North Vietnamese agreement to meet with the United States in Warsaw in early December on the basis of his proposals. Lodge subsequently sent Lewandowski's plan back to Washington for review. Now seeing the possibility of real negotiations and alarmed that the ten points, in William Bundy's words, were a "perfectly wretched draft" of the U.S. bargaining position, the State Department insisted on editing them where its own views had been altered and on the right to interpret them once negotiations began. Lewandowski protested but went along, and the first meeting was set for Warsaw on December 5.[48]

Bureaucratic blunders and gross mismanagement may have doomed that meeting. Once Lewandowski's channel appeared to take on promise, a nervous Johnson administration took steps to ensure secrecy. Not without reason, the president had a veritable "phobia" about leaks.[49] The State Department respected North Vietnam's sensitivity about publicity and its desire to keep any peace moves under wraps. Earlier initiatives like La Pira had been destroyed by leaks. It seemed therefore more than expedient to protect a channel that had suddenly taken on possibilities. Thus in mid-November the State Department's executive secretary, Benjamin Read, reduced to a mere six people access to the file now officially code-named MARIGOLD. The new list excluded a number of people with specific responsibility for coordinating military and diplomatic actions. Among the six officials, only Leonard Unger and Read himself knew of the diplomatic channel and simultaneous military operations.[50]

The omission turned out to be crucial. In mid-November, about the time the State Department sent its proposals to Saigon and Read cut the distribution list, the president approved a new batch of bombing targets that included the first attacks on Hanoi since the POL strikes in late June. The strikes were delayed by several weeks because of bad weather. In such circumstances, they did not have to be reauthorized, however, and on December 2, the very day Lewandowski informed Lodge that a meeting had been set for Warsaw December 6, U.S. planes hit fuel dumps, radar sites, anti-aircraft missile installations, and truck depots around Hanoi. Two days later, American aircraft hit the same and new targets around the North Vietnamese capital.

Ironically, the steps taken to protect the secrecy of MARIGOLD rendered inoperative a fail-safe system established to ensure diplomatic-military coordination. Foreign Service officers had been stationed at most military installations to monitor major ground and air operations and make sure that they did not jeopardize diplomatic initiatives, and in at least several cases they were able to do this.[51] In addition, each day local commanders responsible for bombing missions had to send up the chain of command a list of targets they would strike in the next twenty-four hours. The State Department liaison officials stationed at CINCPAC headquarters in Honolulu and at the Pentagon did not know of MARIGOLD, however, and could not raise warning signals. Only Unger and Read had access to the target lists and MARIGOLD cable traffic. Either they did not see the bombing cables or they did not make a connection between the two.[52] Cooper was cut out of the traffic flow; Harriman was apparently left in, but he was out of the country.[53]

The December 2 and 4 attacks by themselves may not have done in MARIGOLD. Lewandowski was upset, but he agreed to proceed as planned. Ambassador to Poland John Gronouski met with Polish foreign minister Adam Rapacki on December 6. The North Vietnamese were not present, and Rapacki expressed grave concern about the impact of the bombing on MARIGOLD, but at this point there was still a possibility that the talks would proceed.

Additional U.S. air attacks settled the issue. Gronouski pleaded with Washington to hold off further bombing until it was determined whether MARIGOLD would produce something, and Lodge, Undersecretary of State Katzenbach, and even McNamara urged the president to halt the bombing around Hanoi for the time being. Still perhaps influenced by the Christmas pause, Johnson rejected all such proposals, arguing that a cessation of the bombing had not been required by Lewandowski's formula and that a bombing halt at this point might be interpreted in Hanoi as a sign of weakness.[54] Thus on December 13 and 14, U.S. planes again hit railroad yards and vehicle depots around Hanoi. North Vietnam even claimed that some bombs hit the embassy area, damaging, among other things, the Polish embassy. On December 15, Rapacki informed Gronouski in no uncertain terms that the U.S. bombing had ruined the talks. The ambassador made a frantic effort to save MARIGOLD, even securing from Washington pledges not to bomb within a circle ten miles in radius around Hanoi, but he was too late. When he brought the proposal to Rapacki, the foreign minister indicated that the initiative had been broken off.[55]

Whether the U.S. bombing actually prevented serious negotiations will probably never be known. Johnson later insisted that Hanoi had not been interested in negotiations and that what was portrayed as a promising channel was in fact a "dry creek."[56] Since cessation of the bombing had never been a requirement for negotiations, he added, the December attacks on Hanoi could not in any event be held responsible for the breakdown of the contact. Katzenbach agreed that MARIGOLD was probably a "phoney," but he conceded that it should have been pursued more carefully.[57] Harriman thought that the Poles acted in good faith, but he also was skeptical they had anything firm from Hanoi.[58] Hungarian diplomat Janos Radvanyi agreed that the Poles had nothing of substance from Hanoi and thought the whole affair a Rapacki "ploy," "masterfully executed" to embarrass the United States.[59]

Some scholars have argued that serious damage was done by U.S. policy. Wallace Thies has speculated that the apparent promise of a coalition government in point two of Lewandowski's ten points may have been sufficiently enticing to encourage Hanoi's "doves" to consider negotiations, but their position was undercut by the U.S. insistence on interpreting the ten points, which may have placed the coalition in jeopardy, and the U.S. bombing on December 2, 4, 13, and 14. Thies further contends that MARIGOLD may have been the last best hope for a negotiated settlement, and its demise led directly to North Vietnam's decision to launch an all-out military offensive.[60]

What is beyond question is that, once again, the Johnson administration's credibility suffered when, inevitably, news of MARIGOLD broke. Remarkably, the initiative was kept secret the entire time it was in operation. In early February, however, Robert Estabrook reported in the *Washington Post* that a "promising" initiative had been "bungled" when U.S. planes accidentally hit nonmilitary targets around Hanoi in December.[61] Estabrook's story came in the wake of a series of sensational first-hand reports from Hanoi by Harrison Salisbury of the *New York Times* detailing in graphic and highly critical terms the impact of the December bombing.

Once again, the Johnson administration took a public relations beating. To be sure, hawks such as columnist Joseph Alsop and administration defenders such as the *Washington Post* speculated that North Vietnam was sending out false signals to try to trick the United States into stopping the bombing.[62] Doves, on the other hand, insisted that the signals were serious and should have been considered such by the United States. Labeling Rusk's continued public demands for mutual deescalation a "chilling response to an atmosphere of faint hopes," the *New York Times* insisted that the administration in the interest of peace should take the risk and stop the bombing altogether.[63]

In the meantime, the United States had launched other peace moves that produced perhaps the biggest debacle yet. The so-called SUNFLOWER initiative of early 1967 actually involved three separate contacts, a direct approach to the North Vietnamese embassy in Moscow, a personal letter to Ho Chi Minh from President Johnson, and an effort on the part of British prime minister Harold Wilson working through Soviet premier Alexei Kosygin to initiate negotiations. Predictably, the U.S. initiatives produced nothing, and confusion as to Washington's position on deescalation, in part the result of yet another bureaucratic mixup, snarled Wilson's efforts, producing at least a minor crisis in Anglo-American relations.[64]

Acting on signals conveyed to Salisbury by North Vietnamese premier Pham Van Dong and assurances from Moscow that Hanoi would respond to a positive move, the United States in late January tried to contact North Vietnam through its embassy in Moscow. The move may have been designed to convey to Hanoi that, despite MARIGOLD, the United States was interested in negotiations, and Washington was certainly eager to ascertain whether, as the Poles had alleged, North Vietnam had been ready to talk in December. The North Vietnamese may have responded for much the same reason. Their curiosity piqued by MARIGOLD, they were probably interested in learning the extent to which the United States had been prepared to negotiate on the basis of Lewandowski's ten points.

In view of the apparent motives of the belligerents, it is not surprising that the Moscow channel led nowhere. U.S. chargé d'affaires John Guthrie met with his North Vietnamese counterpart, Le Chang, on six separate occasions and presented detailed expositions of the American bargaining position. Guthrie offered nothing that was new, however, and his restatement of earlier U.S. stands on such issues as the political future of South Vietnam may have persuaded Hanoi that nothing could be gained from negotiations at this time. Moreover, the two nations quickly reverted to the old impasse on deescalation. Le Chang flatly rejected Guthrie's renewed offer of the Phase A–Phase B formula originally proposed during MARIGOLD. On January 29, North Vietnamese foreign minister Nguyen Duy Trinh issued with considerable fanfare a statement indicating that talks "could begin" if the United States stopped the bombing unconditionally. The tone of the statement, as well as its wording, hinted at a greater North Vietnamese willingness to negotiate and aroused widespread speculation in the press that talks might be imminent. In fact, the two nations were back where they had started, the United States insisting on some form of mutual deescalation, North Vietnam demanding that the bombing be stopped without condition.[65]

In the final stages of the Moscow contact, moreover, the American position on mutual deescalation hardened. Sometime in late January, perhaps in response to the Trinh statement, Johnson decided to address a personal appeal for peace to Ho Chi Minh. Early drafts of the proposed letter apparently contained the standard Phase A–Phase B formula, leaving a time lag between stoppage of the bombing and an end to North Vietnamese infiltration.[66] By the time the letter to Ho was actually delivered in Moscow on February 8, however, the United States was insisting that it would terminate the bombing only after infiltration "had stopped."[67]

The reason for this important change of policy remains unclear. William Bundy later recalled that Washington had received "very reliable, sensitive intelligence" that North Vietnam had moved three full divisions into the area just north of the demilitarized zone. Ever suspicious of its adversary, the administration feared that Hanoi might send these troops into South Vietnam and then accept the Phase A–Phase B formula, insisting that the United States stop the bombing and cease reinforcing its own troops in the South. "We weren't going to sit still for that," Bundy affirmed.[68] At an NSC meeting on February 8, top administration officials privately made clear their exasperation with North Vietnam and their determination to extract concessions. Rusk expressed concern that the numerous rumors of peace might persuade Hanoi that the United States was "panicking [sic]," reinforcing its determination to secure sanctuary for the north without giving up anything. "We will keep on until we get something from the North Vietnamese," Johnson insisted.[69]

Before the letter to Ho had been delivered, Wilson had initiated his ill-fated peace move. The prime minister had long thought of himself as a potential Vietnam peacemaker. Britain's role as co-chairman of the Geneva Conference gave him formal justification to intercede, London's "special relationship" with Washington appeared to give him some influence with the United States, and he seems to have cherished exaggerated notions of his influence with Moscow. Certainly, like other would-be mediators, he was enticed by the prestige that could be gained from successful intercession. Perhaps most important, by early 1967, he was under considerable pressure from members of his own Labour party who felt he had attached Britain too closely to U.S. policy on Vietnam. He therefore decided to use the occasion of a Kosygin visit to London to try to bring about peace talks.[70]

Although notably unenthusiastic about Wilson's move, the Johnson administration had to go along. Having just been burned in a third-party initiative, American officials much preferred to operate through the direct channel already opened in Moscow. They profoundly distrusted Wilson, moreover, and feared that his overeagerness might trap them into negotiations on unfavorable terms. At the same time, they could hardly appear to oppose a serious peace initiative and they hesitated to antagonize the one nation that had consistently supported them. Reluctantly and with considerable skepticism and suspicion, they gave Wilson the go-ahead.

The recent change in the American position on deescalation hopelessly snarled the Wilson initiative. Ironically, to ensure maximum clarity of communication, the administration had sent Harriman's assistant, Chester Cooper, to England to brief Wilson on U.S. policy. Incredibly, however, the American position on deescalation was communicated to London in a manner sufficiently vague to cause major confusion.[71] Perhaps, as Benjamin Read later speculated, the letter to Wilson was written "with midnight oil and without the presence of the lawyers and the tense slipped."[72] Or, the policy may have changed after the letter to Wilson had been drafted and no one caught the contradiction. In any event, the letter to Wilson left unclear the sequence in which the various acts of deescalation would take place. From the standpoint of Cooper and Wilson in London it seemed consistent with the Phase A–Phase B proposal, which called for the United States to stop the bombing with nothing more than assurance that at some later point North Vietnam would cut back infiltration. To those in Washington, it appeared to state the current position that the United States would not stop the bombing until infiltration "had stopped."

Whatever the cause, the result was a minor diplomatic crisis. After nearly a week of pleading, Wilson persuaded a wary Kosygin to deliver to Hanoi a slightly modified version of the Phase A–Phase B proposal and, before securing formal approval from Washington, actually gave the Russian a written statement of what was assumed to be the official American stance. When horrified administration officials learned what had happened, they insisted that the earlier statement be retracted immediately and Kosygin informed of the actual and much tougher U.S. policy.[73]

The misunderstanding produced Anglo-American recriminations comparable to the Suez crisis of 1956 and the Skybolt affair of 1962. U.S. officials were outraged that Wilson had acted without consulting them. Wilson and Foreign Secretary George Brown were "incredulous and irate," Cooper later recalled, and the prime minister later complained of the "hell of a situation" in which he had been placed by Washington.[74] Wilson's subsequent efforts to retrieve something from the mess only added to the bad feeling. The United States grudgingly approved a last-minute Wilson proposal to extend a bombing pause put into effect over the Tet holiday and to present Kosygin yet another formula for a mutual pullback of forces and a cease-fire. But it gave him less than twenty-four hours to put together a complicated transaction. What Wilson later described as a "historic opportunity" broke down under this "utterly unrealistic timetable."[75]

Once again, mismanagement contributed to a major diplomatic disaster. To be sure, in his eagerness to promote peace, the well-meaning Wilson was guilty at least of impropriety in passing to the Russians what was presumed to be an American offer without first securing clearance from Washington.

And Wilson's later claim that the United States destroyed a promising initiative appears an overstatement. Even if Kosygin was committed to using his influence to get North Vietnam to the conference table, which cannot be certain, his leverage was limited. North Vietnam had already rejected the original Phase A–Phase B proposal, and there is nothing to suggest that it was prepared to accept Wilson's only slightly altered version, much less the tougher position stated in Johnson's letter to Ho.

Still, Washington's failure to state clearly its change of policy to an ally undertaking an important initiative stands as a classic example of diplomatic bungling. As in numerous earlier cases the administration paid a high price. Mercifully, word of SUNFLOWER did not leak out at once, thus adding to the bad aftertaste of MARIGOLD. Nevertheless, relations with a major and heretofore supportive ally were fouled and confusing signals were sent to the North Vietnamese and Soviets.

IV

Even as the administration braced to handle the fallout from MARIGOLD and SUNFLOWER, it was fending off a veritable barrage of private peace feelers. All sorts of people visited Hanoi in those days, Rusk later recalled. Unfamiliar with the lingo of diplomacy, they heard things they thought were important and returned home "eight months pregnant with peace," perhaps with visions of the Nobel Prize dancing in their heads.[76]

The administration found itself in a no-win situation. U.S. officials were certain that the feelers were dead-ends, and they were duly and properly wary of working through amateurs. But they recognized from past experience that for political reasons they could not turn a deaf ear even to the most far-fetched proposals. In addition, Rusk was convinced that, as in Berlin in 1948 and Korea later, negotiations might actually start through a secret contact, and the administration must not be so blind and deaf that it could not pick up a subtle signal when it was given.[77] Thus the United States checked out all the feelers with care, and with the exception of the one brought back from Paris by Johnson's nemesis, Robert Kennedy, handled them rather well, minimizing the public relations damage without compromising its position. Whether pursuit of these will-o'-the-wisps convinced Hanoi that the United States was overeager for peace, as Walt Rostow later suggested, will probably never be known. What is clear, as Rusk observed, is that handling of them was a time-consuming, frustrating, and generally unrewarding experience.[78]

In mid-January, Harrison Salisbury of the *New York Times* produced the first of a series of 1967 peace feelers. The first American journalist to get a visa to go to North Vietnam, Salisbury went to Hanoi in December, sending back a sensational and controversial series of columns detailing the impact of the bombings in and around the North Vietnamese capital.[79] In addition, he had a private interview with Pham Van Dong that produced the tantalizing hint of a willingness to negotiate. Much of what Pham said comprised the standard North Vietnamese line, denunciations of the "criminal action" of the United States and accusations of an "aggressive war." After reiterating the usual demand for the cessation of U.S. air attacks on North Vietnam, however, he added that if the bombing were stopped North Vietnam "will take an appropriate stand." Later, he repeated that if the United States showed "good will" and stopped "doing harm to the North, we know what we should do."[80]

The administration treated the feeler seriously, but with the utmost caution. Salisbury was miffed that he could not take his message directly to the president, and he later complained that Rusk was so busy debating him that he seemed unreceptive to the apparent signal.[81] In fact, the administration was more receptive than the journalist could have known. The State Department scrutinized with the utmost care the memorandum of Salisbury's talk with Pham, noting the slightest word change from previous North Vietnamese statements and paying special attention to the differences between Salisbury's private notes of the interview and the official text as approved by the North Vietnamese foreign ministry. The foreign ministry, for example, deleted the key phrase about an "appropriate stand," adding mystery and possibly significance to it. Administration officials disagreed as to the possible meaning of the signal. Rusk and Bundy concluded that Pham's unreported statements were "interesting as mood music" but added little to signals received from other sources. Rostow, on the other hand, thought the Salisbury interview confirmed the "possibility—if not probability" that the North Vietnamese were "looking for a way out." Both agreed that Hanoi would insist on secret, direct talks without an intermediary.[82] Unknown to Salisbury, the administration therefore followed up his signal with two separate overtures to North Vietnam in early February. In light of the MARIGOLD fiasco, the generally hawkish Rostow even urged the president not to expand the bombing because "at this particular moment" we should not "take operational risks which might weaken our negotiating record."[83]

The administration exercised similar caution in responding to another initiative conducted by journalists and peace activists Harry Ashmore and William Baggs. The two men journeyed to Hanoi in early 1967 under the auspices of the Center for the Study of Democratic Institutions. While there, they met with Ho Chi Minh, and they later reported to the State Department that they found him in a conciliatory mood. He continued to insist that there could be no talks until the United States stopped the bombing, but he hinted at mutual deescalation and invited continued contact with them or with American officials through a channel in Phnom Penh.

Recognizing the diplomatic and public relations minefields ahead, the administration handled Ashmore and Baggs with the same care shown Salisbury. Like Salisbury, the two men later sharply attacked the government, but in retrospect it is difficult to see how U.S. officials could have done more.[84] Indeed, even before they left for Hanoi the State Department briefed them thoroughly on its negotiating position and helped them maintain secrecy. As with Salisbury, the president refused to see them upon their return—if he saw Baggs, he would have to see "every American, crackpot or otherwise, who has been to Hanoi," he instructed Harriman to tell Fulbright.[85] But he did arrange for them to meet with top State Department officials, including Katzenbach, and to cover himself suggested that Fulbright might attend. State Department officials then joined Ashmore and Baggs in drafting a letter to Ho. As conciliatory as any U.S. "signal" to this point, the letter responded with "particular interest" to the North Vietnamese suggestion that private talks could begin if the United States stopped the bombing and refrained from escalating the ground war. It asked for nothing more than "some reciprocal restraint to indicate that neither side intended to use the occasion of the talks for military advantage," saying this would "provide tangible evidence of the good faith of all parties in the prospects for a negotiated settlement."[86] By the time Ashmore's letter arrived in Hanoi, it had been overtaken by events, and he and Baggs were refused a second visit to Hanoi.

The only flaw in the administration's otherwise effective short-run handling of these merchants of peace involved Robert Kennedy. Kennedy's agonizing break with the Vietnam policies of his brother was well under way by early 1966, and while on a European tour, he had spoken with Etienne Manac'h, the Quai d'Orsay's Asian expert. Kennedy understood French poorly and he was not well versed on the negotiating positions of the major belligerents. The conversation therefore revealed nothing that was new to him. But a U.S. embassy official who accompanied him, John Gunter Dean, concluded from Manac'h's report of a conversation with the ever present and ever mysterious Mai Van Bo that North Vietnam had now dropped its insistence on U.S. prior acceptance of the National Liberation Front's four points and was demanding only a bombing halt. Dean subsequently dispatched a cable to the State Department emphasizing the importance of the apparent concession.[87]

Upon returning from Europe, Kennedy found himself in the middle of a political firestorm. A State Department official apparently leaked to *Newsweek* word that Kennedy had received a feeler in Paris, and the *New York Times* printed a lead story along these lines on February 6, less than a week after Estabrook's revelations of MARIGOLD. Long convinced that the Kennedys were out to get him, an enraged Johnson was equally certain that Kennedy had leaked the story. Although confused as to what happened, the senator agreed to meet with the president. "God, it was an unpleasant meeting," Katzenbach later recalled.[88] At his profane, sarcastic worse, Johnson angrily accused Kennedy of leaking the story. When Kennedy blamed the leak on "*your* State Department," the president responded hotly, "It's not *my* State Department, God damn it. It's *your* State Department." According to Kennedy's report of the meeting, the president threatened to destroy him and all the doves. The senator pleaded with Johnson to do what was necessary to start negotiations. LBJ refused, blaming Kennedy and his dovish colleagues for prolonging the war. At Rostow's and Katzenbach's urging, Kennedy finally agreed to say publicly he had brought home no peace feelers. Most commentators agreed that the incident said more about domestic politics than the search for peace. Representative Rogers Morton (R-MD) took Kennedy to task for setting himself up as a one-man State Department, and columnists Rowland Evans and Robert Novak attacked him for undermining the president at a critical period.[89] But the administration also suffered. The dovish *Nation* even blamed the White House for a leak designed to kill yet another initiative, suggesting that a Kennedy "peace coup would be about as welcome to President Johnson as a nuclear bomb dropped on 1600 Pennsylvania Avenue."[90]

V

Writing to Harriman in July 1967, Chester Cooper identified some of the major problems that had bedeviled the administration in waging peace. "Our effort is unnecessarily diffused, duplicative and, consequently, less efficient and effective than it should be," he observed. Some matters had been adequately handled through existing informal networks among top administration officials. But "major problems arise when we must work out a government-wide approach . . . and, in particular, when we attempt to mesh the political and military aspects." Cooper proposed the establishment of a "command relationship" through the appointment of a presidential special assistant, with powers comparable to those exercised by Komer in pacification, to coordinate the negotiations effort.[91]

Ironically, in the latter half of 1967, the man LBJ had frequently assigned responsibility for conduct of the war—his strong right fist—assumed in the peace initiative code-named PENNSYLVANIA much the role outlined by Cooper. As early as December 1965, Robert McNamara appears to have concluded that the war could not be won militarily, and by the spring of 1966 he was privately talking of a political settlement and a coalition government. In October 1966, he pressed Harriman to pursue every conceivable channel to open negotiations, and his May 1967 draft presidential memorandum had proposed scaling back U.S. objectives.[92]

After returning from a visit to Vietnam in July 1967, McNamara and Katzenbach committed themselves to a "concentrated, 'all-out'" effort to secure a negotiated settlement. Pressures for drastic escalation were building in Saigon and in Washington. Thus, at the same time he was squaring off with the Joint Chiefs in the Stennis hearings, McNamara, with Katzenbach's support, used an ongoing peace initiative to launch a desperate, last-ditch attempt to head off further expansion of the war and perhaps extricate the United States through negotiations.[93]

PENNSYLVANIA took place in the late summer and early fall of 1967 in an atmosphere of confusion and growing controversy. In Vietnam itself, the situation was more murky than usual. The military command continued to talk of victories and progress, but the enemy showed no sign of quitting, and the extent to which North Vietnamese and Vietcong main forces had actually been "attrited" became an issue of raging controversy within the U.S. intelligence community. South Vietnam held its first democratic elections in September, rightly hailed as a sign of progress, but the government, however chosen, remained incompetent and riddled with corruption.

In the United States, the most obvious fact was declining public support for the war and especially for the president's conduct of it. In the press, the Congress, and the public at large, there was growing talk of a stalemate, and among hawks and doves alike noisy demands for decisive action to break it. Hawks insisted on an all-out bombing campaign to win a war that had already dragged on too long. Doves demanded negotiation, in some cases as a way of getting the United States out of a quagmire, in others seemingly as an end in itself.

Whipsawed between hawk and dove, still precariously clinging to the shrinking center, Lyndon Johnson during this period was clearly a man at war with himself. Always more sensitive to demands from the right and burned in the Stennis hearings, he keenly felt the pressure from the hawks. Frustrated by the self-imposed restraints, he ached to pound his tormentors in Hanoi into submission. He was painfully aware, on the other hand, that to do so risked the larger and more dangerous war that he so feared and might provoke a greater upheaval among the already considerable antiwar forces arrayed against him. "How are we going to win?" he asked plaintively at the Tuesday Lunch on October 16. Anticipating his dramatic decision of March 31, 1968, he even wondered aloud how the war might be affected if he were to announce that he would not run for reelection.[94]

Learning from its previous mistakes, the administration handled PENN-SYLVANIA with great care.[95] The United States had generally spurned third party initiatives in the past, but with all other avenues closed in the summer of 1967, U.S. officials saw little choice but to encourage reliable third party contact. The two French intermediaries, Herbert Marcovich and Raymond Aubrac, although critical of American policy and eager for peace, turned out to be discreet and dependable messengers. The United States worked closely with them from the outset, briefing them extensively on its own negotiating position and cuing them what to look for in North Vietnamese statements. The American who dealt with them most closely, Henry A. Kissinger, also proved highly effective in this his first major venture in diplomacy. Johnson worried that the then relatively obscure Harvard professor might be a dove, and Walt Rostow feared he might "go a little soft when you get down to the crunch."[96] In fact, he would turn out to be a tough, shrewd negotiator. According to the authors of the *Pentagon Papers*, he handled the delicate assignment with "consummate skill," displaying caution when needed and toughness when required, continually "clarifying points and making interpretations that could lead to a continuing dialogue."[97]

In his first intrusion into the management of peace initiatives and in what turned out to be his swan-song as a presidential adviser, McNamara oversaw the entire effort. Unlike MARIGOLD, the initiative was regularly discussed at Tuesday Lunches and other top-level meetings between August and October, permitting a careful monitoring of progress and coordination with military operations. Desperate to commit the administration to negotiations and persuaded that bombing and military policy must be more closely tied to diplomacy, McNamara carefully orchestrated peace moves and bombing missions. He personally dictated the message Kissinger took to Aubrac and Marcovich. Recalling MARIGOLD and fearful that the bombing of targets of "no real value" in the early stages of the initiative—those targets authorized by LBJ to appease the JCS and the Stennis committee—might have jeopardized the contact, he fought hard to hold back the bombing during especially sensitive periods.[98]

The United States used the PENNSYLVANIA contact to develop a new formula for deescalation. Aubrac and Marcovich brought back from Hanoi messages sufficiently enticing to encourage keeping the channel open. Kissinger sought to arrange their return to Hanoi, and when that failed he presented through them to Mai Van Bo in Paris a new proposal on deescalation, in fact a modification of the Phase A–Phase B scheme originally proposed in MARI-

GOLD. The United States would stop the bombing with the understanding that this would lead to "prompt and productive discussions" and that North Vietnam would not take military advantage. The United States took considerable care in presenting its proposal. It assured Hanoi that it would keep the offer confidential and urged it to do the same. Without any hint of apology, it explained that recent bombing of dikes in North Vietnam had been accidental and did not represent a deliberate step of escalation. To establish the "authenticity" of the offer and avoid MARIGOLD-like problems, the United States indicated that it would stop bombing around Hanoi for a ten-day period while the proposal was being considered.[99]

When its first proposal was rebuffed, the administration persisted. After a delay of two and one-half weeks, Bo gave Aubrac and Marcovich Hanoi's response: the bombing must be stopped without condition. The administration debated at length its own response, McNamara arguing for an unconditional bombing halt with the understanding that the bombing could be resumed later if negotiations were not productive, Rusk and the president preferring to stick with the original proposal. Rostow eventually worked out a compromise that spoke in more conciliatory tones without altering the substance of the original proposal.[100] To give added credibility to the proposal and perhaps also to score points in the public relations game, the president in a speech in San Antonio on September 29 went public with his proposal, giving rise to what became known as the San Antonio formula.

Throughout much of September and October, PENNSYLVANIA was the subject of intense debate in top-level meetings. An increasingly impatient Wheeler pressed for the bombing of bridges and power plants in Hanoi irrespective of the diplomatic consequences. Literally grasping at straws, McNamara and Katzenbach, sometimes with help from Rusk, pleaded for military restraint and urged keeping the channel open for another month, calling a singularly unproductive contact "an important dramatic change of attitude" and "the closest thing we have yet had to establishing a dialogue with North Vietnam."[101] They later proposed that it be used as a vehicle to launch an extended bombing pause, the unspoken idea being to move toward a settlement.

A weary and uncertain president wavered before following his usual middle-of-the-road path. Emotionally, without question, he leaned toward Wheeler. He expressed anger that the United States had held back on the bombing of Hanoi "just because two professors are meeting." Whatever the reports said, he was certain that the bombing was hurting the North Vietnamese—"I feel it in my bones." He expressed eagerness to "pour the steel on," to get the enemy down and keep him down. Yet while fussing and fuming in top-level meetings, he listened to McNamara and Katzenbach, delaying for weeks before making any decision. With the support of his kitchen cabinet, Clifford, Fortas, and Taylor, and of the Wise Men, he rejected McNamara's proposal for an extended pause and eventually permitted PENNSYLVANIA to die. As before, however, he did not go the full route proposed by Wheeler, refusing to approve several major targets.[102]

PENNSYLVANIA manifested with stark clarity the no-win situation the Johnson administration faced in managing peace initiatives in a limited war setting. From the U.S. standpoint, the initiative was handled with exemplary skill. The administration framed a new and more conciliatory proposal, presented it with the most scrupulous care, monitored it closely, coordinated it with military operations, and maintained its secrecy. If nothing else, PENNSYLVANIA marked a giant step away from the complacency that had undercut the U Thant initiative and the bungling of MARIGOLD and SUNFLOWER.

Nevertheless, skill in execution did not ensure results. Bo repeatedly protested that the steady escalation of the bombing during the course of the Paris discussions undermined the value of the new proposal on deescalation. In fact, Hanoi was already committed to a major military offensive, the first phase of which was just weeks away. It seems unlikely that anything short of a complete and unconditional bombing halt would have enticed North Vietnam into negotiations, and negotiations under those circumstances would most likely have been a tactical ploy, an integral part of North Vietnam's strategy of "fighting while negotiating." In any event, the Johnson administration would not—perhaps could not—go that far at this time. And the president may well have been right in speculating that the North Vietnamese were "playing us for suckers," keeping the Paris channel open merely to secure a respite from the bombing of Hanoi.[103]

The administration was not even able to extract public relations advantage from the Paris contact. The president briefly considered leaking the details of PENNSYLVANIA to prove his commitment to peace, but he ultimately decided against it, probably for fear of jeopardizing the channel's possible use in the future. Going public with the San Antonio formula won the administration few points. Commentators admitted that the speech contained the "gentlest phrasing" and "softest tones" the president had yet used, but they were quick to add that his "weekend riposte actually was an almost ritualistic reiteration—and reaffirmation—of his war policy." They went on to note that the soft tones scarcely concealed his determination to prevail. The harshest critics simply demanded more. Senators Fulbright, Mansfield, and John Sherman Cooper (R-KY) pressed for a full bombing halt. The *New York Times* agreed that the logic that had brought Johnson to San Antonio should "impel" him to a full and immediate bombing halt. Even those who supported the substance of the San Antonio speech warned that it should raise no "undue hopes." If, as *Time* surmised, Johnson's San Antonio speech was a "public move to stanch the nation's unrest," it failed badly.[104]

VI

"I chase every peace feeler, just as my little beagle chases a squirrel," Lyndon Johnson proudly told a group of White House Fellows in February 1967, and in a narrow, literal sense, at least, he was right.[105] Learning the price of indifference from the U Thant initiative of 1964 and 1965, the Johnson administration between 1965 and 1967 pursued, often with painstaking care, countless private and third-country peace moves and launched numerous major and minor initiatives of its own. After several major snafus and despite the difficulty of coordinating the activities of an enormous bureaucracy, the United States also greatly improved its skill at managing peace initiatives, demonstrating with PENNSYLVANIA considerable finesse in handling a delicate diplomatic ploy.

Despite the intensity of its efforts and the sharpening of its skills, the Johnson administration never quite mastered the art of managing the initiatives. Peace was not really the issue, of course. Most top U.S. officials doubted that serious negotiations were possible, and their skepticism was probably justified. Given the irreconcilable bargaining positions of the two major belligerents and the apparent faith of both sides in the efficacy of military means, there was little chance of a negotiated settlement. The task rather was to appear committed to a peaceful settlement and willing to negotiate without conveying the wrong signals to the other side and without taking positions that would be harmful should negotiations actually start.

The Johnson administration had numerous disadvantages in this sort of endeavor. Part of the problem undoubtedly came from the president's own reputation as a wheeler-dealer and the steadily widening credibility gap that vexed all his activities by 1967. Further problems derived from the difficulty of conducting secret diplomacy in an open society. In marked contrast to their North Vietnamese counterparts, it was very difficult for American officials to conceal their activities and virtually impossible for them to cover up their mistakes, and on several occasions, U.S. moves were undercut and U.S. bungling exposed by press leaks. Also unlike North Vietnam, Johnson had few methods to silence his critics and restrain well-meaning seekers of peace, and it proved increasingly difficult for him to appease them. Doves, like hawks, had insatiable appetites, McGeorge Bundy correctly pointed out, and when concessions were made to them "they come right back for more."[106] In addition, a double standard was often imposed, the United States being held to a higher standard of behavior than its enemy. "It is a strange fact," Harriman complained to Thailand's foreign minister Thanat, "that if we do not pick up every single rumor concerning negotiations, we are automatically deemed at fault."[107]

For a variety of reasons, then, the United States, in the Johnson years, fared less well than its adversary in the delicate game of diplomatic one-upmanship. There is nothing to indicate that North Vietnam was any more eager to negotiate except on its own terms than the United States. But in those cases that came to light, Washington usually appeared the culprit. Through sheer cleverness or by exploiting its other advantages, Hanoi was often able to convey the impression that it was willing to negotiate and that its good intentions were foiled by American indifference, incompetence, or cupidity. Even when Johnson took special steps to try to gain an advantage, he was often upstaged.[108] And the concessions he made to prove his commitment to peace, in at least some cases, played into North Vietnam's hands, as with the suspension of the bombing around Hanoi during the PENNSYLVANIA initiative. The Johnson administration thus learned the hard way that managing "peace" was one of the most difficult and thankless elements of waging limited war.

"Without Ire"

FIVE

Management of Public Opinion

"The greatest contribution Vietnam is making," Secretary of Defense Robert S. McNamara observed in the early days of the conflict, "is developing an ability in the United States to fight a limited war . . . without arousing the public ire. In that sense," he added, "Vietnam is almost a necessity in our history because this is the kind of war we'll likely be facing for the next fifty years."[1] McNamara's statement appears in retrospect both naive and tragically ironic. Vietnam ultimately provoked the public ire as no other American war. But this anger was directed at the nation's leaders rather than its enemies, and public frustration contributed significantly to the failure of Johnson's policy. The backlash from Vietnam put restraints on American leaders for the next twenty years.

McNamara's statement is nevertheless quite helpful in understanding the way the Johnson administration fought in Vietnam. It provides at least a partial explanation for the way the administration went to war in 1965. It explains perhaps better than anything else the fundamental dilemma it confronted in waging the conflict. Johnson went to war "in cold blood" to protect his cherished domestic programs but also, in accordance with limited war theory, to ensure that pressures for further escalation could be contained and the war kept limited, thus minimizing the likelihood of a nuclear conflagration. The administration therefore did not seek a declaration of war or even openly attempt to rally the public. In the absence of such efforts and without signs of progress in Vietnam, however, it had no chance of holding popular support. For nearly two years, it clung to an increasingly shaky consensus. Ultimately, its inability to impose a settlement in Vietnam cost it support at home, and its loss of support at home, threatened any possibility of a settlement in Vietnam.

Belatedly recognizing its peril, the administration in late 1967 mounted a vigorous public relations campaign to shore up its domestic base. But this campaign was constructed on a most flimsy foundation—the premise that the United States was winning the war—making the administration especially vulnerable to public disenchantment and criticism after the North Vietnamese Tet Offensive of early 1968.

I

Throughout U.S. history, building and sustaining popular support in wartime has been among the most difficult problems faced by the nation's commanders in chief. Opposition to war has been the norm rather than the exception among Americans, and partisanship has never stopped at the water's edge. Thus, presidents James Madison and James K. Polk faced widespread and potentially crippling opposition in the country and Congress, even, in Madison's case, where the nation's very survival was at stake. In the American Civil War, Abraham Lincoln rigorously suppressed civil liberties to contain possibly damaging dissent.

Growing popular involvement in war in the late nineteenth and early twentieth centuries, as Sir Michael Howard has observed, meant that "management of, or compliance with, public opinion became an essential element in the conduct of war." Mobilizing the nation as it had not been mobilized before to meet a threat that was anything but obvious to most Americans, Woodrow Wilson in 1917 created the Committee on Public Information, a "vast bureaucracy for managing public opinion on a massive scale." Under the energetic and imaginative direction of journalist George Creel, the committee used modern advertising techniques to mount a huge and blatant propaganda campaign to arouse support for the cause and hatred of the enemy. The administration permitted journalists to censor themselves. But it used the Sedition and Espionage acts to enforce conformity, and Creel's committee even encouraged Americans to root out subversives by spying on each other.[2]

Characteristically, Franklin Roosevelt used more subtle—and generally more effective—means in World War II. Popular reaction against Creel's overselling of World War I and the deservedly sinister reputation of Joseph Goebbels's Nazi thought-control machine heightened Americans' traditional antipathy to anything smacking of propaganda. Roosevelt's Office of War Information therefore sought to educate rather than propagandize and offered no more than vague explanations of why the nation was fighting. At the same time, officials throughout the government employed new technologies to pioneer methods of mobilizing support. Policymakers increasingly scrutinized public opinion polls and even conducted their own polls to identify potential sources of support and opposition. Without imposing rigid censorship, the Roosevelt administration skillfully managed the press by using its control of information and setting guidelines under which the journalists censored themselves. Much of the work of selling the war was left to private industry.[3]

When the OWI ran afoul conservative congressmen for its "New Dealism" and alleged partisan activities, the State Department's Bureau of Public Affairs filled the gap, and in the last years of the war it spearheaded a sweeping and generally effective campaign to sell the American people such novel internationalist initiatives as the Bretton Woods proposals and the United Nations. It established ties with internationalist citizens groups and furnished information and speakers. Government officials conducted nationwide speaking tours. The State Department sponsored radio programs and even contracted with filmmakers such as Alfred Hitchcock to produce movies selling the United Nations. The Roosevelt administration and especially the president continued to come under sometimes bitter attack, and even in the "good war" leaders such as Gen. George C. Marshall feared that American impatience might threaten Allied victory. Nevertheless, the government successfully employed modern techniques of mass communications and advertising to win broad support for the war and for peace programs that departed sharply from tradition.[4]

In the Cold War, the executive branch fine-tuned these instruments. The government kept a potentially troublesome press in line by appealing to its patriotic instincts, by flattery and favors, and, when these failed, by pressures or threats of reprisal. Politicians and bureaucrats became increasingly sophisticated in their understanding of public opinion. They learned that a normally apathetic or indifferent public could be rallied with scare tactics or quieted by downplaying problems. They came to recognize, as political scientist Gabriel Almond put it, that a generally permissive public would "follow the lead of the policy elites if they demonstrate unity and resolution."[5] Perceiving the importance of elites, the government used various means to sway them, giving interest group leaders special briefings, inviting them to conferences, offering them spots on consultative bodies, and appointing them to offices. The Central Intelligence Agency subsidized citizens groups and even funded scholarly work.

On especially urgent issues, the government mobilized ostensibly independent citizens groups to conduct public relations campaigns in support of specific policies or programs. The classic example was the Committee for the Marshall Plan, modeled on the prewar Committee to Defend America by Aiding the Allies, which raised over $100,000, sent out press releases, took out advertisements, sponsored radio shows, maintained a speakers bureau, and lobbied the mass public and Congress, rallying the opinion leaders so that they in turn could influence the mass public and Congress. Postwar administrations were never free of criticism, but rarely was a major foreign policy venture frustrated by lack of public support.[6]

The Korean War was a major exception. At the outset, the public rallied around the flag with unprecedented unanimity. Expecting the war to be short and hoping to keep it limited, Truman did not seek a declaration of war, took no special steps to mobilize support, and permitted the press to report military operations without restriction. This changed dramatically within six months. The new war resulting from Chinese intervention, the partisan attacks following the firing of Gen. Douglas MacArthur, and the peculiar frustrations of fighting a limited war in a remote corner of the world changed Korea into a "sour little war." Censorship was belatedly imposed, more rigorous and tightly controlled than in World War II, provoking sustained conflict with the press. The administration's efforts to quietly regain public support through such instruments as the Advertising Council were unavailing. More than anything else, the Korean War cost the Democrats the election of 1952.[7]

As the Korean experience suggested, limited war exacerbated what had always been a major problem in the American system. Limited wars by their very definition were undeclared wars which did not provide the sort of controls that could be used to contain dissent. In a limited war setting, moreover, it was essential not to arouse public emotions to the extent that they threatened the government's ability to keep the war limited. Yet as Korea again suggested, it might be difficult to sustain public support without doing something to sell the war.

Those political scientists who developed the theories of limited war so much in vogue in the 1950s and 1960s all but ignored the obvious "lessons" of Korea. After considerable discussion, Robert E. Osgood conceded that because of their traditional approach to issues of war and peace, Americans might have difficulty accepting limited war. Without indicating how the problem could be resolved, he went on to assert that limited wars must be fought because they provided the only viable military alternative in the nuclear age.[8]

II

Recognizing growing popular anxiety with the worsening situation in Vietnam and its potential danger as a political issue, Johnson during his first year handled the problem with great caution. In general, as presidential aide Bill Moyers put it, the administration dealt with Vietnam by keeping the public debate at "as low a level as possible."[9] The exception, of course, was the Tonkin Gulf incident of August 1964, which the president skillfully used to rally public support and secure a sweeping congressional resolution giving him carte blanche to proceed as he saw fit.

The administration's public relations activities escalated as the war itself escalated. "We have an education problem that bears close watching and more work," McGeorge Bundy warned the president on February 9, 1965, two days after the administration initiated reprisal bombing attacks against North Vietnam.[10] Indeed, although public opinion polls continued to show strong support for the president's handling of Vietnam, the bombing provoked protests that gained momentum during the spring of 1965, especially on college campuses.[11]

While escalating the war from January to July 1965, Johnson employed a variety of methods to sustain public support. To counter charges that he was inexperienced in foreign affairs, protect his flanks against partisan attack, and cement ties with foreign policy elites, he created a panel of foreign policy consultants—later to become known as the Wise Men—made up of such establishment luminaries as Eugene Black, Allen Dulles, Robert Lovett, and John McCloy.[12] Behind the scenes, the administration also encouraged the formation of an ostensibly private citizens committee, headed by Arthur Dean, to rally support for its foreign policies.[13] The president, McNamara, and Rusk made numerous speeches and statements defending the administration's policies in Vietnam, policies, they insisted, they had inherited from their predecessors. "Lyndon has been hammering away this month on TV, in press conferences, with individual columnists, in groups of Congressmen, to every forum he meets, trying to put Vietnam in true perspective," Lady Bird Johnson confided to her diary in April.[14]

The administration also moved quietly and unobtrusively to counter the growing dissent. U.S. officials plainly underestimated the importance of the early protests, comparing them to the generally ineffectual antinuclear movement of the 1950s. Still they were sufficiently concerned to take countermeasures. Top civilian leaders carefully monitored speeches to eliminate bellicose statements that might inflame critics.[15] The president masked escalatory military actions with peaceful rhetoric. To undercut those critics who claimed that he was relying exclusively on military methods, he publicly committed himself in a major speech at Johns Hopkins University on April 7, 1965, to "unconditional discussions" and proposed a massive TVA-like program for the Mekong valley that might include aid for North Vietnam. He followed up with the MAYFLOWER bombing pause and peace initiative.[16]

Perceiving, as Averell Harriman put it, that the protestors on campus were only a "vocal minority" whose actions gave the administration a "unique opportunity" to get across its message, the White House worked actively to counter them.[17] It sent representatives to participate in some of the early teach-ins. Presidential aides also organized a program called "Target: College Campuses," dispatching some of their "best young troops" to speak at universities and bringing professors and student leaders to Washington for seminars.[18] The president authorized the Democratic National Committee to mobilize through the Young Democrats a cadre of student leaders to speak out in defense of U.S. policy.[19]

Turning to citizens groups, as its predecessors had so many times before, the administration also established close ties with the American Friends of Vietnam, a nonpartisan lobby group founded a decade earlier to support the fledgling South Vietnamese government. Administration officials helped raise private funds to support AFV activities and encouraged the group to conduct rallies to counter the teach-ins and release publications defending U.S. policy.[20]

In typical Johnsonian style, however, the president relied primarily on stealth and subterfuge to implement his policies. Throughout his political career, indeed throughout his life, Johnson had preferred indirection to confrontation, deviousness to candor. "In dealing with people," Clark Clifford later recalled, "I often had the feeling that he would rather go through a side door even if the front door were open."[21] Johnson's style meshed with the tenets of limited war theory, which called for quiet, step-by-step expansion of military pressures in ways that minimized the risks of an expanded conflict.

Thus LBJ escalated the war without appearing to do so. He moved slowly and cautiously, always ensuring that he did not get too far out in front of the nation. "The president felt that he must not force the pace too fast," Rusk observed in April 1965, "or Congress and public opinion, which had been held in line up to now through the president's strenuous efforts, would no longer support our actions in Vietnam."[22]

In Brian VanDeMark's apt phrase, Johnson also sought to "minimize political dangers by minimizing public awareness and debate."[23] While instituting major changes in policy in 1965, he and his top advisers continued to insist that there had been no change. After committing himself to reprisal air strikes against North Vietnam in January 1965, the president rejected Bundy's proposal to announce the measure publicly. Instead, he instructed Ambassador Maxwell Taylor to reveal it through "inconspicuous background briefings." Again, in February, when he initiated regular bombing attacks against North Vietnam, he declined to explain candidly to the nation the risks and possible costs of the move, characterizing it as an effort to blunt North Vietnamese escalation "without escalating the war." He obscured from all but his closest advisers the change of mission of U.S. ground forces and pressed them to implement it in "ways that should minimize any appearance of sudden changes in policy." In fact, the change was so effectively concealed that it crept out only by accident in a State Department briefing several months later.[24]

The administration also contained a potentially threatening problem with the press. The Cold War alliance between government and media had started to come apart in the early 1960s. A "credibility gap" had first opened in Vietnam in the Kennedy years, skeptical journalists like David Halberstam and Neil Sheehan increasingly challenging official reports of progress and bitterly protesting the obstacles placed in the way of their reporting by the Saigon government. Relations between the press and the U.S. mission steadily deteriorated.[25]

To head off an increasingly dangerous problem the Johnson administration in the summer of 1964 instituted a policy of "maximum candor." By being more open and candid with information and by helping rather than hindering journalists' coverage of the war, U.S. officials hoped that reporters would present a more "positive" and "balanced" view of American involvement. The Pentagon spent some $50,000 to assist reporters to gain better access to information. The U.S. command instituted a series of carefully orchestrated backgrounders and a daily briefing—later to become the notorious "Five O'Clock Follies."[26]

"Maximum candor" had mixed results. Most correspondents saw it for what it was—a thinly disguised effort at manipulation. They were not taken in, and they continued to report honestly and critically the weakness of the South Vietnamese government and the lack of U.S. progress. The greater access and information provided in Vietnam also conflicted directly with Johnson's efforts to keep a low profile on escalation of the war. Press reporting from Vietnam made clear that U.S. involvement was increasing, whether the president admitted it or not. U.S. officials also feared the publicity given the bombing would make it more difficult for North Vietnam to back down and might increase pressures on the Soviet Union and China to intervene. The U.S. command increasingly worried that extensive reporting of military operations would divulge information useful to the enemy.[27]

Despite continuing problems, government-press relations improved even while the war escalated. The administration continued to exercise restraint. Although deeply annoyed by the critical reporting of Peter Arnet, the White House refused to pressure the Associated Press to recall him.[28] At several points during the spring and summer of 1965, officials seriously considered the imposition of censorship. Each time, however, they rejected it as impolitic and impractical, recognizing, as Assistant Secretary of State James Greenfield observed, that attempts to withhold information would provoke charges of news management that might do more harm than the stories being published. They would go no further than ask journalists to accept ground rules requiring them to withhold information to protect military security. For their part, journalists benefited from the increased access made possible by maximum candor and willingly followed the government's guidelines. If sometimes critical of the methods being used and skeptical of official claims of progress, the media still generally supported the war.[29]

From a short-term perspective, Johnson handled the public relations dimension of escalation with consummate skill. Polls taken in the summer of 1965 showed that 62 percent approved his handling of the war and 79 percent believed that South Vietnam would fall unless the United States stood firm. The poll results so impressed the State Department that it sent them to U.S. embassies across the world to prove that the nation backed the war. Antiwar protest continued, but the critics, while irritating, seemed manageable, and the administration's modest program of damage control seemed to contain them.[30] Yet LBJ's success bore the seeds of long-term failure. By obscuring the degree to which he was Americanizing the war, he prevented immediate problems but caused big problems for himself later.

In addition, he fared less well with the press at home than in Vietnam. Johnson believed that the news was to be managed rather than reported, a view very much at odds with that of journalists. His modus operandi, especially his impulsiveness and secretiveness, made it difficult for reporters to do their work and left them resentful and angry. Unusually sensitive to criticism, he responded in a way that was often counterproductive. Joseph Alsop complained in 1965 of the "vigorous reprisals" meted out against those who wrote stories that angered the "Emperor" and of LBJ's "obvious desire to write every story about public matters that appears in every newspaper in the United States."[31] Johnson was less accessible to the press than Kennedy and much less skilled in repartee with them, and the harder he tried to put forth a favorable image the more he came across as sinister and manipulative. The phrase "credibility gap" was already a household word in Washington by the summer of 1965. Despite his success at home and abroad, the president was increasingly obsessed with his worsening image.[32]

III

What seems most striking, in retrospect, about the administration's July 1965 decisions for war is the almost negligible attention given to domestic opinion.

At a meeting on July 21, Undersecretary of State George W. Ball, the major opponent of escalation, resorted to the obvious analogy, using an elaborate set of charts from the Korean War to warn of possible dangers ahead. Ball admonished that a protracted war would generate powerful, perhaps irresistible, pressures to strike directly at North Vietnam, risking dangerous escalation. He also reminded the group that as casualties had increased in Korea between 1950 and 1952, public support had dropped from 56 percent to 30 percent. "We can't allow the country to wake up one morning and find heavy casualties," Ball warned. "We need to be damn serious with the American public."[33]

Interestingly, no one responded to Ball's warning, but on those few other occasions when the issue came up the tone was much more optimistic. At another point in the same meeting, McGeorge Bundy observed that the nation "seemed in the mood to accept grim news." In another meeting, Marine Corps Commandant Gen. Wallace Greene predicted that the nation would support the commitment of as many as 500,000 men for as long as five years.[34]

The issue also received a brief and revealing hearing at a meeting on July 27. Himself playing the role of devil's advocate, Johnson asked his advisers if Congress and the public would go along with 600,000 troops and billions of dollars being sent 10,000 miles away. Only Secretary of the Army Stanley Resor responded, laconically observing that the Gallup Poll showed that Americans were "basically behind our commitment." But, Johnson persisted, "if you make a commitment to jump off a building and you find out how high it is, you may want to withdraw that commitment," a remarkably prescient observation. No one responded, however, and nothing more was said. His mind apparently made up, the president dropped a crucial question and went on to something else.[35]

Some administration officials appear to have been complacent about holding public support. Drawing a sharp distinction between the political liabilities that had bedeviled France in the First Indochina War and the political advantages of the United States in 1965, McGeorge Bundy assured Johnson that the American public, although unenthusiastic, was reconciled to the U.S. role in Vietnam. "While there is widespread questioning and uneasiness about the way in which we may be playing that role," Bundy concluded, "the public as a whole seems to realize that the role must be played."[36]

Such complacency was reinforced in the summer of 1965 by clear signs of continuing public support. Polls even suggested a hawkish mood, a solid plurality of 47 percent favoring sending more troops to Vietnam, more than double the 23 percent who expressed uncertainty what to do, two and one-half times the 19 percent wanting to keep the same number, and four times the 11 percent who wanted to pull all U.S. troops out of Vietnam.[37]

Top administration officials seem also to have dismissed Ball's Korean analogy. Bundy speculated that the American people might have developed greater patience in the twelve years since the end of the Korean War.[38] Johnson and his advisers seem also to have felt they could get what they wanted in Vietnam without the travail and agony of Korea. They acted in the expectation that "reason and mutual concessions" would prevail, Bill Moyers later conceded, that Hanoi could be enticed or intimidated into negotiating and a drawn-out war avoided.[39] A fatal miscalculation about North Vietnam's response to U.S. escalation may therefore have been behind an equally fatal miscalculation about U.S. public opinion.

The administration clearly misread the significance of the budding peace movement. Rusk compared the campus protest of the spring and early summer of 1965 to the Oxford Union debate, observing that most of those who "took the pledge" in 1938 subsequently entered the military without protest.[40] Bundy later admitted that "we simply hadn't estimated the kinds of new forces that were loose in the land in the middle 1960s. I don't think anybody foresaw in 1964 and 1965 the overall cresting of feeling which had begun in 1964 at Berkeley."[41]

Some administration officials were sufficiently concerned about public opinion or sensitive to the importance of the July decision to urge forceful steps. Originally anticipating that the president would at least call up the reserves and declare a national emergency, some advisers in June 1965 had proposed a "full scenario" of actions to prepare the nation for war. A presidential message was to be drafted and plans laid for consultation with Congress. McNamara proposed creating a blue ribbon task force to explain the war and generate public support. Presidential aides even suggested the formation of a citizens committee like the Committee for the Marshall Plan to build elite support. White House adviser Horace Busby urged Johnson to go out and rally the public in the mode of a Franklin Roosevelt or Winston Churchill. The Wise Men encouraged him to explain to the public the need for more troops. "How do you send young men there in great numbers without telling why?" former ambassador to South Vietnam Henry Cabot Lodge, Jr., asked.[42]

The president rejected all these proposals. He undoubtedly feared that a public debate on Vietnam at this crucial time might jeopardize major pieces of Great Society legislation then pending in Congress. And he did not want to risk what he later called "the woman I really loved" (the Great Society) for "that bitch of a war on the other side of the world."[43]

But there were other, perhaps equally important, reasons intimately connected to prevailing theories about the way limited wars should be fought.

Johnson also feared that mobilizing the nation for war would set loose irresistible pressures for escalation and victory that might provoke a larger war with the Soviet Union and China, perhaps even the nuclear confrontation that the commitment in Vietnam had been designed to deter in the first place. At the very least, Rusk warned, a provocative U.S. move might push the Soviet Union and China to give greater support to North Vietnam and contribute to the healing of their rift. The administration thus concluded, as Rusk later put it, "that in a nuclear world it is just too dangerous for an entire people to get too angry and we deliberately . . . tried to do in cold blood what perhaps can only be done in hot blood."[44] "I don't want to be dramatic and cause tension," the president told his National Security Council on July 27.[45]

For a variety of reasons, then, Johnson gambled that without taking exceptional measures he could hold public support long enough to achieve his goals in Vietnam. "I think we can get our people to support us without having to be provocative," he told his advisers.[46] The United States thus went to war in July 1965 in a manner uniquely quiet and underplayed—in "cold blood." The president ordered his decisions implemented in a low key way. He announced the major troop increase at a noon press conference instead of at prime time and even lumped it in with a number of other items in a way that obscured its significance. Although he had approved the immediate deployment of 100,000 troops followed by another 100,000 in 1966, he revealed publicly only that he was sending 50,000, and he made this move as palatable as possible by not calling up the reserves and asking for a tax increase. It was a far cry from the parades and fanfare of World War I or the resigned determination of World War II or Korea. The public and elites may even have viewed the July 28 decisions with relief rather than grim acquiescence. In no real sense did the nation appear to be going to war.

IV

With the exception of several hastily arranged, typically Johnsonian public relations blitzes, the administration persisted in this low-key approach until 1967. It created no special machinery to monitor and manipulate public opinion. It took only a few modest steps to promote public support, leaving much of the work to nominally private groups. More often than not, its public relations efforts were reactive and defensive—and as the war wore on increasingly vindictive.

The administration's understanding of its public relations problems at the outset of the war combined naiveté and myopia with a good measure of perceptiveness. The problem with the South Vietnamese government, some officials reasoned, was its "mushy" public relations program rather than its chronic instability and palpable incompetence. Popular uneasiness with the war was attributed to misunderstanding. The American people and elites, even editors and publishers, did not comprehend how this "twilight war" differed from earlier wars, officials lamented. "We are still looking for the 'front,' still talking largely in terms of battles, number of casualties, tonnage of bombs."[47]

On the other hand, some of Johnson's advisers clearly perceived that public support, although broad, was perilously thin. There seemed little understanding of the larger policies upon which intervention in Vietnam was based. The public was "extremely vulnerable to rumor, gossip, and quick reverses," and each new initiative fed exaggerated expectations for a settlement that when not quickly realized led to disillusionment.[48] The administration seemed always on the defensive. "We only plug holes and run as fast as we can to stay even," Greenfield conceded.[49] Some lower-level officials also shrewdly perceived that the key to ultimate success was not the skill of their public relations activities but signs of progress in Vietnam. "What we need more than anything else is some visible evidence of success for our efforts to defeat the Viet Cong, deter Hanoi, and . . . bring peace to the Vietnamese countryside."[50]

Assuming that in "twilight war" education rather than exhortation was the key to public support, administration officials mounted a quiet, behind-the-scenes campaign. In keeping with limited war theory, no Office of War Information was established and no dramatic programs undertaken to rally the public to the cause. Organizationally, the administration would go no further than create a Vietnam Public Affairs Policy Committee, chaired by McGeorge Bundy and made up of representatives from the State and Defense departments, the Agency for International Development (AID), and the United States Information Agency (USIA). The committee met weekly, its assigned task to discuss public relations problems and coordinate the activities of the various agencies involved.[51]

Recognizing that if they did not fill the vacuum in public opinion it would be filled against them, administration officials took a number of steps to deal with problems and build support. The president directed top officials to make major speeches and personally targeted certain areas of the country for attention.[52] A New York public relations firm was hired to improve the image of the Saigon government. The booklet *Why Vietnam?* was sent to every member of Congress and every major newspaper, and a film by the same name, originally designed for military recruits, was sent to nearly five hundred high schools and colleges and shown on a number of commercial television stations.[53] Administration officials conducted briefings for state governors and compiled packets of materials that could be used to defend the war. They closely monitored press and congressional debates, watching for and answering criticisms.[54]

To avoid blatant propagandizing, the government to a considerable degree privatized its selling of the war. With administration advice and assistance, the Young Democrats mounted drives on college campuses in support of U.S. policy. The Junior Chamber of Commerce arranged half-time ceremonies at local and nationally televised football games to include salutes to America's "fighting men" in Vietnam.[55] The elite citizens committee, headed by Arthur Dean, ran full-page ads in the *New York Times* and thirteen other newspapers endorsing the president's Vietnam policy.[56]

With hidden-hand support from the administration and private funding arranged by White House staffers, the American Friends of Vietnam through the last six months of 1965 continued to spearhead the prowar drive. It established a speakers bureau to make available speakers for teach-ins and other forums. It made contact with friendly student, labor, and business groups and worked through civic clubs. It published a periodical, *Vietnam Perspectives*, conducted seminars, instituted people-to-people programs through which American groups would "adopt" Vietnamese villages, and sponsored newspaper advertisements.[57]

Administration officials remained deeply concerned about the reporting of the war. From the government's perspective, journalists did not seem well prepared for this new kind of conflict. Either they lacked experience in war altogether or their experience in World War II blinded them to what was going on in Vietnam. The press put too much emphasis on the military aspects of the war, too little on the political; too much on the American role, too little on the South Vietnamese. "We may not know how to fight the war," Greenfield observed, "but the correspondents don't know how to report it either."[58]

An incident at Cam Ne less than a week after Johnson's decisions for war highlighted the incipient problems with the press, made clear the special problems created by television coverage, and sparked a debate among administration officials on how best to respond. In early August, CBS ran on its evening news report, complete with film, correspondent Morley Safer's account of the burning of the village of Cam Ne by U.S. Marines. Pentagon public affairs officer Arthur Sylvester bitterly complained of unfriendly journalists, many of them, like Safer (a Canadian), foreigners "who miss no chance to embarrass us." Greenfield retorted that in limited war it was necessary to get accustomed to "fighting in the open" in the full glare of television cameras. The key was to ensure that such things as Cam Ne did not happen, not to keep them from being reported. It was not primarily a question of public relations but rather how the war should be fought. "You can't win the people in Vietnam by burning their villages," he insisted.[59]

For the most part, in dealing with the press, the administration continued to rely on persuasion rather than coercion. Sylvester did try to get Safer replaced by an American reporter who, in his view, better understood the new kind of war. On occasion, administration officials read the riot act to the media. Harriman told the editorial board of the *New York Times* in "very blunt" language that the more people opposed the president's policies the longer it would be before North Vietnam came to the conference table.[60] Still, although some officials continued to advocate censorship, the administration stuck to the policy of "maximum candor." Large numbers of correspondents were admitted to Vietnam and given maximum feasible access to information while being asked only to protect the security of U.S. personnel and operations. Administration officials considered conducting a course for journalists on the nature of guerrilla war. They sought to provide better briefings for journalists. To get more balanced reporting, military and civilian spokesmen were directed to draw attention to nonmilitary matters and highlight enemy atrocities.[61]

The administration used similarly low-key tactics in dealing with the growing antiwar protests. In the beginning, at least, top officials seem not to have taken the movement seriously. More concerned with the right wing in American politics, what he labeled the "great lurking monster," the president probably agreed with Marine Commandant Greene that the antiwar movement constituted little more than a "small, misguided and misinformed element of our citizenry."[62] Publicly, the administration maintained a low profile, going out of its way to avoid "any impression of an overly worried reaction" to major demonstrations in November.[63] To neutralize the protestors, the president designated November 28 a day of dedication and prayer honoring those who were risking their lives to bring about a just peace in Vietnam.[64]

In keeping with its larger public relations approach, the administration left to private groups major responsibility for responding to the antiwar movement. Freedom House sponsored an advertisement in major newspapers urging Americans to "shout" their approval of U.S. policy so that it would ring "as loudly in Peking as in Peoria" and be understood in "Hanoi as in Houston."[65] With administration advice and assistance, the Young Democrats tried to use their national convention to launch a drive on university and college campuses in support of Vietnam policy. Working through the AFV, student organizations, including the CIA-funded National Student Association, agreed to issue public statements disassociating themselves from campus protest.[66]

Despite its considerable efforts, the White House could not have been comforted by public opinion surveys taken at the end of the year. Administration policies continued to enjoy general support, but officials recognized that its backing was soft in a number of crucial ways. A significant portion of those supporting the president on Vietnam thought he should do more faster to defeat the NLF and North Vietnam. In addition, as Greenfield observed, although there was popular support for the war the war was not popular.[67] No one better captured the public mood than old New Dealer David Lilienthal. To "judge by the people on the streets and in the restaurants," he noted in his journal, there was no way to tell that a war was on, "parties . . . , Park Avenue glittering with lighted trees." Yet beneath the surface insouciance, Lilienthal detected a growing "angst" over the war, anxiety no longer over whether the United States could win, a hope already abandoned, but whether it could extricate itself from the tangle.[68]

The great danger, opinion analyst Hayes Redmon warned, would be the inability, as in Korea, to secure a settlement. Thus he advised Moyers in December 1965, "If we are to have public support for our policies—if we are to blunt mounting frustration—it is absolutely essential that the public be constantly reassured that we are doing all we can to get an honorable settlement." Redmon thus proposed a series of moves, "preferably dramatic," to reassure the nation that every imaginable effort was being made to secure peace.[69]

V

At the beginning of 1966, Johnson did take several dramatic steps to rally public support. To make clear that everything possible was being done to attain a peaceful settlement, in part to prepare the way for another escalation of the war, the administration stopped the bombing for thirty-seven days and staged its noisy "peace offensive." To preempt from a public relations standpoint the Fulbright committee's hearings on Vietnam, Johnson in February hustled off to Honolulu for the impromptu "summit" meeting with South Vietnamese leaders.[70]

Following this burst of activity, the president reverted to the low-key approach adopted earlier. Throughout much of 1966, he maintained an uncharacteristically low profile, spending three months at the LBJ Ranch, holding few press conferences, and making even fewer speeches. At first, his silence was justified in terms of strategic necessity, aides confiding his fear that statements of optimism might sway hawks to press for victory and doves for negotiations. Journalists later speculated that he was lying low as a way of dealing with his sagging popularity. Increasingly, he was criticized for being the most aloof chief executive since Calvin Coolidge and for being unable to communicate to the nation a sense of what it was doing in Vietnam and why it was necessary.[71]

While carefully remaining behind the scenes, Johnson did orchestrate, often personally, a wide-ranging effort to sustain public support for the war. Administratively, several changes were made. The Vietnam Public Affairs Policy Committee was replaced by a Vietnam Public Affairs Working Group, chaired first by Moyers and then by Assistant Secretary of State Harold Kaplan, which met weekly to discuss Vietnam public relations issues and coordinate the activities of the various agencies and departments.[72] In the spring of 1966, an increasingly worried White House began a more systematic tracking of public opinion polls, the press, speeches in Congress, and statements by important public figures.[73] In April, the president appointed veteran journalist Robert Kintner as a general adviser on press relations, giving him, along with Moyers, the formidable assignment of trying to improve relations with an increasingly skeptical and hostile media.[74]

In the quiet, low-key manner directed by the president, administration officials carried out a full range of activities to sell the war. The State Department put together a poster exhibit, "The Faces of Freedom in Vietnam," sent out five-minute audio-tapes to radio stations, made available "kits" to high school and college debate teams, and distributed to various audiences "Fact Sheets" on Vietnam, short statements of the official position on the war, "deliberately concise, easily absorbed, and written in basic English."[75] Teams of briefers from various agencies spoke to state legislatures and other elected officials. Military and civilian officials just returned from Vietnam discussed their experiences before civic groups and public service organizations. Top officials such as Rusk, William Bundy, and Vice-President Hubert H. Humphrey made speeches, appeared on television programs such as "Meet the Press," and held regular backgrounders for journalists. Kintner did a lot of what he called "missionary work" among critical journalists like James Reston and Joseph Kraft, chastised NBC news for its hostility to the president and its sensationalist and inaccurate coverage of the war, and urged his media colleagues to report the conflict with greater balance.[76] Even in-house dove George Ball, most likely with the president's encouragement, met with prominent opponents of the war such as columnists Walter Lippmann and Reston and Senator George McGovern, insisting that the administration had no choice but to do what it was doing and must see the war through to a successful conclusion.[77]

Hypersensitive to the political implications of anything that concerned the war, the president oversaw the entire effort with almost microscopic attention to detail. He grew concerned early in the year that critics might highlight the brutality of the war by seizing upon the designation "MASHER" given a major offensive in the Central Highlands. McGeorge Bundy therefore quietly urged Gen. Wheeler to tell the military command in Saigon to use for operations "neutral" and "innocuous" designations which even the most biased person could not exploit. Perhaps with tongue in cheek, the military changed MASHER to WHITE WING and afterwards named operations for American cities, historic places, and important persons.[78] Fearful later in the year that rising casualty figures might erode public support for the war, Johnson directed his aides to determine how many of the reported casualties were serious and how many only moderate and slight.[79]

Taking their cue from the commander in chief, military leaders in Washingthon showed equal sensitivity to public opinion. A *Playboy* show for the troops in Vietnam was canceled for fear of possible negative publicity, and the military command in Saigon quickly corrected an erroneous report that the lst Cavalry Division had constructed at An Khe a twenty-five-acre spread of officially supervised "boom-boom palaces."[80] When the administration launched a new bombing offensive against North Vietnam in late 1966, Wheeler instructed the military in Vietnam not to use the word "escalation," a "dirty word" that imposed "further inhibitions here against moving ahead to win this war."[81]

Increasingly on the defensive, administration officials responded to criticism in a way that was typically Johnsonian and generally counterproductive. If Ronald Reagan was the "teflon president," to whom nothing stuck, Johnson—to a large degree by choice—was the "flypaper president," to whom everything clung. A compulsive reader, viewer, and listener who took every criticism personally and to heart, he was at first intent on and then obsessed with answering every accusation, responding to every charge. "Unless prompt replies are given," he once instructed his aides, "those who criticize get up a head of steam; it is like taking dope."[82]

When Gen. Matthew Ridgway came out against the war, the president ordered Army Chief of Staff Johnson to get statements of support from two leading World War II generals, Omar Bradley and J. Lawton Collins.[83] When a group of lawyers charged that U.S. intervention in Vietnam was illegal, speechwriter Harry McPherson tried to get another legal organization to uphold its legality.[84] Harried White House staffers spent hours answering line for line criticism from journalists and congressmen. Reams of paper were devoted to proving how wrong Lippmann had been on so many occasions. Thousands of hours were wasted compiling dossiers on persistent critics like Fulbright and the despised Kennedy brothers.[85]

The president personally—and closely—monitored the speeches of his advisers. In July, he pressed Harriman to cool what he saw as a dangerous optimism building in the country, urging him to go no further than emphasize the administration's "determination to see it through." He also unleashed Harriman to go after the antiwar forces, instructing him to underline in a speech in Omaha that dissent encouraged North Vietnam.[86] At about the same time, the White House issued a set of guidelines for speeches, themes that were to be "elaborated and driven home systematically." Cabinet officials should be "confident," not "optimistic," should not promise "too much, too soon" but should affirm that the United States would persist and would succeed.[87]

The president constantly struggled with the public relations dilemmas of trying to fight what had become a full-scale war in cold blood, seeking to find the happy but elusive middle ground between too much attention to the war and too little. Fearful that if the United States did not "get out its story" the accounts of its enemies would "preempt the news," he pushed Lodge and Westmoreland in July to conduct regular briefings and to keep the media informed "seven days a week, 24 hours a day."[88] Just a short time after, the White House squelched a State Department press release that highlighted the war on the grounds that the president needed to show "he is *not* wholly preoccupied with Vietnam."[89]

Despite the size and scale of their public relations campaign, administration officials by mid-year were increasingly concerned. Privatization of selling the war accomplished little because groups such as the American Friends of Vietnam were too small and poorly funded to have great influence. White House aides fretted that the president desperately needed to "freshen his image." Gallup and Harris polls also made clear that inflation, race relations, and especially Vietnam had the public "frustrated" and in a "foul mood." Support for the war persisted, but advocates of increasing or terminating the bombing spoke out with a new urgency, and Senator Richard Russell's "get it over with or get out" approach appeared to be gaining in popularity. There was growing "distaste" for what appeared an "indecisive stalemate" in which increasing numbers of American lives were being spent but uncertainty what should be done to break it. The "isolated island in the middle" on which the president was standing might shrink smaller and smaller. He could still count on solid support for whatever initiative he might undertake, and he had to offer the nation hope. If nothing materialized, however, "we would be in a more disastrous position than we are now."[90]

White House staffers pressed Johnson to take the lead in dealing with these problems. He could best improve his image, they said, by letting his natural toughness and aggressiveness show through. He must develop a more persuasive argument for American involvement in Vietnam, shifting the emphasis from altruism to hard-nosed realism and self-interest. Rostow urged him to "get off the defensive" and "rally the sound 60% of the country."[91] Valenti pressed him to warn voters that his defeat in the critical, off-year elections would play into the hands of the enemy and thwart peace, thus, at least "by inference," charging those who opposed him with prolongation of the war. The administration's refusal to arouse the public, Valenti warned, left a vacuum television was filling against him. Until the "home front, as it used to be called, is given a role, however small—until the people have a sense of participation and sacrifice," Horace Busby added, "confusion will increase, frustration will spread, irritation will rise hazardously."[92]

Responding to the pleas of his advisers, Johnson emerged from his self-imposed isolation in the summer and fall of 1966. In a much-publicized speaking tour of the Midwest, he employed some of the arguments recommended to him, emphasizing enemy atrocities and complaining that U.S. forces were not getting the support they deserved. Just before the elections, he donned the hat of commander in chief, flying off to Manila to preside over an assemblage of the leaders of the seven nations fighting in Vietnam, then visiting each of the nations and using the publicity thus generated to drum up support for his policies.[93]

These efforts were no more than modestly successful, however, and by the beginning of 1967 the administration was beginning to perceive that its most urgent problem might be at home. Relations with the press had deteriorated drastically. As the American role expanded, complaints of the journalists in Vietnam grew louder. Despite the liberal policies adopted by the U.S. government, journalists complained that the South Vietnamese were restricting their ability to cover the war. U.S. civilian and military officials, on the other hand, dismissed the journalists in Vietnam as second-rate, accused them of being one-sided, and complained that they covered the war from the bars.[94]

The war within the war was worse in the United States. Journalists bitterly protested the "McNamara flak screen" that surrounded the Pentagon, resulting in a form of censorship that had not been imposed in Vietnam, and blamed it on the president, McNamara, and Sylvester.[95] After being shut off from the White House, Alsop bitterly complained that the government had sunk to "depths in which glints of espionage alternate with hints of suspicion and persecution, of a sort I had not expected to encounter in American society in my lifetime."[96] Throughout much of the year, the president engaged in a running feud with the *New York Times*. Journalists complained louder and louder of the credibility gap. Administration officials griped about biased and inaccurate coverage of the war.

The public mood was even more worrisome. Polls made clear the persistence of solid support, and public opinion remained permissive, eagerly endorsing any initiative "offering even the slightest promise of peace." On the other hand, the president's job approval rating declined steadily, and his personal credibility gap widened.[97] Whatever he said was "ignored, made fun of, rejected, and worst of all not believed," a sympathetic Lilienthal observed.[98] Perhaps more ominous, the number of those who thought a mistake had been made sending troops to Vietnam increased sharply, raising the parallels to Korea that Ball had warned of in July 1965.[99] Still more unnerving was the mood of the nation, anxious, frustrated, increasingly divided. This "pinpoint on the globe," Lilienthal observed of Vietnam, was "like an infection, a 'culture' of some horrible disease, a cancer where the wildly growing cells multiply and multiply until the whole body is poisoned."[100]

Warnings from friends and advisers grew more ominous. Attacking the very concept of limited war, former general and president Dwight D. Eisenhower, whom Johnson had cultivated with the utmost care, curtly dismissed the McNamarian notion that "small wars" like Vietnam could go on indefinitely and society must be prepared to support them. Americans "eventually get tired of supporting involvements of this kind," the former president insisted, and the war must be ended as soon as possible.[101] Journalist Drew Pearson expressed personal distress at the drastic change in public attitudes toward the president and warned that in any vote "the odds would be against your reelection." Komer urged Johnson to mount a "major information campaign" to combat the looming danger. Rostow advised the creation of a special task force to inform a confused and uncertain public.[102]

Perhaps no one better captured the public frustration and the president's dilemma than his wife. "A miasma of trouble hangs over everything," Lady Bird Johnson confided to her diary early in 1967. "The temperament of our people seems to be, 'you must either get excited, get passionate, fight and get it over with, or we must pull out.' It is unbearably hard to fight a limited war."[103]

VI

Johnson's position worsened dramatically in 1967. Expansion of the war brought increased casualties and new taxes, and as the cost grew with no apparent end in view public frustration mounted. Rioting in the cities, a spiraling crime rate, and noisy demonstrations in the streets suggested that violence abroad had produced violence at home. Increasingly divided against itself, the nation appeared on the verge of an internal crisis as severe as the Great Depression, and by late 1967 the war had become for many observers the most visible symbol of a malaise that seemed to afflict all of American society. The president himself was a man under siege in the White House, the target of vicious personal attacks. His top aides had to be brought surreptitiously into public forums to deliver their speeches.

Signs of opposition appeared everywhere. By mid-1967, for the first time a near majority of Americans began telling pollsters that involvement in Vietnam had been a mistake. Only slightly more than 25 percent approved Johnson's handling of the war. The antiwar movement gained prominent new adherents like Dr. Martin Luther King, Jr., and the pace of protest quickened, culminating with a massive march on Washington in October. The Saigon press corps was more antagonistic than ever, relentlessly attacking the South Vietnamese for inaction and incompetence and proclaiming in banner headlines that the war had degenerated into a stalemate. In the United States major newspapers and periodicals that had supported the war began to question it or at least criticize the president's conduct of it. Rumblings of opposition in Congress grew louder, and there were major defections among key Democrats and Republicans. Friendly politicians began to warn of a possibly disastrous defeat at the polls in 1968.[104]

Persuaded that the United States was at last making some progress in Vietnam, Johnson increasingly feared that the war might be lost at home. He expressed great frustration with his inability to get across his message. "It is hell," he complained, "when a president has to spend half of his time keeping his own people juiced up."[105] He was particularly worried by the charge that the war had become a stalemate, and he groped for some magic formula to reverse the spread of disillusionment. On several occasions, he expressed almost wistful longing for "some colorful general like McArthur [sic] with his shirt neck open" who could dismiss as "pure Communist propaganda" the talk of a stalemate and could go to Saigon and take on the press. We "have no songs, no parades, no bond drives," he lamented, "and we can't win otherwise." "We've got to do something dramatic."[106]

Still refusing to "get emotional," as some of his advisers now urged, Johnson, in the last five months of 1967, did launch a wide-ranging program to rally support for the war. As so often in the past, he designed major military and diplomatic initiatives with an eye toward the home front. To appease the increasingly restive hawks, he authorized major new bombing targets in August and again in September. The San Antonio formula, announced in a speech on September 29, was intended to placate the doves and was timed to take the steam out of the October march on Washington.

Belatedly perceiving that the doves posed at least as great a threat as the hawks, Johnson took the offensive against them.[107] Publicly, the administration continued to act with restraint. Top officials refused to attack the protestors, going no further than to avow that the movement did not represent majority opinion and warn that it was sending the wrong signals to Hanoi. The administration treated the march on Washington with great care, scrupulously upholding the protestors' right to dissent while desperately attempting to maintain order and protect government property. [108]

Behind the scenes, however, Johnson ordered a number of measures to discredit and limit the effectiveness of the movement. He instructed the CIA and FBI to institute surveillance of antiwar leaders to prove his suspicions that they were Communists acting on orders from foreign governments. The president repeatedly insisted that he "did not want to be like a McCarthyite," but he was true to himself only in the most literal sense. When the CIA was unable to prove the links he was certain existed, he told friendly congressmen he had the proof, leaving it to them to issue reckless charges that the peace movement was being cranked up in Hanoi. He also confided to congressional allies that draft card burners were "crazy people," many of whom had been in mental institutions, and warned vaguely and ominously that "the country was in greater danger than we think." [109]

The war against the movement included harassment and disruption. Law enforcement agencies began to indict antiwar leaders such as pediatrician Dr. Benjamin Spock for such things as counseling draft resistance. The FBI and CIA investigated critical journalists like Peter Arnet and Joseph Kraft and antiwar groups such as Students for a Democratic Society, SANE, and Women's Strike for Peace. They sent phony letters to editors of major newspapers defaming the movement and its leaders and leaked information to friendly journalists detailing the alleged subversive activities of antiwar groups. They infiltrated the movement to disrupt its activities and provoke its members to do things that would discredit them in the eyes of the public. [110]

Recognizing that it might lose the war unless it could "get its story told," the administration employed both carrot and stick in a desperate effort to preserve some influence with an increasingly hostile media. Johnson made up with prowar journalists like Alsop and even invited Alsop to assist in the drafting of a major presidential statement. [111] The administration showered favors on friendly journalists while denying interviews to those deemed hostile. [112] When it was learned that *Time-Life* publications might be jumping off a sputtering bandwagon, top editors were given free access to U.S. military commanders to get a private, first-hand report on the war. [113] In the meantime, national security adviser Rostow unleashed a full barrage against critics such as *Newsweek* for their "shallow journalism." [114]

The military command persisted in its futile effort to win over the Saigon press corps. Although top military and civilian officials admitted they would have liked to impose censorship, they continued to resist the temptation for the obvious reason that the political costs would be much higher than any possible gains. Westmoreland rejected even McNamara's modest proposal to bar journalists from going on air combat strikes.[115] Still hoping as in past wars that the media could be used as a channel to the public, the White House pushed officials in Saigon to improve their daily briefings and in particular to present the "big picture" more effectively. Westmoreland and Ambassador Ellsworth Bunker were instructed to provide more backgrounders.[116] In Saigon, the Mission Council gave highest priority to the "press effort" and implored military and civilian officials to be more open and forthcoming with correspondents. MACV attempted to find briefers who could work more effectively with the press and to keep well-informed briefers close to journalists at all times.[117]

To deal with public relations problems more systematically and effectively, the administration established in August 1967 a Vietnam Information Group. Comprised of representatives of the various agencies involved in Vietnam, housed in the White House, and given a staff of its own, the VIG met weekly with Rostow and Press Secretary Christian. It was to serve as a "quick reaction team" that could seize any opportunity to "strike a positive note" and, by dealing with problems before the administration was thrown on the defensive, break out of the "counter punching, siege mentality" that had thus far dominated Vietnam public relations. Its specific tasks included identifying public relations issues and setting priorities for handling them, coordinating public relations activities, collecting data about the war, compiling publications, providing briefing materials, assisting public affairs offices in the State and Defense departments, and monitoring the flow of information. It was no Creel committee or even Office of War Information, but the VIG did represent a first, belated effort to assign administrative responsibility for an increasingly urgent problem. Calling public opinion the "X factor" in the Vietnam equation, Director Harold Kaplan emphasized to his colleagues that the group's work must not be permitted to lapse like the committees before it. Perceiving the sensitivity of the media and public to anything resembling propaganda, it went about its task with notable caution. At its first meeting, Kaplan impressed upon participants the need for "discretion" since the press had already criticized the VIG as a "miniature Office of War Information."[118]

The Vietnam Information Group coordinated a full-scale public relations campaign in the late summer and fall of 1967. White House staffers tried to minimize the damage of the credibility gap by showing that even the greatest of American presidents had similar "gaps." They sought to spread doubts about the validity of public opinion polls that ran against the president. At Johnson's direction, they assigned top-level people like Lodge and Gen. William Depuy to conduct off-the-record briefings "for key persons in those areas that particularly need some religion." They closely monitored statements in Congress, helping friendly congressmen make speeches, ignoring critics who were "beyond redemption," and spending considerable time and effort trying to influence those who still might be swayed.[119]

Following Cold War precedents of twenty years, the administration in the fall of 1967 also made a calculated effort to hold the foreign policy elite and through it the "vital center" in American politics. With considerable publicity, Johnson in early November, for the first time in nearly two years, called in for counsel the Wise Men to make clear to a worried nation that he was getting the best advice and to secure validation from these experts for his policies.[120]

From behind the scenes, administration officials also orchestrated the creation of a citizens committee modeled on the Committee for the Marshall Plan to promote support for the war. The formation of such a committee had been discussed for over two years, and it is a measure of White House concern that in late 1967 talk finally gave way to action. Called the Committee for Peace with Freedom in Vietnam, the group was headed by former Democratic senator Paul Douglas of Illinois, with former presidents Eisenhower and Harry S Truman as honorary chairmen. Its avowed purpose was to "raise a banner to which the silent center can repair," to appeal to the presumed majority of Americans who opposed capitulation on the one hand and drastic escalation on the other.

With considerable fanfare, the so-called Douglas committee went public on October 23, the day after the antiwar march on Washington. Employing means similar to those of its illustrious predecessors, it set out to offset antiwar propaganda and mobilize grass roots support so that the majority voice would be heard "loud and clear" and a distinct signal sent to Hanoi. Its numbers quickly increased to around 1,500, and Douglas was heartened by the early response, excitedly informing Acheson that his office was "literally flooded" with requests for information and offers of support, confirming his view that there was a "silent center" in this time of polarization.[121]

In addition to holding the "silent center," the 1967 public relations campaign sought to combat the perception, fed by the Saigon press corps, that the South Vietnamese Army (ARVN) was not doing its job. To convey the notion that, despite the size of the American presence, the conflict remained a Vietnamese rather than an American war, MACV in late 1967 began using Vietnamese names to designate major military operations. Westmoreland assigned a U.S. information officer to each ARVN commander to try to improve South

Vietnamese relations with the American press. The military command made particular efforts to get more favorable coverage of ARVN operations. When a battle broke out in Chuong Thien province late in the year, MACV airlifted journalists to the scene of the action, and the administration later rejoiced at the favorable coverage.[122]

The centerpiece of the 1967 public relations campaign was a calculated, multifaceted effort to dispel the notion that the war had become a stalemate and persuade an increasingly skeptical nation that the United States was making "steady if slow progress." Throughout the summer of 1967, the press was filled with articles proclaiming that the war had become a stalemate and that victory, if indeed it could be achieved, was still years, maybe decades away.[123] The articles particularly troubled Johnson, and as the summer wore on he became obsessed with answering them. Washington officials devoted great attention to responding to the charges. The president instructed top officials in Saigon to "search urgently for occasions to present sound evidence of progress in Viet Nam."[124]

In both Saigon and Washington in the last months of 1967, great efforts were made to dispute the stalemate charge. The president formed a task force, headed by the director of Central Intelligence, to review the means used to measure progress and come up with new instruments to meet the "urgent need for reliable, useable data."[125] MACV worked up comparisons going back to 1965 to show progress in such areas as village security, government control of territory and population, and ARVN training and performance. U.S. officials identified subjects about which the press had doubts and sought to present "concise, hard-hitting briefings" to allay "credibility problems." Briefers especially stressed that there were signs of winning "where it counts, that is, in the minds of the people."[126]

Sympathetic opinion-makers were brought into the campaign. Information was leaked to Alsop for a series of columns elaborating official claims of progress and predicting that it would continue unless the home front failed the troops just "when the great turning point has been reached."[127] New York Times military analyst Hanson Baldwin spent three weeks in Vietnam, visiting various bases and talking to GI's and generals alike. In a series of articles in late November and early December, he dutifully reported that "there are clear signs of progress."[128] To enable opinion leaders to see for themselves the progress that had been made, the president dispatched to Vietnam at government expense "selected private citizens," legislators, educators, and clergy, people who were "basically sympathetic to national policy" and would presumably come home and persuade others.[129]

The campaign focused especially on the enemy. "The trouble has been,"

Kaplan observed, "that the American public has seen the enemy's problems through a glass darkly, while ours are pitilessly spotlighted and magnified by the enormous press corps in Saigon."[130] Using interrogations and captured documents, MACV conducted intensive studies, some later leaked to the press, showing a decline in VC/NVA morale, difficulties in recruiting and raising taxes, and loss of control of the people.[131]

U.S. officials relied heavily on captured documents to prove their point. From the hundreds of thousands of documents taken from the enemy, experts selected and translated those items that most graphically demonstrated the growing problems of the NLF and NVA. They added introductions in the form of "low key comments" to put the documents in context. These Vietnam Documents and Research Notes were then released to the USIS, editors and journalists, scholars, and libraries. The first issue, "The Diary of an Infiltrator," highlighted the increasing hardships suffered by enemy forces in the south.[132]

In November, Johnson began to inject into the campaign the sort of emotion to this point he had so carefully refrained from using. Support for the war dropped to an all-time low in October, and *Time* observed that the "only audible consensus" in the nation was the one building against the president.[133] Certain by this time that "the main front of the war is here in the United States," lamenting that his people were not as "solid in support of my soldiers as Ho's people are solid in support of his troops," he wondered aloud at one meeting about the possible impact on the nation should he decide not to run again.[134]

By mid-October, depression and self-pity had given way to a fighting mood. On October 17, he enjoined his top aides to "pull their gloves off" in speeches and press conferences. "Too many signs are bad now," he warned. "We need to be a little more outspoken."[135] He himself took the lead. In a 5,100-mile tour of U.S. military bases and in a fighting Veterans Day speech, he went on the attack. Vietnam was not "an academic question," he insisted. "It is not a topic for cocktail parties, office arguments, or debate from some distant sidelines." The lives of American troops were tied by "flesh and blood to Viet Nam." Victory would be possible only if the home front stood firm.[136]

At a press conference on November 17, he abandoned the stiff, formal style that had become his trademark, defending his policies in a conversational manner and with great emotion. In war or football, he noted, Americans wanted quick decisions—"get in or get out"—but this was not the kind of conflict the nation was fighting in Vietnam. Admitting that "we take two steps forward and we slip back one," he reiterated claims of progress. In the still supercharged aftermath of the March on Washington, he reserved special comment for dissent. Reminding his listeners that there had been protest in every American war, he defended "responsible dissent," adding, with rare self-deprecation, that if he had done anything as president it was to "insure that there are plenty of dissenters." But he condemned the "storm trooper" tactics of some antiwar protestors, chided the press for not defending the first amendment on which it depended, and warned that "storm trooper bullying," "rowdyism," and suppression of free speech were "extremely dangerous to the national interest and harmful to America's fighting men in Vietnam."[137] Kintner labeled the press conference a "masterpiece," and even the president's most bitter critics were impressed with his performance. Last week the "real Johnson" reemerged, *Time* observed, "combative, spontaneous, self-assured," ready to reassert his leadership and face the opposition head-on.[138]

To sustain the momentum, the administration brought back to Washington Ambassador Bunker and General Westmoreland for the first of a projected series of reports to the nation. The move was designed to meet the need for a "comprehensive presentation" on the war in a form that would have "the greatest possible positive impact on current public questions on progress of [the] war." It was stage-managed with all the care of a Broadway opening, even to the point of orchestrating the answers to likely questions. The emphasis, Rostow said, should be on the "solid progress" being made "in the right direction."[139] At a press conference on November 13, Bunker reported "steady progress" and "every prospect" that it would "accelerate." At a joint appearance on "Meet the Press" on November 19, Bunker reiterated his claims of progress and Westmoreland proclaimed that the United States was "winning" a war of attrition. In a much publicized speech to the National Press Club on November 21, Westmoreland reiterated this generally optimistic view of the war, proclaiming, "We have reached an important point where the end begins to come into view."[140]

At a top-level meeting at the White House the following day, U.S. officials agreed on a full agenda of moves to sustain public support. Civilian casualties should be reduced as much as possible. To mitigate rising public concern about U.S. casualties, briefers, in reporting the figures, should carefully differentiate between those actually hospitalized and those with only minor wounds. More influential visitors should be sent to Saigon to observe the progress first-hand. To counter the notion that the United States was fighting the war alone, everything possible should be done to put ARVN "center stage," improve its image, and correct the mistaken impression that it would not fight. Westmoreland and Bunker should make periodic reports to the nation.[141]

The 1967 public relations campaign had mixed results. Whatever its value, the dispatch of dignitaries to Saigon was also a burden, the embassy complaining by January 1968 that it was "drowning under the load of visitors." The more the military command sought to demonstrate ARVN's improvement, the more the Saigon press corps sniffed out deficiencies. Among most media, indeed, distrust of government pronouncements was by this time so deeply ingrained that official claims of progress were instinctively greeted with skepticism. Cricitism of the war and Johnson's handling of it continued in the country and Congress, and there were more crucial defections like moderate Republican senator Thruston B. Morton of Kentucky and Massachusetts Democratic congressman Thomas P. O'Neill.[142]

The campaign did pay some dividends, however. For the first time in months, Gallup and Harris polls showed dramatic increases in approval of Johnson's handling of the war, and for the first time since the summer, his approval rating exceeded the disapproval. His popularity surged by eleven points in early December, and there was another smaller upswing in early January. Although criticism continued, moreover, Johnson himself was pleased with what he regarded as an overall improvement in media coverage. He thus concluded that his hard sell had worked and that the nation was rallying around its leaders. Possibly, indeed, had the situation developed differently in the winter of 1968, the public relations campaign might have bought him some vital time by stabilizing public support at least temporarily.[143]

In fact, in one of the most cruel ironies of a war rich in irony, it merely deepened his problems. On January 31, 1968, the North Vietnamese launched massive coordinated attacks against the cities and towns of South Vietnam. As perhaps nothing else could have, the so-called Tet offensive put the lie to the administration's year-end claims of progress, forcing Johnson after a period of soul-searching to withdraw from the presidential race and alter his methods in Vietnam if not his fundamental goals.

VII

Johnson's ill-fated efforts to manage public opinion in the Vietnam War illustrate most graphically the difficulties of fighting a war in cold blood. Unlike his counterpart in total war, the president cannot drape himself in the flag and rally the nation to the war and himself. Yet he must have public backing for his policies. How to balance these conflicting demands especially vexed Johnson, and as the war grew more unpopular, anything he did or did not do opened him to ridicule, abuse, indignation, or outrage. If he attempted to raise morale, as with his infamous injunction to the troops to "nail that coonskin to the wall," he was pilloried by those who opposed the war. If he did nothing, he was charged with failing to lead. Johnson never resolved this dilemma.

Perhaps complacent at the outset, he and his advisers played it low-keyed, hoping to hold public support without exciting popular passions. This did not happen, of course, and by late 1967 they had to mount a desperate, rearguard action to prevent the total collapse of the home front.

Johnson and his advisers also faced enormous problems in trying to sell this particular war. A once compliant media was abandoning its role as accomplice in the national security state for its more traditional role as adversary. Television coverage of the war, however primitive, posed new and difficult problems that policymakers did not perceive clearly, much less come to grips with. In addition, Vietnam was by any accounting a difficult war to sell. There was no perceivable threat to America's security or even its vital interests, and it was not easy to make a case on grounds of altruism when the Saigon government was so palpably corrupt and undemocratic, North Vietnam's role so cleverly disguised, and Ho Chi Minh the one legitimate national hero. Cold War rhetoric appeared increasingly shopworn, moreover, at a time when the Soviets and Chinese were shouting and shooting at each other.

Johnson's personality and leadership style posed still further problems. His wooden television manner, especially as contrasted with his legendary predecessor, continually afflicted his ability as a political pitchman, and his image as the master manipulator rendered even his most innocent pronouncements automatically suspect. His obsessive urge to control everything and his near pathological craving for approval exacerbated an already serious problem. Subsequent experience suggests that he might have done better to stand above the furor, blithely ignoring his critics rather than trying to win them over, but this was only clear in retrospect and in any event it was totally out of character for him.

Operating within the parameters set by limited war theory, the Johnson administration did take steps to build and sustain public support. Until the establishment of the Vietnam Information Group in 1967, administrative responsibility was not clearly designated nor people given exclusive responsibility for this crucial area, and for this, as well as its initial complacency, the administration can be faulted. Seeing themselves in the role of educators rather than exhorters, the president and his top advisers tried to get across why the nation was fighting and persuade an increasingly skeptical public that it was succeeding. Administration officials closely tracked polls and the press and monitored Congress. Cautiously at first, more vigorously as the war wore on, the administration sought to answer its growing list of critics. It employed time-tested methods, used by presidents since Truman to sell their Cold War policies, relying heavily on the private sector and using elites to sway the mass public.

Given the difficulties it faced and the limitations and handicaps under which it operated, it is not surprising that the Johnson administration ultimately failed. Indeed, it is perhaps remarkable that it held public support as long as it did. In any event, Vietnam was not primarily a public relations problem, and it seems unlikely in the absence of military or diplomatic success that a more vigorous and successful public relations campaign, initiated at the outset of the war, could have stemmed the tide of public dissatisfaction, thereby giving the administration more time to apply military pressure against North Vietnam and the National Liberation Front. Indeed, there is no certainty that, as some commentators have insisted, a declaration of war, call-up of the reserves, and partial or full mobilization would have held public support long enough for the administration to achieve its goals. As Johnson and Rusk repeatedly pointed out, moreover, the risks of such actions were considerable, and there was no reason to incur them as long as it seemed unnecessary to do so.

In the final analysis, the key, as some officials recognized in the beginning, was not the skill of their public relations activities but "visible evidence of success for our efforts to defeat the Viet Cong, deter Hanoi, and . . . bring peace to the Vietnamese countryside."[144] As late as the end of 1967, the hard-sell campaign based on perceptions of progress bought some time, suggesting the ability of the executive branch even under the most adverse circumstances to sway the public. The shock of the Tet offensive ended all that, forcing on the administration a whole new set of even more intractable problems.

"Fighting while Negotiating"

SIX   *The Tet Offensive and After*

On March 4, 1968, in the frenzied aftermath of the North Vietnamese Tet offensive, Secretary of State Dean Rusk gave President Johnson a memo given him by British ambassador Sir Patrick Dean and originally prepared by a group of British intellectuals. Seeking to help their beleaguered ally find an answer to the Vietnamese riddle, the Britishers rejected the extreme alternatives of withdrawal and massive escalation that Johnson had steadfastly resisted from the beginning of the war. They proposed instead a variant of what the Communists called "fighting and negotiating." The United States should stop the bombing of North Vietnam and conduct a major "peace offensive," announcing that it was prepared to talk at any time, appointing negotiators, and appealing to world opinion. At the same time, to strengthen its negotiating position, it should reinforce its armies in South Vietnam and intensify the pacification program.[1]

Johnson seized on the idea, and throughout the remainder of his term the United States attempted, after a fashion, to fight and negotiate. The shock of Tet forced the administration to admit its strategic failure and to examine its alternatives in a way it had not before. After a long and agonizing reappraisal, the United States stopped the bombing above the twentieth parallel (and subsequently throughout all of North Vietnam). In his March 31, 1968, speech, Johnson repeated his earlier offers to negotiate, named Harriman chief negotiator, and, to give force to his words, withdrew from the presidential race. At the same time, during the remainder of 1968, the United States mounted the largest ground operations yet undertaken in the war, launched a furious air offensive in South Vietnam, initiated an Accelerated Pacification Campaign, and began the process of what would later be called Vietnamization.

Like the approaches tried before, fighting while negotiating did not solve Johnson's problems. The war became much more complex after March 31, 1968, and formulating and implementing such a subtle and sophisticated strategy proved a difficult if not impossible task for the ponderous American bureaucracy. In terms of Johnson's management of the conflict, moreover, the change after March 31, 1968, was more apparent than real. Even under the pressure of Tet, the president refused to take control of the war. He continued to evade rather than confront the fundamental strategic issues. His dramatic March 31, 1968 speech, often cited as a major change of policy, appears to have been designed to quiet the home front as much as anything else. Like most of his earlier decisions, it was driven by a quest for consensus, picking and choosing from conflicting approaches rather than forming a coherent strategy to achieve a clearly defined objective. In the aftermath of that speech, the ambiguity persisted, the president's advisers more divided than ever, the lame duck Johnson less certain. The result, among other things, was perpetuation of the stalemate to the end of Johnson's term in office.

I

On the eve of Tet, Lyndon Johnson was firmly fixed on the course he had staked out in 1965 and maintained at such cost thereafter. The public relations campaign of late 1967 seemed to be working, and the administration took growing comfort from its gains in the polls. In December 1967, the president privately committed himself to review the ground strategy at some later unspecified time, but in January 1968 he showed no inclination to do so. When Senator Edward Kennedy (D-MA) attacked the search and destroy strategy and proposed a shift to the "population security" approach so fashionable among critics of the war, Johnson mounted a vigorous defense of Westmoreland, asking the Joint Chiefs and several of his top civilian advisers to submit written responses to Kennedy's charges.[2]

LBJ's major concern in early 1968 was the embattled marine base at Khe Sanh near the demilitarized zone. Persuaded by intelligence reports that the North Vietnamese were concentrating for a major attack and increasingly concerned that the base might be overrun, perhaps resulting in an American Dienbienphu, a worried commander in chief nervously stalked the White House halls and haunted the Situation Room to stay abreast of the latest developments. Increasingly distrustful of those military advisers who had not brought him success, the president on January 29 asked for and received verbal assurances from the Joint Chiefs that everything possible had been done to ensure the defense of Khe Sanh.[3]

Johnson himself was responsible for a minor public flap on the issue. In-dulging in the hyperbole for which he was famous, he revealed that he had asked the Joint Chiefs to sign a letter saying they were ready for the antici-pated enemy offensive. "I told them I thought I almost had to have them sign up in blood," he informed congressional leaders, "because if my poll goes where it has gone, with all the victories, I imagine what I would do if we had a . . . major defeat." When pressed to confirm the untrue story he himself had leaked, Johnson quickly backed off, denying that he had made the Joint Chiefs sign a paper and subsequently denying even that a firm decision had been made to hold Khe Sanh.[4]

While American attention was focused on Khe Sanh, the enemy launched the Tet offensive. On January 30, 1968, North Vietnamese and NLF units unleashed a series of attacks extending from the demilitarized zone to the Ca Mau peninsula. In all, they struck thirty-six of forty-four provincial capitals, five of the six major cities, sixty-four district capitals, and fifty hamlets. NLF sappers penetrated the compound of the U.S. embassy in Saigon, assaulted Tan Son Nhut airport, and hit the presidential palace. In Hue, enemy forces took control of the ancient citadel, once the seat of the emperors of the king-dom of Annam.

Although caught by surprise, the United States and South Vietnam recov-ered quickly. In Saigon, American and ARVN forces held off the initial at-tacks and within several days had cleared the city, inflicting huge casualties, taking large numbers of prisoners, and forcing the remnants to retreat into the countryside. The result was much the same elsewhere except in Hue. The liberation of that city took nearly three weeks and required heavy bombing and artillery fire. The United States and South Vietnam lost an estimated 500 killed, while enemy killed in action have been estimated as high as 5,000. The savage fighting around Hue also caused huge numbers of civilian casualties and created an estimated 100,000 refugees.[5]

Tet caused a tremendous shock in the United States. Early wire service reports exaggerated the success of the NLF raid on the embassy, some even indicating that the enemy had occupied several floors of the building. Tele-vised reports of the bloody fighting in Saigon and Hue made a mockery of Johnson and Westmoreland's year-end reports of progress, widening the credi-bility gap. The battles of Tet raised to a new level of public consciousness basic questions about the war that had long lurked just beneath the surface.[6]

The attacks left Washington in a state of "troubled confusion and uncer-tainty."[7] Westmoreland insisted that the offensive had been repulsed and there was no need to fear a major setback, and administration officials publicly echoed his statements. Johnson and his advisers were shocked by the suddenness and magnitude of the offensive, however, and some intelligence appraisals were more pessimistic than Westmoreland. Some officials feared that Tet was only the opening phase of a larger communist offensive. Some felt that Khe Sanh was still the primary objective, a fear that seemed to be borne out when the besieging forces renewed their attack on the marine base in early February. Others feared a major offensive in the northern provinces or a second wave of attacks on the cities. An "air of gloom" hung over White House discussions, Maxwell Taylor noted, and General Wheeler likened the mood to that following the first battle of Bull Run. Harry McPherson later described February 1968 as "the most dismaying month I ever remember in the White House."[8]

In the immediate aftermath of Tet, the Johnson administration could do little more than respond on a day-to-day basis to a situation deeply enshrouded in the fog of war. Rusk, McNamara, Clifford, Rostow, Wheeler, Christian, on occasions CIA director Richard Helms, McPherson, and Taylor comprised a sort of war council to deal with the crisis, and the president met almost daily, sometimes more than once a day, with these senior foreign policy advisers.

Tet raised new and even more complex problems in the area of public relations. The shock effect of the enemy attacks reinforced the doubts of those who had already come to oppose the war and raised new doubts among others, sending support for the war and Johnson's handling of it on another downward spiral. An increasingly militant Rostow urged the president to take the public relations offensive by making a "war leader" speech that would slay the "credibility gap dragon with one blow." Others urged a more cautious approach. The State Department warned against overplaying U.S. success and making "excessive claims prematurely." Clifford agreed that the situation was so fluid that any comment was inadvisable and would merely increase public concern.[9]

With some reluctance, Johnson deferred to the latter point of view. Privately, he lamented that the United States "was letting the other side have the floor and saying nothing," and while visiting troops aboard the USS *Constellation* he affirmed that it was time for America to "make a stand." Burned by his excessive optimism in November 1967, however, he hesitated to go further and in general took a cautious approach.[10]

The military command in late February did institute a major change in news policy. Concerned that published reports of the number of enemy rounds hitting Khe Sanh and precise U.S. casualty figures would permit the NVA to determine the accuracy of its artillery, the military began providing correspondents generalized figures on rounds, described casualties only in terms of light, moderate, and heavy, and withheld reports of damage to equipment, vehicles, and aircraft. The number of journalists visiting Khe Sanh was also restricted.[11]

Tet exposed as nothing before the flaws in the U.S. command system. The president handled the air war much as before, splitting the differences among his advisers. Within days after the onset of the Tet offensive, the Joint Chiefs pressed to expand the bombing closer to the center of Hanoi and Haiphong. Incoming Secretary of Defense Clark Clifford supported them, arguing that Tet represented a ringing enemy answer to the generous U.S. proposals set forth in the San Antonio formula. As in the past, McNamara stood firmly against the Chiefs, arguing that the military gain would not be worth the price and that civilian casualties would be high. The president's "just a minute man," Rusk, proposed a compromise that would permit the bombing of designated targets within the previously restricted area but would defer a decision on armed reconnaissance. Preferring, as always, to select items from opposing positions rather than support one or the other, the president concurred.[12]

Post-Tet discussions of additional ground forces set off a replay of the cat-and-mouse game that had characterized relations between the president, the Joint Chiefs, and civilian defense officials from the start of the war. Less concerned with the immediate crisis in Vietnam than with America's larger, long-range ability to meet its global military commitments, the JCS and especially Wheeler sought to use the emergency of Tet to secure the reinforcements needed to meet contingencies in Vietnam and elsewhere. Using the same methods of indirection he had applied in the past, Wheeler pried from a confident and initially indifferent Westmoreland a request for the 82nd Airborne Division and a marine brigade (40,000 troops). The troops were needed, the military claimed, to offset a weakened ARVN, contain the enemy in the embattled northern provinces of I Corps, stave off possible new NVA attacks, and facilitate execution of Westmoreland's 1968 campaign plan. When Westmoreland's initial "requests" for the additional forces seemed to lack urgency, Wheeler pushed him to strengthen the tone. The JCS chairman warned the president that provision of the additional forces would leave the United States with no strategic reserve and thus proposed an extension of tours in Vietnam and a reserve call-up.[13]

Johnson's civilian advisers responded skeptically. In his last days in office, McNamara, as so often before, opposed Westmoreland's request, arguing that to send additional U.S. troops would perpetuate the shopworn pattern of compensating for South Vietnamese deficiencies. Hawkish on the bombing, Clifford had been dovish on the ground war from the outset. Displaying the skepticism that would soon lead him to sharply question the JCS and seek extrication from the war, he noted the "very strange contradiction" between the military's claims of victory at Tet and its request for sizeable additional forces. Rusk was typically reticent, but when the president asked if a declaration of war would be necessary to implement a reserve call-up the secretary of state spoke out forcefully. Defending limited war as vigorously in 1968 as he had in 1965, he warned that a declaration would be a direct challenge to Peking and Moscow and might have a "very severe" international impact.[14]

The president was clearly troubled. He agreed with Clifford that the United States must get South Vietnam to do more, and he was deeply concerned with the political implications of a reserve call-up. He was confused by the uncertainty in Vietnam and perplexed by Westmoreland's strange requests. One week the general needed nothing; the next he needed 40,000 troops. Johnson was uncertain whether or not Westmoreland was requesting troops and wondered aloud whether the same person had written the two cables. Old Cold Warrior Dean Acheson had profoundly shaken his confidence in his military advisers, informing him on one occasion that "with all due respect, Mr. President, the Joint Chiefs of Staff don't know what they're talking about." In contrast to Wheeler, the Joint Chiefs, and Westmoreland, the president was most concerned with the immediate crisis in Vietnam and terrified at the possibility of a military defeat. "I don't want them to ask for something, not get it, and then have all of this placed on me," he fretted at one meeting in February. Responding to the short-term crisis rather than the long-term problems that troubled the military, he decided to dispatch to Vietnam immediately one brigade of the 82nd Airborne and a marine landing team. The reserve call-up was deferred, and Wheeler was sent to Vietnam to take a first-hand look.[15]

Wheeler's report created a shock in Washington almost as great as the Tet offensive itself, and the way it was framed and the impact it had starkly reflected the inability to communicate and the lack of candor that had afflicted the command system from the start of the war. Both Westmoreland and Wheeler later claimed that their recommendations of February 1968 were merely contingency plans developed to meet the various uncertainties that loomed ahead. It was unclear what the enemy might do, they insisted, and how the South Vietnamese might respond. South Korean troops might be withdrawn from Vietnam in response to the *Pueblo* incident. In any event, Westmoreland later observed, North Vietnam's shift to a "go-for-broke" strategy provided an opportunity for the United States to reevaluate its own conduct of the war. As confused by the mysterious signals emanating from Washington as Washington was confused by his cables, Westmoreland claimed to read in them signs that a strategic reappraisal might be in the offing.[16]

Among the various contingencies they considered, Wheeler and Westmoreland developed proposals for an aggressive, offensive strategy. Reviving their spring of 1967 plan, they called for intensified ground operations in South Vietnam, an expanded air war against North Vietnam, and operations to cut the Ho Chi Minh Trail and against North Vietnamese sanctuaries in Laos, Cambodia, and across the demilitarized zone. Their plan called for the raising of a strategic reserve of 206,000 troops. Westmoreland insisted that it was not a formal request for 206,000 men, as it was widely interpreted, but a "prudent planning exercise designed to generate the military capability to exercise tactical and strategic options if permitted by a reappraisal of national policy." The full 206,000 troops would be provided only if the new strategy were approved.[17]

In large part because of the way it was presented, the report was viewed very differently in Washington. Wheeler also saw it as a contingency plan. By this time, however, he was deeply frustrated with the constraints that in his view kept the United States from winning the war.[18] He was also concerned about America's global military posture and the depletion of the strategic reserve. And he was more worried than Westmoreland about the immediate situation in Vietnam. All units were presently committed, and there were no reserves available to meet a second round of enemy attacks and help make up the losses in pacification. Employing the subtle, indirect approach he had applied throughout the war, he sought to use the shock of Tet to force the president's hand.

Wheeler's report thus struck a tone of urgency. Describing Tet as a "very near thing," he warned that the margin of U.S. victory had been very thin in many areas. ARVN had been hit hard and might take many months to regain its equilibrium. The enemy had also suffered heavy losses, to be sure, but it had always demonstrated a capacity to recover quickly, and the United States must be ready for a new wave of attacks. Large-scale reinforcements were thus needed to protect the cities, drive the enemy from the northern provinces, and pacify the countryside. There was no theater reserve to meet other global contingencies. Labeling 1968 a "critical year," Wheeler warned that without additional forces the United States must be "prepared to accept some reverses," a line undoubtedly calculated to sway a president who had expressed terror at the political implications of defeat and had vowed not to accept it.[19]

Wheeler's report deeply disturbed Johnson's civilian advisers. Joseph Califano later described the meeting called to consider it as the "most depressing three hours of my public life." McNamara, Katzenbach, and William Bundy had gone from pessimism to the verge of despair. Rusk seemed exhausted. McNamara estimated that the manpower would cost $2.5 billion in 1968, $10 billion in 1969, and $15 billion in 1970, causing inflation, a large tax increase, or both. The increasingly skeptical Clifford could not understand the reasoning behind a request that seemed "neither enough to do the job, nor an indication that our role must change." He also wondered how such a request could be justified publicly when the United States had repeatedly claimed that it was doing well in Vietnam and how the administration could avoid creating the feeling that it was "pounding troops down a rathole." Agreeing with Clifford, speechwriter McPherson dismissed the proposals as "unbelievable and futile." In what amounted to his swan song, McNamara punctuated a notably gloomy discussion. Speaking with a faltering voice and "between suppressed sobs," he implored his colleagues: "We simply have to end this thing." Looking at his successor, he added, "I just hope you can get control of it. It is out of control." [20]

Civilian concern about the implications of Wheeler's report provoked the sort of full-scale review of strategy that the administration had thus far scrupulously avoided. The president was plainly alarmed by the magnitude of the request. Rostow and Clifford insisted even before Wheeler returned that his proposals must be examined with care. Thus after meeting with Wheeler and his top civilian advisers on February 28, the president announced that he would not make an immediate decision. Indicating that he wanted to subject the proposals to a "new pair of eyes and a fresh outlook," he asked Clifford to chair an interagency group to conduct a full-scale review of U.S. policy. In one breath, he suggested the sort of integrated approach that had not been tried before, a study that would "reconcile the military, diplomatic, economic, congressional, and public opinion problems involved." In the next, he reverted to form. "Give me the lesser of evils," he concluded, verbalizing the approach he had employed from the outset of the war. [21]

II

In the frenetic five days during which it completed its work, the Clifford task force began raising questions that had been avoided for years. Clifford's civilian advisers in the Pentagon, Townsend Hoopes, Paul Nitze, and Paul Warnke, urged an overhaul of U.S. strategy. Tet confirmed, Warnke later recalled, that the United States was engaged in a war that could not be ended in a reasonable time. The Pentagon civilians thus insisted that even with the additional troops requested by Westmoreland, the prevailing strategy promised no end to the conflict. Further Americanization of the war would reinforce the South Vietnamese tendency to do nothing. The costs would be heavy, moreover, and additional escalation would bring increased U.S. casualties and require new taxes, risking a "domestic crisis of unprecedented proportions." The civilians thus recommended that Westmoreland be given no more than a token increase in troops and that existing limits on military operations be retained. [22]

They went further, however, proposing once again a shift from a search and destroy strategy to population security. American forces would be deployed to protect the major population centers, and the South Vietnamese would be forced to assume greater responsibility for the war. The object of the new approach would be a negotiated settlement rather than military victory. American goals should be scaled down to a "peace which will leave the people of SVN free to fashion their own political institutions."[23]

Doubts raised in Clifford's mind by the Pentagon civilians were reinforced and greatly strengthened by his conversations with the Joint Chiefs. In a discussion he later described as "often confused and emotional," the secretary of defense cross-examined the nation's top military leaders like witnesses in a courtroom, using his newness and presumed ignorance to raise questions he hoped would break the stalemate in decision making. Would the troops requested by Westmoreland be able to do the job? If not, how many troops would be needed? Could the enemy respond with a buildup of its own? Could bombing end the war or reduce American casualties? In answer, the military would offer no assurance that 206,000 additional troops could end the war and could not estimate how many more might be required. The enemy could match U.S. escalation, they conceded, and bombing would probably not have a decisive impact. When Clifford asked the Chiefs to present their plan for victory, he was told there was none. "I was appalled," he later wrote; "nothing had prepared me for the weakness of the military's case."[24]

In the area of public opinion, as with military strategy, the Clifford task force addressed the hard issues in a way they had not been confronted before. Officials conceded that no one had worked full-time on public relations and that little had been done to rally the public. "The limited application of force for limited objectives has demanded that we avoid the emotion-rousing steps taken by governments in earlier wars," one paper observed, and the author noted numerous anomalies. The United States had scrupulously avoided killing the enemy on his own soil—and bragged about it! It had apologized for accidental overflights of China, one of the enemy's major suppliers. It had concealed the possible torture of Americans being held captive.

Administration officials remained painfully aware of the dangers of a campaign to rally the people. They could not "unleash the emotions of the people and continue to leash the military who are doing the fighting. One of the prices of this war must be restraints on the public opinion front." Thus, ironically, if the 206,000 additional troops were provided, the administration would have to take steps to "*hold down* the people, not to arouse them."

The task force study did offer some modest proposals. A special assistant should be established in the White House with his own staff to devise and administer a "rally" plan and to coordinate the public relations activities of the various agencies. The public could be rallied, the study concluded, if the nation could be persuaded that the war was in its interests, the government had a plan to win it, and the people were apprised of the costs of victory. The price to be paid for doing this, however, would be the "increased difficulty of withdrawing short of victory," something that should be carefully considered before such a program was launched.[25]

For all the boldness of its scrutiny, the task force was notably cautious in its conclusions. It was clear, Clifford later observed, that the president's top military and civilian advisers could not agree on a response to the military proposals on troops, and Clifford feared that if the issue were debated in Johnson's presence he would approve Wheeler's proposals. New to the game, the secretary of defense was not prepared to take on the big guns after a mere four days in office. He seems to have felt also that he must prepare the president for change gradually rather than confront him with drastic measures immediately.

Thus after what Clifford described as a "chaotic and frantic" day, the task force agreed on a compromise report. Expressing "grave doubts" about continuing down the same road, it recommended that the administration provide Westmoreland only those forces needed to meet the exigencies of the next few months—22,000 troops. A reserve call-up should be instituted so that more forces would be available if needed later.[26]

In its boldest proposal, the Clifford report raised questions about the appropriateness of Westmoreland's strategy and the attainability of military victory. "We seem to have a sinkhole," the secretary reported to the president's top advisers. "We put in more—they match it. We put in more—they match it." Warning of "more and more fighting with more and more casualties on US side and no end in sight," he called for a "whole new look at the whole situation," a strategic reappraisal that went beyond the narrow horizons of the field commander to look at the economic and political implications of the war and its relationship to America's other global commitments. Without formally recommending the population security strategy, Clifford hinted at its desirability. "I am not sure we can ever find a way out if we continue to shovel men into Vietnam," he ominously concluded.[27]

The president pared Clifford's modest proposals down still further. He readily agreed to provide Westmoreland 22,000 men, a move that helped allay his haunting fears of a setback in Vietnam, and he agreed that South Vietnam should be required to do more. But that was as far as he would go. He was no more enthused about a major reserve call-up in 1968 than he had been in 1965, and he would go no further than ask Wheeler and Clifford to discuss it with congressional leaders. More concerned as before with the number of troops than how they were used, he was equally cautious about undertaking the sort of strategic review called for by Clifford. He conceded at one point that it was useful to reevaluate policies from time to time, but, he added, he did not want to be holding a "seminar" on strategy "back here while our house is on fire." When Henry Cabot Lodge, Jr., on March 19 again proposed shifting to the population security approach, the president sharply retorted that to do so would be to comply with Senator Kennedy's demand, reason enough, in his mind, to reject it. A mere review of strategy, he added, might "create doubt" by indicating that "we are doubtful." [28]

In the aftermath of the Clifford report, the Johnson administration patched together in typically improvised fashion an ad hoc and highly politicized post-Tet approach to the war. The president never gave serious consideration to the military's proposals to try to shorten the war by enlarging it. He had been determined from the outset to keep the war limited, and on this point his determination never faltered. Indeed, he eventually approved only 13,500 new ground troops, far less than the Clifford group had recommended. As a way of defusing the growing criticism of Westmoreland and himself, he announced in late March the general's appointment as army chief of staff, thus, in effect, kicking him upstairs. [29]

While removing Westmoreland, however, the president did not challenge his strategy. The Clifford task force's major proposal for a full-scale review of the ground strategy and possible shift to a population security approach died quietly in March, never to be revived. Before returning to the United States, moreover, Westmoreland resumed the offensive in Vietnam, mounting a series of large-scale search and destroy operations throughout South Vietnam. "It will be the side that perseveres and carries the fight to the enemy that wins," he advised Wheeler, and "we are going to do it." In the weeks that followed, 50,000 U.S. and South Vietnamese troops moved out from Saigon in an operation dubbed "Resolved to Victory" and designed to break up the ring of enemy forces that surrounded the city. It was the largest offensive operation thus far conducted in the war. "We're going into every bit of woods—right into the pea patches," one U.S. officer exulted. [30]

In terms of information policy, also, no major changes were made. No one was appointed to handle public relations full time and no "rally" program was initiated. The approach was ad hoc, much as before. Beleaguered officials sought to counter press reports that pacification had collapsed. They encouraged friendly journalists like Joseph Alsop to publicize the contributions of the South Vietnamese and America's other allies. The newly formed Vietnam Information Group grappled with a whole range of old and new issues: how better to publicize NLF terrorism; how to put the best light on the GVN's response to Tet; how to counter charges of corruption in South Vietnam; how to make clear the importance of Vietnam to U.S. global interests.[31]

The most difficult public relations issue was the handling of Westmoreland's ground offensive. The general himself wanted to play it up to indicate to a troubled nation that the United States was no longer on the defensive.[32] Clifford staunchly opposed him. Tet had the impact it did, the secretary argued, because of Washington's excessive optimism of late 1967. If Westmoreland's offensive did not come off or if there were new enemy attacks in its wake, the credibility gap might be "virtually unbridgeable." Rusk agreed, noting that the United States should not emphasize what it had done until it was over, and the president concurred that it would be best not to promise more than could be delivered.[33] Wheeler thus instructed Westmoreland to be "conservative" in assessing the impact of Tet and speaking of the new offensive. He cautioned especially against predictions of victory. MACV should make clear that tough fighting lay ahead and that the enemy was still strong. If there were reverses, the nation would not be shaken. If successes were attained, the military could "claim and receive some kudos." A reluctant Westmoreland agreed only to conform "consistent with intellectual honesty as to my appraisal of the situation and in consideration of an essential attitude of command requiring a reflection of confidence."[34]

A dramatic new peace "move" rounded out the administration's post-Tet "strategy" of fighting while negotiating. Rusk first proposed a partial bombing halt on March 4 as part of the package suggested by the British. The secretary of state continued to push the idea over the next four weeks, mainly as a way of quieting the home front, arguing that it would cost nothing militarily since the weather would prevent heavy bombing anyway and that it would run little diplomatic risk since it was unlikely to lead to serious negotiations. Clifford and McPherson endorsed the Rusk proposal, but for very different reasons, seeing it as a crucial first step in a process of deescalation that in time might get the United States out of Vietnam. McGeorge Bundy, UN representative Arthur Goldberg, and Harriman preferred a full bombing halt but, at least in the case of Bundy, saw the Rusk proposal as a step in the right direction. The impetus to do something got crucial support from the Wise Men, who reconvened in Washington in late March and with a few exceptions agreed that the United States should move toward extrication.[35]

Throughout much of March, Johnson wavered. He was "more in a swivet" than Wheeler had ever recalled seeing him before, his manner very different, obviously upset emotionally.[36] He worried, as he put it, that standing down the bombing would get the hawks "furious." He feared he would be "nixing things" if his war moves included a peace initiative. "Let's make it troops and war," he exclaimed on one occasion. "Later we can revive and extend our peace initiatives." The bombing, he insisted on another occasion, would help keep "lead out of men's bodies." He seemed to sympathize with Bunker's proposal to "pour steel" into an embattled enemy. In a speech at Minneapolis on March 18, he appeared to lean toward war, calling on the nation to join him in a "total national effort to win the war. . . . We will—make no mistake about it—win." [37]

Eventually, a seemingly reluctant commander in chief gave in to the growing pressures for a peace move. The Wise Men persuaded him that something dramatic must be done, and the partial bombing halt proposed by Rusk seemed likely to meet several needs. It would help quiet the home front, as the secretary of state pointed out, and would cost nothing militarily. It would neutralize the doves without inciting the hawks. It was the sort of compromise, halfway measure that had appealed to him from the start of the war, the "lesser of evils."

In a truly remarkable session with Wheeler and Abrams on March 26, an embattled commander in chief sought to stifle potential military criticism of his peace moves by playing to the generals' sympathy. Obviously torn with emotion, he lamented an "abominable" fiscal situation, the panic and demoralization in the country, near universal opposition in the press, and his own "overwhelming disapproval" in the polls. "I will go down the drain," he conceded. In his dramatic March 31, 1968, speech, the product of nearly a month of frenzied deliberation, he publicly set forth the Rusk proposal for a partial bombing halt and joined it with a new appeal for negotiations and the appointment of Harriman as his personal representative to peace talks. To the shock of the nation, he went a step further, withdrawing himself from the presidential race. [38]

Johnson's decisions, however dramatic, represented a perpetuation of the old approach rather than a new departure and did not get near the heart of the problem. Success in the battles of Tet reinforced the conviction of some U.S. officials that an independent, noncommunist South Vietnam could yet be salvaged from the rubble of war, and the president's post-Tet decisions appear to have been designed to buy time to attain this result. They seem to have derived from wishful thinking. Militarily, the means were scaled back without modifying the ends, and it is impossible to see in retrospect how U.S. officials hoped to achieve with the application of less force aims that had thus far eluded them. The United States had taken over the war in the first place because of the poor performance of the South Vietnamese, and the concept of Vietnamization was equally illusory. Negotiations were desirable from a do-

mestic political standpoint, but in the absence of a military advantage the
United States did not have and concessions it was not prepared to make, they
could not achieve anything. And the mere fact of negotiations could soften
U.S. resolve and limit the administration's ability to prosecute the war.

III

An already difficult war became much more complicated after March 31,
1968. The profound political impact of the Tet offensive in the United States
combined with a presidential campaign and the other stunning events of a
notably traumatic year to make the home front an even more vital and volatile
factor in the war. The opening of negotiations in Paris in May added a new
and uncertain element to an already bewildering mix. In particular, it opened
a rift with the South Vietnamese, who increasingly feared an American sell-
out and to preserve their very existence began to be more independent and
assertive. Thus after March 31, any action that was taken on any of the three
major fronts of the war had to be calculated in terms of its possible impact on
the others. That stage of the war the North Vietnamese called "fighting while
negotiating" required the most delicate, fine-tuned strategy and the most careful and precise implementation.

Johnson made no changes in the decision-making process to adapt to this
new phase of the war. Like others before him, McPherson in early April proposed the appointment of someone in the White House or State Department
to oversee and coordinate the "peace talks–military scenario" in this highly
intricate stage of the war.[39] LBJ would have none of it. He kept control tightly
in his own hands and continued to operate through the same machinery as
before. The National Security Council still met because people expected it to
meet, but its role remained unimportant.[40] The nongroup also continued to
function, although its precise role is impossible to determine because no records were kept and any actions taken went through regular channels. As before, LBJ worked mainly through the group now formally known as his senior
foreign policy advisers, the Tuesday Lunch group that met at least weekly
during much of the year and far more frequently in times of crisis.[41]

Not surprisingly, divisions within the U.S. government grew even sharper
in this new phase of the war. The central issue was implementation of the
president's March 31 speech. Was it intended to extricate the United States
from a war now conceded unwinnable or had it been designed to achieve
at a lower cost the original goal of an independent, noncommunist South
Vietnam?

On the one side were Rusk, Rostow, Bunker, and the military. Certain, as

Westmoreland put it, that the enemy had suffered a "colossal" defeat and that in any negotiations the United States would "hold four aces," North Vietnam "two deuces," they were uninclined to make concessions and sought to sustain maximum military pressure. They were most concerned that the North Vietnamese might use negotiations to divide the United States from its South Vietnamese ally. Borrowing from the civil rights revolution a loaded phrase that had come to be synonymous with foot-dragging, Bunker therefore urged that the United States in any negotiations move with "deliberate speed." "We can afford . . . to be tough, patient and not too anxious in our negotiating stance," he insisted. Rostow concurred, suggesting that if the president could shore up the home front and the United States could improve its military position in Vietnam, North Vietnam would be forced to make major concessions to secure a settlement.[42]

Clifford, Harriman, Katzenbach, Nitze, and Warnke, on the other hand, had abandoned hope of military victory. Clifford, Harriman, and Nitze were all architects of the original containment policy, and they had long since concluded that Vietnam was crippling America's ability to deal with world problems, diverting its attention from more important areas and undermining its position as "standard bearer of moral principle in the world." Through what Clifford described as a "winching down" process, they sought mutual deescalation and disengagement through negotiations, even at the expense of South Vietnam. An accomplished bureaucratic infighter, Clifford, without opposing Johnson directly, sought to move him to positions he had not yet reached. At an April 11 press conference, for example, he affirmed that a ceiling had been imposed on U.S. ground troops, a position the president had not yet approved but did not challenge and that therefore became policy.[43]

The battle raged throughout 1968. The two sides fought bitterly over such issues as the negotiating position to be taken in Paris, the scale and intent of ground operations, and resumption or curtailment of the bombing. The stakes were high, the participants exhausted, nerves frayed. Clifford remembered 1968 as the most difficult year of his life, a year that lasted five years.[44] Rusk recalled only a "blur" and claimed to have survived on a daily regimen of aspirin, scotch, and cigarettes.[45] Personal attacks descended to unprecedented levels. Harriman found Rusk's behavior in one battle "contemptible." Rusk charged that Clifford had lost his nerve.[46] "The pressure grew so intense that at times I felt that the government itself might come apart at the seams," the secretary of defense later observed. "There was, for a brief time, something approaching paralysis, and a sense of events spiralling out of control of the nation's leaders."[47]

Johnson was no more able than before to extract a workable strategy from the conflicting positions of his advisers. He had always abhorred conflict in his official family, and he was distressed with the warfare that raged in 1968, literally pleading with Rostow on one occasion to get Rusk and Clifford together.[48] He too was exhausted and dispirited from four years of an exceedingly frustrating war, and his impending retirement from the presidency removed an element of urgency. While finding occasional "flashes" of the "old vigor," *Time* also reported an "unfamiliar atmosphere of tranquility" in the White House, even signs that Lyndon Johnson had "placed himself in the past tense."[49] Torn between wanting out of Vietnam and his fear of losing, he veered erratically between a hard line and a softer position. For the only time he worked with Johnson, William Bundy later recalled, he was unsure "what his line was," what "he was really trying to do."[50]

Although emotionally he leaned toward the Rusk-Rostow position, the president, as before, refused to adopt either of the conflicting approaches pushed by his advisers. He would not escalate to break the deadlock. Only under extreme pressure would he finally in late 1968 approve a bombing halt as a way to produce substantive negotiations and perhaps salvage Hubert Humphrey's faltering presidential campaign. He continued to act, Clifford observed, more like a "legislative leader, seeking a consensus among people who were often irreconcilably opposed than like a decisive commander-in-chief giving his subordinates orders."[51]

Not surprisingly, the administration in the fight-talk phase of the war lurched along the crooked path staked out after the March 31 speech. The debate was joined as soon as the president's top advisers began to discuss the position to take in negotiations with North Vietnamese representatives in Paris. Harriman and Clifford wanted to move as quickly as possible into the winching-down process. Although they muted their views in front of the president, they sought to check any escalation that might threaten the Paris talks, work back from the generous proposal set forth in the San Antonio formula, and use the prospect of a full bombing halt to engage the North Vietnamese in substantive negotiations. Their preferred approach was one of mutual deescalation. By reducing the level of violence, the United States might get the North Vietnamese to do the same. Their ultimate goal, Clifford conceded to Gen. Andrew Goodpaster, was to "bring this thing to an end on the best terms we can get."[52]

The president's more "hawkish" advisers took a much tougher position. Rostow pressed for a major escalation of the war on the eve of the peace talks to make clear to the enemy that the United States could not be stampeded into a settlement. He and Rusk advocated a retreat from the San Antonio formula and reversion to earlier U.S. demands for a cessation of North Vietnamese infiltration in return for a full bombing halt. They also took a hard line on the peace settlement. They were so opposed to any premature move that Rusk instructed the negotiating team not to prepare or even discuss a fallback position or look for areas of compromise, a step that infuriated Harriman. The secretary of state insisted that minimum U.S. terms must include North Vietnamese compliance with the 1962 Geneva accords on Laos, withdrawal of NVA troops from South Vietnam, and respect for the demilitarized zone. The goal, he conceded on one occasion, should be restoration of the status quo ante bellum.[53]

As before, the president sought a middle ground between his advisers. Although Rostow's proposal to escalate appealed to what Clifford called his "coonskin mentality," LBJ rejected it out of hand. He also resisted any move toward mutual deescalation and agreed that maximum military pressure should be sustained in South Vietnam. In his approach to the negotiations, he was much closer to Rusk and Rostow. Conceding that he was not at all optimistic about the outcome, he agreed with his secretary of state that there was no need to hurry the negotiating process. He also insisted that U.S. representatives should not feel compelled to make concessions to influence the upcoming election. They should be "hard traders," he averred, and should not put their minimum conditions on the table first.[54]

With some difficulty, the president and his advisers finally hammered out a vague compromise that leaned toward the Rusk-Rostow position. On a bombing halt, they would seek "prompt and serious substantive talks looking toward peace in Vietnam, in the course of which an understanding may be reached on a cessation of bombing in the North under circumstances which would not be militarily disadvantageous." They also agreed on the essentiality of some kind of control mechanism to oversee a cease-fire or peace settlement, held out for reestablishment of the DMZ, and insisted on full inclusion of the Saigon government in any talks on the future of South Vietnam.[55] The agreement on instructions barely masked fundamental disagreements. When Clifford privately stressed the importance of ending the war quickly, Goodpaster retorted that this was not the president's position and "quite an argument" ensued. Leaving nothing to chance, a nervous president sent Cyrus Vance and William Jorden to Paris to keep an eye on the dovish Harriman.[56]

While taking a firm negotiating position, the administration also quietly endorsed the maintenance of maximum military pressure on enemy forces in South Vietnam. After Tet, as before, MACV appears to have operated with minimal direction from Washington. Vividly recalling the "lessons" of Korea and fearing that the gains made since Tet might be squandered at the peace table, military commanders insisted that the United States must not again be victimized by the talk-fight strategy of the wily communists. They staunchly resisted any move toward mutual deescalation and insisted on harassing the enemy until the North Vietnamese Army was removed from the South.[57]

As a consequence, before and immediately after the opening of peace talks, the war in South Vietnam reached its most intense and destructive phase. After March 31, the focus of the bombing shifted to South Vietnam and Laos. U.S. pilots mounted more than 3,000 B-52 strikes in South Vietnam in 1968, three times the number in 1967, and the tonnage of bombs nearly doubled.[58] The ground war reached a new level of fury. On April 4, Westmoreland made clear to his corps commanders that the president's speech changed nothing, enjoining them to "march forward with even greater zeal and aggressiveness." A week later, MACV launched the largest offensive operation of the war, hoping to cripple the North Vietnamese and thereby restore security to the major cities and recoup losses in pacification. Throughout April and May, there was heavy fighting in the areas around Saigon and in I Corps. "We are winning," one officer proclaimed. "We are smashing" the enemy "wherever he appears. Peace talks be damned."[59]

The only area where MACV applied restraint—and that with real reluctance—was in the publicity given its operations. The term "search and destroy" was dropped from the official military lexicon in late March because of the bad reputation it had acquired in "lay circles" at home. The same sort of operations were now referred to in such relatively innocuous terms as "reconnaissance in force." When the press made much of the fact that the largest operation of the war, code-named *toan than*, or "final victory," had been launched in the aftermath of Johnson's March 31 "peace move," Wheeler pressed Westmoreland to adopt a more subdued public relations approach.[60]

The field commander grudgingly assented. Westmoreland and other military leaders in fact wanted to play up the operations to boost morale among American and South Vietnamese forces and to exploit for maximum propaganda advantage the heavy losses inflicted on the enemy. The general conceded, however, the "dilemma" posed between maintaining the momentum of offensive operations and "doing as little as possible to give aid and comfort to our critics by rocking or appearing to rock the negotiations boat." He therefore reluctantly agreed that MACV, while pushing offensive operations "unabated," would "low key" its press announcements provided that such an approach did not play into enemy hands by giving the appearance the United States was doing nothing or the war was winding down.[61]

Throughout April and much of May, top administration officials also debated, sometimes quite bitterly, the bombing of North Vietnam. When the Paris talks quickly and predictably deadlocked, pressures began to build from the military and the president's more hawkish civilian advisers to remove the March 31 limits. Admiral Sharp urged resumption of bombing throughout all of North Vietnam. Westmoreland proposed bombing enemy sanctuaries in Cambodia and holding North Vietnamese cities "hostage," striking Haiphong or Hanoi in retaliation for North Vietnamese and NLF attacks on Danang or Saigon. At various times in April and May, Wheeler and the Joint Chiefs recommended armed reconnaissance or the resumption of full bombing between the 19th and 20th parallels, or, if the peace talks broke down, full resumption of the bombing of North Vietnam.[62]

On this, as on other issues, the president's civilian advisers disagreed sharply among themselves. Rusk and Rostow endorsed on various occasions as a way of sending signals to Hanoi removal of the self-imposed limitation at the 19th parallel. Clifford and Katzenbach retorted that escalation at this critical stage might threaten the peace talks in Paris or undermine the crucial support at home and in world opinion that the president's March 31 speech had secured.[63]

Johnson wavered. He clearly sympathized with his more hawkish advisers and yearned to hurt his tormentors. "We can't sit back and let them hit us without letting them have it," he complained on one occasion. He also feared that the self-imposed limits on the bombing would put U.S. troops at risk. Ever cautious, however, he could not ignore the warnings of Clifford and Katzenbach and he would go no further than to authorize a study of what the United States should do if there was no progress in the peace talks. In the meantime, Harriman dropped not so subtle hints to a Soviet contact in Paris that if the deadlock persisted the United States might resume bombing up to the 20th parallel or beyond.[64]

In terms of public relations, administration officials continued to struggle with old problems such as how to get maximum public relations advantages from enemy atrocities, how to expose the enemy's growing weaknesses, and how to make a persuasive case for continued prolongation of the war. They also wrestled with the new and even more complicated problems of how to prepare Americans for peace talks and a possible settlement, how to strike a "delicate balance" between "our sincere interest in productive talks" and "our unwillingness to seek 'peace at any price,'" and how to coordinate public relations activities in a bafflingly complex war with fronts now on three continents.[65]

In general, the administration reverted to the soft-sell, low-key approach employed before late 1967. In Paris, U.S. officials eschewed a hard-line propaganda campaign, feeling that it might produce a "plague on both your houses" response from the world press that would dissipate some of the good will the United States had gained since March 31. In both Washington and Paris, the emphasis was on avoiding polemics and understating when possible. In Saigon, too, the approach was low-key. Before returning to Washington to become army chief of staff, Westmoreland made some "carburetor adjustments" in press policy, encouraging briefers to use more frequently the "no comment" response to sensitive questions. His successor, Gen. Creighton Abrams, went further in that direction, insisting that MACV must not involve itself in useless propaganda. "The overall public affairs policy of this command will be to let results speak for themselves," Abrams proclaimed. "Achievements not hopes will be stressed."[66]

The post-Tet middle-of-the-road approach, as those before it, provided no means to break the military and diplomatic stalemate in Vietnam. Johnson's March 31 peace move, the opening of negotiations, and the administration's low-key, generally effective public relations program eased the domestic pressures that had developed from the shock of the Tet offensive, generating by mid-June among Americans a mood of patient resignation.[67] The president's hard-line, no-concessions approach to the Paris talks, on the other hand, offered no incentive to the North Vietnamese to enter into substantive discussions, and the talks dragged into the summer with no discernible progress.

Without any direction from Washington, Abrams significantly modified the ground war shortly after arriving in Vietnam. He continued to employ conventional forces and in April launched another massive offensive. The goal of ground operations changed from search and destroy to a form of population security, however. Abrams abandoned the much-maligned body count and sought to reduce indiscriminate violence and civilian casualties. He shifted from large-unit sweeps to small-unit patrols with the object of eliminating enemy local forces so that villages and hamlets could enjoy some security. His "One-War" strategic concept eliminated the artificial barriers between South Vietnamese and U.S. military operations and pacification, integrating all of them in a way they had not been before. His Accelerated Pacification Campaign put renewed emphasis on achieving Komer's 1967 goals and sought to expand government control of the countryside in the event serious negotiations began.[68]

Abrams's intensified military pressure was not sufficient to force a settlement. It was easier to proclaim a change in the ground strategy than implement one, and in many areas operations continued much as before. The offensive launched in April blunted the enemy's "mini-Tet" campaign of May, inflicted huge casualties, and drove North Vietnamese and NLF forces back into their sanctuaries. In the process, however, the already battered cities of South Vietnam suffered yet more devastation. Despite crippling losses, the enemy retained the ability to carry out harassing actions, mount deadly rocket attacks on the cities, and revert to guerrilla warfare. The United States also incurred near-record casualties in the bloody campaigns of April and May 1968, and if North Vietnam was running low on manpower time remained on its side.[69]

I V

Throughout the long, hot summer of 1968, the president clung stubbornly to the approach that had served him so poorly to this point. Beset by pressures from both directions, he refused to move decisively in either. In early June, Soviet premier Alexei Kosygin indicated that North Vietnam was ready to negotiate if the United States would stop the bombing. Obviously trying to lock the president into their winching-down process, Clifford and Harriman urged him to test Kosygin's initiative.[70] On the other side, certain after nearly three years of frustration that they were finally on the verge of victory, military leaders pressed relentlessly for an expansion of the bombing. Any North Vietnamese escalation of the war, they argued, should be used as an occasion to resume bombing between the 19th and 20th parallels, then in all of North Vietnam, and eventually in Laos and Cambodia as well.[71]

Characteristically, the president rejected both approaches. Although deeply frustrated by the stalemate in Paris and eager to strike back at North Vietnam, he appears never to have seriously considered resuming the bombing above the 19th parallel. At the same time, he stubbornly resisted pressures for a bombing halt. He seems to have agreed with Wheeler that a complete bombing halt would undermine the morale of U.S. troops, and he certainly concurred with Wheeler, Rostow, and Rusk that the United States should not make a concession without getting something in return. Like his military advisers, he appears to have concluded that the United States was doing well in the fight-talk stage. "We have them beaten now," he declared in early June. "The only thing that will stop us is ourselves." He therefore responded to Kosygin's initiative by inquiring of the Soviet leader what North Vietnam would do in return for stopping the bombing, initiating an extended and unproductive exchange of cables with Moscow.[72]

The president quashed even more forcefully another peace move in July. He "was more irritable than he had been in months," Clifford later recalled, "and spoke in a low, depressed, and muffled voice." "He seemed to disagree with everyone."[73] He may have sensed by this time that any hope for peace was slipping away. He may, as Clifford speculated, have recognized that he was presiding over a disintegrating administration. Whatever the case, when

Harriman and Vance late in the month proposed a bombing halt, he would have none of it. "This is just absolutely no dice!" he told William Bundy.[74] He angrily denounced the proposal as "mush" and complained that it was part of a conspiracy to force him to stop the bombing. "The enemy is using my own people as dupes," he snarled.[75] He ordered Rusk to hold a hard-line press conference reaffirming America's position and then chastised his most loyal lieutenant for not making it tough enough. At the Tuesday Lunch on July 30 he expressed a wish to "knock the hell" out of the enemy. At a press conference the following day he issued an only slightly veiled threat to reescalate the bombing if North Vietnam launched new attacks on U.S. forces. He became so annoyed with Clifford's relentless efforts to get the bombing stopped that he cut the secretary of defense off from the cable traffic dealing with negotiations.[76]

After months of hesitation, the president in late October finally agreed to a full bombing halt, taking the fight-talk stage of the war to the next level. He acted only after being persuaded that stopping the bombing would lead somewhere. In private talks with Harriman and Vance, North Vietnamese negotiators affirmed in mid-September that serious discussions would begin immediately after a bombing halt. A month later, they made a major concession by indicating that the Saigon government could participate in such talks. Soviet diplomats in Paris subsequently reaffirmed the North Vietnamese pledges.[77] Armed with these assurances, Harriman, Vance, and Clifford redoubled their efforts to move the president off dead center. The doves were more eager than ever to extricate the United States from a war they deemed unwinnable, and they increasingly worried that time was running out on them. They also feared that if something dramatic were not done soon, Hubert Humphrey's faltering campaign would collapse, resulting in the election of the despised Richard Nixon. Clifford insisted that the risk of a full bombing halt was "minimal," and that if nothing else it would lower the cost of the war at home. He also sought to tempt Johnson by telling him he should not risk leaving to Nixon the "honor" of ending the war. Long-time dove George Ball joined the chorus. "We are needlessly continuing the bombing and the war," he warned, "without testing the chances for a settlement."[78]

The president remained dubious. He and Rusk profoundly distrusted the North Vietnamese and the Soviets, and he vividly recalled being taken in on the December 1965 pause. "A burned child dreads a fire," he averred. "I am that child."[79] His most trusted adviser, the secretary of state, worried that stopping the bombing without getting anything in return would undermine the confidence of the Saigon government. LBJ feared being accused of a "cheap political trick," of risking the lives of American boys simply to get

Humphrey elected. Indeed, at times he seemed to go so far out of his way to avoid doing anything to help Humphrey that his dovish advisers privately wondered if he preferred the election of Nixon.[80]

Ultimately he relented. The Joint Chiefs conceded that because of approaching bad weather the military effects of a bombing halt would be negligible. Most important, LBJ seems to have been convinced that the United States had at last gained the upper hand. U.S. forces had blunted the long-anticipated enemy "third offensive" in September. Abrams's One-War concept and Accelerated Pacification Campaign seemed to bring results and especially to improve the government's position in the countryside. "The tide of history now seems to be moving with us and not against us," Bunker reported from Saigon in mid-October. Bunker, Abrams, Wheeler, and Rusk concurred that the North Vietnamese concession was an admission of weakness and a "real turning point." In effect, Wheeler affirmed, "the military war has been won."[81]

The president thus seems to have acted on the assumption that the enemy was hurting badly and might prefer to deal with him rather than an unknown successor. He remained fearful of being lured into a trap and suffering the stigma of being duped. He hedged his bets by agreeing to maintain maximum military pressure on the enemy after the bombing of North Vietnam was stopped. He conceded on one occasion that much hard fighting lay ahead and that he could not wave a magic wand and end the conflict. Buoyed by the estimates of his more bullish advisers, on the other hand, he entertained vague hopes that through a combination of the bombing halt and increased military pressure he might yet persuade the North Vietnamese to match their record at Geneva in 1954 and end the war in thirty days.[82]

Johnson stage-managed the October bombing halt decision with all the care he had given to his July 1965 decisions for war. For one of only a handful of times during the entire war, he consulted with the Joint Chiefs of Staff as a group, permitting each to have his say *and* give his assent. He consulted with congressional leaders, the presidential candidates, and former president Eisenhower, then ill in Walter Reed Army Hospital. Appearing to remain uncommitted to the very end, he even called Abrams back to Washington for a hurried, secret, last-minute consultation. Once assured by his field commander in a dramatic 2:45 A.M. meeting that enemy compliance with the terms of the agreement would more than compensate for stopping the bombing and that American troops would not be put at risk, he agreed to go ahead.[83]

In terms of its substance as well as its staging, the October bombing halt decision was vintage Johnson. As before, the president adopted a piecemeal approach rather than a coordinated, integrated strategy to end the war. While acceding to Clifford and Harriman's proposal, he did not accept their approach to the war. He agreed to the bombing halt to get negotiations going, but his goals for the negotiations were at best ambiguous and he remained opposed to any concessions. Persuaded by his advisers, as on so many earlier occasions, that the United States was winning the war, he agreed to cut back the application of air power. And in moving toward substantive negotiations, he failed to take into account yet another obstacle to success—opposition from an increasingly nervous Saigon government.

In agreeing to stop the bombing to get negotiations under way, the president and his advisers did not agree on the goal to be sought in Paris. Clifford had long since concluded that the war could not be won militarily and that the United States could not build a stable South Vietnamese government in the time the American people were prepared to allow it. He had also persuaded himself that by preventing a North Vietnamese takeover, building up the South Vietnamese armed forces, and giving South Vietnam the tools for self-determination, the United States had met its obligations to its ally. Thus he saw the bombing halt as a first step on the road to extrication.[84] Rusk's views on a settlement, on the other hand, were "very simple." The United States must not give North Vietnam any part of South Vietnam. North Vietnamese troops in South Vietnam and Laos must go home.[85] The president seems to have been much closer to Rusk. Whatever the case, the issue was never really discussed at the top levels, much less resolved. The administration headed toward possible negotiations without any clear sense of what it wanted or was prepared to accept.

The president continued to join conciliatory diplomatic moves with intensive military pressure. In the aftermath of the bombing halt, Clifford proposed a token withdrawal of U.S. forces as a move toward mutual withdrawal. Rusk and Wheeler strongly objected, preferring "to pour it on" in South Vietnam after the bombing was stopped. The president concurred. After October 31, the brunt of the bombing shifted to Laos, U.S. pilots flying more than 12,000 sorties in November 1968 compared to 4,400 in November 1967. Abrams carried back to Vietnam a letter from the president authorizing him to apply "the manpower and resources at your command to maximum effect." Follow the enemy in "relentless pursuit," Johnson instructed his field commander. "Don't give them a moment's rest. Let the enemy feel the weight of everything you've got." U.S. troops thus continued to pour it on in South Vietnam. "They're going after the enemy hammer and tong," Wheeler boasted in early December.[86]

Whether this approach would have worked can never be known, but it made no difference, for in moving toward substantive negotiations the administration had failed to take into account another possible roadblock—the Saigon government. Clifford had perceived as early as the summer of 1968 that the United States and its ally were heading in different directions. The secretary of defense returned from a visit to Saigon in July shocked and outraged at the size of the requests for aid and "depressed" with the discovery that South Vietnam seemed not to want the war to end. The secretary urged Johnson when he met with President Nguyen Van Thieu in Honolulu shortly after to put his ally on notice that compromise would be necessary. Rusk and Rostow sharply disagreed.[87]

As always, the president refused to resolve the issue. He did not accede to Thieu's demand that North Vietnamese withdrawal from South Vietnam be a precondition for a bombing halt. But he demanded nothing of the Saigon government either, and from Clifford's perspective the South Vietnamese were the clear winners. McPherson agreed, observing shortly after that "the American Gulliver is tied down by the South Vietnamese Lilliputians. We have no freedom of action."[88]

McPherson's lament turned to prophecy in October when Thieu obstructed the U.S. move toward negotiations. His intransigence was no doubt encouraged by Republican leaders, who feared being undercut by a Democratic "peace gimmick" and secretly urged him to stall until after the election. A wily and increasingly nervous politician, Thieu probably concluded without any prompting that he might do better with the Republicans than the Democrats and that delay was a good risk. He thus made demands neither North Vietnam nor the United States could accept. When the United States initiated the bombing halt without his assent, he delayed several weeks before sending representatives to Paris. Once in Paris, the South Vietnamese raised procedural objections that prevented the opening of substantive discussions. By the time the procedural issues had been resolved, the Johnson administration was in its last days and any hopes for substantive negotiations had passed.[89]

Even in its dying days, the wrangling and indecision continued. In December, there was mounting pressure to resume the bombing and step up other kinds of military pressure. Abrams specifically asked to put a battalion of U.S. troops in the demilitarized zone in response to an enemy attack on a U.S. patrol. Wheeler, Rostow, and Rusk supported him, the latter making an impassioned plea to protect U.S. troops and insisting that all-out military pressure was the best way to get results in negotiations. "Rusk and Rostow still seem to be in a mood that we are about to win the war if only given a little more time," a disgruntled Harriman wrote.[90]

Harriman and Clifford feared that all-out military pressure would lead only to increased fighting and that Americans should not be asked to die for that. They pressed instead for "negotiations for mutual reduction of violence, for reduction in American casualties and [to] begin movement of troops home." President Johnson would then be acknowledged by history "as the man who was primarily responsible for bringing this unhappy conflict to a close."[91]

Once again, in this last debate between his torn advisers, the president refused to choose. To the end, a man at war with himself, he alternated between outrage with Thieu for blocking a peace settlement and anger with Harriman and Clifford for pushing him in a direction he did not want to go. He seems not to have given serious consideration to resuming the bombing or beginning troop withdrawals. He would go no further than permit Abrams to send a company into the demilitarized zone. The deadlock in Paris thus remained unbroken and the war in Vietnam raged. Upon leaving office, the president could content himself only with the realization that, as he later put it, his service had ended "without my having to haul down the flag, compromise my principles, or run out on our obligations, our commitments, and our men who were upholding their obligations and commitments in Vietnam."[92] As veteran Washington correspondent Chalmers Roberts observed, the reluctant warrior left office "bloody but unbowed."[93]

V

For the Vietnamese, *Danh va dam, dam va danh* (fighting and talking, talking and fighting) comprised a sophisticated, tightly integrated approach to warfare. The term appears to have been borrowed from Mao Tse-tung's Chinese revolutionaries, but the technique itself was deeply rooted in Vietnamese history, an approach to war "refined over centuries of confrontation" with more powerful enemies.[94] The approach closely coordinated military, diplomatic, and political moves with the overall objective of stimulating the enemy's internal contradictions and, in the case of the United States in particular, weakening its internal support. The aim of talking was not necessarily to reach a settlement but to feed the enemy's hopes for peace and heighten divisions in the enemy camp. The goal of fighting was to maintain or even intensify the pressure that had brought the adversary to the conference table in the first place. Every move was carefully calculated with regard to its impact on the different dimensions of the war.

Although it claimed after Tet to be following a strategy of fighting while negotiating, the United States was never able to operate at a level of sophistication comparable to the Vietnamese. The objectives of fighting and negotiating were never precisely defined, and indeed among Johnson and his advisers there was little agreement on what they should be. The several dimensions of U.S. strategy were not integrated and continued to work against rather than reinforce each other. For Johnson, the fighting while negotiating approach suggested by Rusk proved an expedient rationale for doing what he preferred to do. From the beginning of the war, he had refused to choose between conflicting approaches, instead selecting from each as a way of neutralizing possible political opposition and silencing critics. He persisted in this highly politicized approach in the tumultuous period after Tet. As a consequence, neither his peace moves nor his military actions produced the outcome he wanted. In part at least as a direct result of the approach he had taken toward its management, the president left the war in January 1969 much as he had found it in November 1963—a bloody, destructive stalemate.

SEVEN   Conclusion

Of the two great questions concerning involvement in Vietnam—why did the United States intervene and why did it fail—the latter has provoked the most emotional controversy. Historically, as a nation, America has been uniquely successful, so much so that its people have come to take success for granted. When failure occurs, scapegoats are sought and myths concocted to explain what is otherwise inexplicable. In the case of Vietnam, many critics of America's conduct of the war have thus insisted that a different approach would have produced the "proper" results.[1] Such arguments can never be proven, of course, and they are suspect in method. As Wayne Cole observed many years ago of a strikingly similar debate in the aftermath of World War II, the "most heated controversies . . . do not center on those matters for which the facts and truth can be determined with greatest certainty. The interpretive controversies, on the contrary, rage over questions about which the historian is least able to determine the truth."[2]

By examining the Johnson administration's conduct of the war—without presuming that it should have been won—this book seeks to help explain why the world's greatest power was unable to impose its will on a "backward" Third World country. The outcome of the war was not exclusively or even primarily the result of bad management. Still, by looking at the formulation and implementation of strategy, the organization of pacification programs, the handling of various peace initiatives, the perception and manipulation of public opinion, and the post-Tet strategy of fighting while negotiating, this study has exposed various flaws in the administration's running of the war.

The most glaring deficiency is that in an extraordinarily complex war there was no real strategy. President Johnson and Secretary of Defense Robert S. McNamara provided no firm strategic guidance to those military and civilian advisers who were running programs in the field. They set no clearcut limits on what could be done, what resources might be employed, and what funds expended. Without direction from the top, each service or agency did its own thing. Strategy emerged from the field on an improvised basis without careful calculation of the ends to be sought and the means used to attain them.

Perhaps equally important and less generally recognized, despite widespread and steadily growing dissatisfaction among the president's top advisers with the way the war was being fought and the results that were being obtained, there was no change of strategy or even systematic discussion of such a change. Not until the shock of the 1968 Tet offensive compelled it were the basic issues of how the war was being fought even raised. Even then, they were quickly dropped and left largely unresolved. Despite talk among the president's top advisers of borrowing a page from the communists' book and fighting while negotiating, the administration after Tet replaced one makeshift strategy with another, perpetuating and in some ways exacerbating the problems that had afflicted its management of the war from the beginning.

Closely related to and to some extent deriving from the absence of strategy was the lack of coordination of the numerous elements of what had become by 1966 a sprawling, multifarious war effort. Johnson steadfastly refused to assume overall direction of the war, and he would not create special machinery or designate someone else to run it. In Vietnam, therefore, each service or agency tended to go about its own business without much awareness of the impact of its actions in other areas or on other programs. The air war against North Vietnam operated separately from the ground war in South Vietnam (and the air war in Laos was run separately from both). Through the first years of the war the various civilian programs in South Vietnam competed with each other for resources. Even after the establishment of CORDS brought some order to pacification, village-level activities were not closely integrated or harmonized with military operations. Abrams's "One-War" concept represented a serious attempt to coordinate pacification and military operations, but it was not entirely successful in changing deeply entrenched ways of doing things. In any event it was too little, and it came too late. MARIGOLD and SUNFLOWER were only the most glaring examples where poor management and lack of coordination destroyed possibly promising peace initiatives or caused the United States serious public relations problems. Even the most modest and limited efforts to better coordinate the war effort through such mechanisms as the proposed Komer/Rostow NSAM of late 1966 came to naught.

It is more difficult to determine why these problems existed. In part, no doubt, institutional imperatives were at fault. The rule in bureaucracy, as Robert Komer has pointed out, is that when an organization does not know what to do—or is not told what to do—it does what it knows how to do. Thus, in the absence of strong leadership from the top, the various services and agencies acted on the basis of their own standard operating procedures whether or not they were appropriate or compatible. CIA operative William Colby recalls warning McGeorge Bundy during the U.S. buildup in 1965 that the growing militarization of the war was diverting attention from the more urgent problems in the villages of South Vietnam. He pleaded with the presidential adviser to refocus the administration's attention toward the proper area. "You may be right, Bill," Colby remembered Bundy answering, "but the structure of the American government won't permit it." "What he meant," Colby concluded, "was that the Pentagon had to fight the only war it knew how to fight, and there was no American organization that could fight any other."[3] This was most true of the army, air force, and navy, but it was also true of the civilian agencies.

Limited war theory also significantly influenced the way the war was fought. Korea and especially the Truman-MacArthur controversy stimulated a veritable cult of limited war in the 1950s and 1960s, the major conclusion of which was that in a nuclear age where total war was unthinkable limited war was essential. McNamara, William and McGeorge Bundy, Rusk, and indeed Lyndon Johnson were deeply imbued with limited war theory, and it determined in many crucial ways their handling of Vietnam. Coming of age in World War II, they were convinced of the essentiality of deterring aggression to avoid a major war. Veterans of the Cuban missile crisis, they lived with the awesome responsibility of preventing nuclear conflagration and they were thus committed to fighting in "cold blood" and maintaining tight operational control over the military. They also operated under the mistaken assumption that limited war was more an exercise in crisis management than the application of strategy, and they were thus persuaded that gradual escalation would achieve their limited goals without provoking the larger war they so feared. Many of their notions, of course, turned out to be badly flawed.

To an even greater extent, Lyndon Johnson's own highly personalized style indelibly marked the conduct of the war and contributed to its peculiar frustrations. LBJ was a "kind of whirlwind," David Lilienthal has observed, a man of seemingly boundless energy who attempted to put his personal brand on everything he dealt with.[4] He dominated the presidency as few others have. He sought to run the war as he ran his household and ranch, his office and *his* government, with scrupulous attention to the most minute detail. As with every other personal and political crisis he faced he worked tirelessly at the job of commander in chief of a nation at war. His approach was best typified by his oft-quoted and characteristically hyperbolic boast that U.S. airmen could not bomb an outhouse in North Vietnam without his approval. In the case of Vietnam, however, the result was the worst of both worlds, a strategic vacuum and massive intrusion at the tactical level, micromanagement without real control. Whether he would admit it or not, moreover, LBJ quickly found in Vietnam a situation that eluded his grasp and dissipated even *his* seemingly inexhaustible storehouse of energy.

In so many ways, the conduct of the war reflected Johnson's modus operandi. The reluctance to provide precise direction and define a mission and explicit limits, the highly politicized, for Johnson characteristically middle-of-the-road approach that gave everybody something and nobody what they wanted, that emphasized consensus and internal harmony over results on the battlefield or at the negotiating table, all these were products of a thoroughly political and profoundly insecure man, a man especially ill at ease among military issues and military people.

Johnson's intolerance for any form of intragovernmental dissent and his unwillingness to permit, much less order, a much-needed debate on strategic issues deserve special note. It was not, as his most severe critics have argued, the result of his determination to impose a hermetically sealed system or his preference for working with sycophants, the so-called Caligula syndrome. LBJ was a domineering individual, to be sure, and he did have a strong distaste for conflict in his official family. As David Barrett and others have pointed out, however, he eagerly sought out and indeed opened himself to a wide diversity of viewpoints.[5] Whatever their faults, the people that worked with him were anything but sycophants.

The problem went much deeper than that. In part, it reflected the peculiar mix of personalities involved, the rigorous standards of loyalty of a Rusk or McNamara, Harriman's determination to retain influence at the cost of principle and candor. From Johnson's standpoint, it was largely a matter of control. "He wanted to control everything," Joe Califano recalled. "His greatest outbursts of anger were triggered by people or situations that escaped his control."[6] He therefore discouraged the sort of open exchange of ideas, free-wheeling discussion of alternatives, or ranging policy reviews that might in any way threaten his control. His admonition to McGeorge Bundy that his advisers must not "gang up" on him reflected his reluctance to permit them to engage in discussions except under his watchful eye.

Johnson's inability to deal effectively with his military advisers posed even more difficult problems. Under fire from the right wing in 1968 for not letting the military run the war, he vigorously and properly defended the principle of civilian control. The brass had been heard, he insisted, but not always heeded, and that was the way it should be. "People who fled to these shores from military atrocities did not want military leadership and rule by Kings." He went on to play down the differences between himself and his military advisers. Traditional military narrow-mindedness had been whittled away, and his own generals and admirals fully appreciated the complexity of military issues in the nuclear age. He conceded that at times they had wanted to do more faster. But, he concluded, "on diplomatic matters an Air Force General doesn't know more than a Johnson City General."[7]

While defending his prerogatives, Johnson also went to great lengths to prove to skeptics his faith in and close consultation with his top military advisers. If he were to list his twenty-five best friends in Washington, he proclaimed to a *Los Angeles Times* reporter in 1968, "Bus" Wheeler and the Joint Chiefs would be on it. Praising his Joint Chiefs of Staff as "restraint" men, "opposite from [Gen. Curtis] LeMay in disposition and temperament," he went on to claim that he had not taken a single major military decision without first securing their assent.[8] On another occasion, he expressed appreciation for his field commander's loyalty and praised his "Marshallesque" refusal to complain. "I like Westmoreland," he told Generals Wheeler and Abrams in February 1968. "Westmoreland has played on the team to help me."[9]

Literally speaking, of course, Johnson was right. He had reason to appreciate Westmoreland's willingness to suppress his convictions about how the war should be fought in the larger interest of team play. He and McNamara had selected for the Joint Chiefs of Staff military officers who were not likely to rock the boat, and the president had taken great pains in the case of each major military decision to consult with the JCS and make sure they were on board.

Yet what Johnson extolled here as virtues were in both cases part of the problem. JCS acquiescence and Westmoreland's team play, however much appreciated by the commander in chief, came at the high cost of an open, candid discussion of fundamental strategic differences. Many of Johnson's aides have conceded that it was difficult, if not impossible, for him to reveal to anyone what he was really thinking, and they were thus forced to figure it out on the basis of what he was doing. LBJ seems to have found it particularly difficult to level with the Joint Chiefs. Indeed, William Bundy has noted, the president may have been at his worst in dealing with his top military advisers. Deferential to them on the surface, he kept them at arm's length and never gave them a real chance to express their views.[10]

Yet as many critics have correctly pointed out, the Joint Chiefs could never really lay it on the line with the president either. Perhaps they were inhibited by their anomalous position in the chain of command, perhaps by a tradition that encouraged deference to civilian authority, perhaps by the "lessons" of Korea and the Truman-MacArthur controversy.[11] Whatever the reason, early in the war they refused to forcefully articulate the advantages of their preferred approach. Had they done so, they might have persuaded LBJ of the virtue of their proposals. More likely, they would have deterred him from going into Vietnam in force. In any event, they did not, opting instead for Wheeler's foot-in-the-door approach, ensnaring themselves and the president in a gradualist approach that caused much grief to all concerned and inflicted enormous destruction on North and South Vietnam without ending the war.[12]

There were other major problems with the Johnson style: the determination to dupe or co-opt advisers and the public rather than confront them candidly and forcefully; the obsessive secrecy; the tendency toward personalization of the domestic debate. The steadily widening credibility gap and the president's own image problems complicated an already impossible public relations problem. Johnson repeatedly denied that Vietnam was his war. It was "America's war," he insisted, and "if I drop dead tomorrow, this war will still be with you."[13] In one sense, of course, he was right. But in terms of the way the war was fought and the agony it caused, Vietnam was far more his than he was prepared to admit or even recognize.

It would be a serious mistake to attribute America's failure in Vietnam solely or even largely to bureaucratic imperatives, the false dogmas of limited war theory, or the eccentricities of Johnson leadership style. Had the United States looked all over the world in 1965 it might not have been able to find a more difficult place to fight. The climate and terrain were singularly inhospitable. More important, perhaps, was the formless, yet lethal, nature of warfare in Vietnam, a conflict without distinct battlelines or fixed objectives where traditional concepts of victory and defeat were blurred. And from the outset, the balance of forces was stacked against the United States in the form of a weak, divided, and far too dependent client lacking in political legitimacy and a fanatically determined and resilient enemy that early on seized and refused to relinquish the banner of Vietnamese nationalism.

American military leaders have left ample testimony of the complex and often baffling challenge they faced in Vietnam and on the home front. Speaking of the "fog of war" in December 1967, Wheeler observed that Vietnam was the "foggiest war" in his memory and the first where the fog was "thicker away from the scene of the conflict than on the battlefield."[14] Marine Gen. Lewis Walt concurred. "Soon after I arrived in Vietnam," he later admitted, "it became obvious to me that I had neither a real understanding of the nature of the war nor any clear idea how to win it."[15] Abysmal ignorance of Vietnam and the Vietnamese on the part of Lyndon Johnson, his advisers, and the nation as a whole thickened the fog of war, contributing to a mistaken decision to intervene, mismanagement of the conflict, and ultimate failure.

A considerable part of the problem also lay in the inherent difficulty of waging limited war. Limited wars, as Stephen Peter Rosen has noted, are by their very nature "*strange* wars." They combine political, military, and diplomatic dimensions in the most complicated way.[16] Conducting them effectively requires rare intellectual ability, political acumen, and moral courage.

Johnson and his advisers went into the conflict confident—probably over-confident—that they knew how to wage limited war, and only when the strategy of escalation proved bankrupt and the American people unwilling or unable to fight in cold blood did they confront their tragic and costly failure.

Deeply entangled in a war they did not understand and could find no way to win, they struggled merely to put a label on it. "All-out limited war," William Bundy called it; "a war that is not a war," some military officers complained. Harry McPherson phrased it in the form of a question. "What the hell do you say? How do you half-lead a country into war?" Westmoreland was prosaic if more explicit in describing Vietnam as a "limited war with limited objectives, fought with limited means and programmed for the utilization of limited resources."[17]

The search for labels suggests the fundamental difficulties of limited war, and it must be conceded in retrospect that there are no easy answers to the problems Johnson and his advisers confronted. The key military problem, Rosen contends, is "how to adapt, quickly and successfully, to the peculiar and unfamiliar *battlefield* conditions in which our armed forces are fighting."[18] That this was not done in Vietnam may reflect the limited vision of the political and military leaders, but it will not be easily done elsewhere.

And the military challenge is by no means the most difficult. Managing peace proved every bit as frustrating for the Johnson administration. If it ignored any of the various peace initiatives launched by third countries or private individuals, it risked missing an opportunity to negotiate or losing a propaganda advantage. If, on the other hand, it responded too eagerly it risked sending the wrong signal to the enemy or to domestic critics. And once involved in the peace process it could not be sure of controlling the results. The management of peace initiatives already under way also posed difficult challenges. If too many people knew what was going on there was the risk of a leak that could blow the initiative or cause embarrassment. If, on the other hand, information was restricted to a handful of people, as in MARIGOLD, peace moves could not be effectively coordinated with military operations.

Nor is there any obvious solution to the dilemma of domestic opinion. Vietnam exposed the enormous difficulties of fighting in cold blood. Without arousing popular emotions and especially without measurable success on the battlefield it was impossible over a long period of time to sustain popular support. Frederick the Great's dictum that war could only be successful when people did not know about it could not possibly work in the age of instant communications and mass media, especially when, as in the case of Vietnam, the size of the U.S. commitment quickly outgrew the presumed parameters of limited war. On the other hand, trying to play down the war also caused major problems. The Johnson and Nixon administrations both went to considerable lengths to maintain the semblance of normality at home. Thus, as D. Michael Shafer has observed, "those fighting [in Vietnam] faced the bitter irony that back in 'The World' life went on as normal while they risked their lives in a war their government did not acknowledge and many fellow citizens considered unnecessary or even immoral." [19]

Johnson's inability to wage war in cold blood produced what appears on the surface a great anomaly—one of the shrewdest politicians of the twentieth century committing a form of political suicide by taking the nation into a war he would have preferred not to fight. To some extent, of course, LBJ was the victim of his considerable political acumen. He took the nation to war so quietly, with such consummate skill (and without getting a popular mandate) that when things turned sour the anger was inevitably directed at him. His inability to manage effectively the war he got so skillfully is typical of his leadership record. He was also much more effective in getting domestic programs through Congress than in managing them once enacted. [20] In the final analysis, however, Johnson's failure reflects more than anything else the enormity of the problem and the inadequacy of the means chosen to address it.

Partial mobilization or a declaration of war provides at best debatable alternatives. George Bush's apparent success in mobilizing support for the Persian Gulf War of 1991 confirmed in the eyes of some critics the deficiencies of Johnson's leadership in Vietnam. In fact, the remarkable popular support for the Gulf War and especially for the troops was in a very real sense an expiation of lingering guilt for nonsupport in Vietnam. It also owed a great deal to perceptions of military success and the rapidity with which the war ended. In any event, Johnson's and Rusk's reservations about the dangers of a declaration of war in the Cold War international system were well taken, and congressional sanction in the War of 1812 and the Mexican War did nothing to stop rampant and at times crippling domestic opposition.

However much we might deplore the limitations of Johnson's leadership and the folly of limited war theory, they alone are not responsible for America's failure in Vietnam. That conflict posed uniquely complex challenges for U.S. war managers both in terms of the conditions within Vietnam itself and the international context in which it was fought. American policymakers thus took on in Vietnam a problem that was in all likelihood beyond their control.

In the new world order of the post–Cold War era, the conditions that appeared to make limited war essential and that made the Vietnam War especially difficult to fight will probably not be replicated, and the "lessons" of Vietnam will have at best limited relevance. There are many different kinds of limited war, however. Korea, Vietnam, the Persian Gulf War (which was, after all, limited in both ends and means) were as different from each other as each was from World War II. What they shared was the complexity in establishing ends and formulating means that is inherent in the institution of limited war itself. Even in this new era, therefore, it would be well for us to remember Vietnam and to recall Lady Bird Johnson's 1967 lament: "It is unbearably hard to fight a limited war."

NOTES

ABBREVIATIONS

LBJP	Lyndon Baines Johnson Papers, all in LBJ Library
AF	Aides Files (with name of aide added)
DSDUF	Declassified and Sanitized Documents from Unprocessed Files
MNF	Meeting Notes File
NF	Name File (with name added)
NSFCFVN	National Security File, Country File, Vietnam
NSFKLF	National Security File, Komer-Leonhart File
NSFMPMB	National Security File, Memos to the President, McGeorge Bundy
NSFMPWR	National Security File, Memos to the President, Walt Rostow
NSFNSCM	National Security File, National Security Council Meetings
NSFRKF	National Security File, Robert Komer File
NSFSF	National Security File, Subject File
PAFDB	President's Appointment File, Diary Backup
TJNM	Tom Johnson Notes of Meetings
VNRF	Vietnam Reference File
WWP	William Westmoreland Papers
BMF, WW/CBSLR	Backchannel Message File, William Westmoreland/CBS Litigation Records, Record Group 407, Federal Records Center, Suitland, Md.
USAMHI	William Westmoreland Papers, U.S. Army Military History Institute, Carlisle Barracks, Pa.

PREFACE

1. Quoted in Brian VanDeMark, *Into the Quagmire: Lyndon Johnson and the Escalation of the Vietnam War* (New York: Oxford University Press, 1991), 178.

I. "A DIFFERENT KIND OF WAR"

1. *Public Papers of the Presidents of the United States: Lyndon Baines Johnson, 1965* (Washington, D.C.: Government Printing Office, 1966), 2: 794–802.

2. *New York Times*, July 29, 1965.

3. *Time*, August 6, 1965, 17–18.

4. *Newsweek*, August 9, 1965, 17–18.

5. Robert Middlekauf, *The Glorious Cause: The American Revolution, 1763–1789* (New York: Oxford University Press, 1982), 297; Ira Gruber, "Toward Limited War in Europe, 1648–1714," and "Limited War in Europe, 1714–1763," draft chapters in author's possession.

6. Daniel Boorstin, *The Americans: The Colonial Experience* (New York: Vintage, 1958), 352; Russell F. Weigley, *The American Way of War* (Bloomington: Indiana University Press, 1977), xxi.

7. For convenient summaries of limited war theory, see Weigley, *American Way of War*, 412–413; Wallace Thies, *When Governments Collide: Coercion and Diplomacy in the Vietnam Conflict, 1964–1968* (Berkeley: University of California Press, 1980), 6–15; and Stephen Peter Rosen, "Vietnam and the American Theory of Limited War," *International Security* 7 (Fall 1982): 84–87. The classic studies are Robert E. Osgood, *Limited War: The Challenge to American Strategy* (Chicago: University of Chicago Press, 1957); Thomas Schelling, *Arms and Influence* (New Haven: Yale University Press, 1966); and Herman Kahn, *On Escalation* (Baltimore: Penguin Books, 1965).

8. Osgood, *Limited War*, 22–27.

9. Quoted in Thies, *When Governments Collide*, 9.

10. Osgood, *Limited War*, 279–284.

11. Dean Rusk as told to Richard Rusk, *As I Saw It* (New York: W. W. Norton, 1990), 246, 498–500; Thomas J. Schoenbaum, *Waging Peace & War: Dean Rusk in the Truman, Kennedy, & Johnson Years* (New York: Simon and Schuster, 1988), 443.

12. Bromley Smith oral history interview, LBJ Library; Barry Rubin, *Secrets of State: The State Department and the Struggle over U.S. Foreign Policy* (New York: Oxford University Press, 1984), 101.

13. McGeorge Bundy to LBJ, August 2, 1965, LBJP, NSFMPMB, box 12.

14. George Christian notes on LBJ conversations with Neil Sheehan, March 24, 1967, and Jack Leacacos, October 14, 1967, LBJP, AF, Christian, box 1; Rusk, *As I Saw It*, 327, 337.

15. Christian notes on conversation with Sheehan, March 24, 1967, LBJP, AF, Christian, box 1.

16. Rusk, *As I Saw It*, 304; Schoenbaum, *Waging Peace*, 411.

17. Max Frankel notes on conversation with LBJ, July 8, 1965, Arthur Krock Papers, Princeton University Library, box 1.

18. Lloyd C. Gardner, "Harry Hopkins with Hand Grenades?" paper presented at Vietnam Symposium, Columbia University, November 1990, 17–18.

19. Schoenbaum, *Waging Peace*, 413.

20. Christian notes on meeting with Leacacos, October 14, 1967, LBJP, AF, Christian, box 1.

21. Schoenbaum, *Waging Peace*, 414.

22. Ibid.

23. David Humphrey, "Tuesday Lunch at the Johnson White House," *Diplomatic History* 8 (Winter 1984): 87.

24. Bromley Smith oral history interview, LBJ Library; Walt Whitman Rostow oral history interview, LBJ Library.

25. Patrick Anderson, *The President's Men* (Garden City: Doubleday, 1968), 340–341.

26. Rostow to LBJ, September 1, 1966, LBJP, NSFMPWR, box 10.

27. Emmette S. Redford and Richard T. McCulley, *White House Operations: The Johnson Presidency* (Austin: University of Texas Press, 1986), 37–38, 110-111; unclassified material in LBJP, NSF, NF, box 7; Walt Whitman Rostow oral history interview; William Jorden memorandum for the record, April 26, 1967, LBJP, NSF, NF, Rostow Memos, box 7.

28. Author interview with Benjamin Read, Washington, D.C., November 16, 1988.

29. Rubin, *Secrets of State*, 116; see also Robert Gallucci, *Neither Peace nor Honor* (Baltimore: Johns Hopkins University Press, 1975), 331.

30. Rostow memo to LBJ, September 2, 1966, LBJP, NSFMPWR, box 10.

31. Schoenbaum, *Waging Peace*, 450–451.

32. Komer to LBJ, agenda for March 11, 1966, meeting, LBJP, NSFCFVN, box 28; also agenda, May 16, 1966, LBJP, NSFMPWR, box 7.

33. Agendas for meetings, March 3, 11, 1966, LBJP, NSFCFVN, box 28.

34. Komer to Vance, Katzenbach, Rostow, November 30, 1966, LBJP, NSFRKF, box 6.

35. U. Alexis Johnson, *The Right Hand of Power* (Englewood Cliffs, N.J.: Prentice-Hall, 1984), 398–400; Bromley Smith oral history interview.

36. Johnson, *Right Hand of Power*, 398–400; Bromley Smith oral history interview; Nicholas deB. Katzenbach oral history interview, LBJ Library.

37. In September 1966, for example, NSC membership included Vice-President Hubert H. Humphrey, Rusk, McNamara, CIA director Richard Helms, General Wheeler, Secretary of the Treasury Henry Fowler, USIA director Leonard Marks, Undersecretary of State George Ball, Deputy Secretary of Defense Cyrus Vance, Ambassador to the United Nations Arthur Goldberg, arms control director William C. Foster, James E. Webb, Joseph Cisco, John McNaughton, Rostow, Moyers, White House aide Robert Kintner, press secretary George Christian, and Bromley Smith. See Rostow to LBJ, September 12, 1966, LBJP, NSFMPWR, box 10.

38. Bromley Smith oral history interview; Rostow to LBJ, April 29, May 11, May 16, May 25, 1966, LBJP, NSFMPWR, box 7. For the complaints of one member about the NSC's nonuse, see Carl T. Rowan, *Breaking Barriers: A Memoir* (New York: Harper Perennial, 1992), 264, 267, 274.

39. Humphrey, "Tuesday Lunch," 88–92.

40. Walt Rostow oral history interview.

41. Ibid.; Bromley Smith oral history interview; Doris Kearns, *Lyndon Johnson and the American Dream* (New York: Harper and Row, 1976), 319–320.

42. Humphrey, "Tuesday Lunch," 98.

43. *Washington Post*, May 21, 1967.

44. Author interviews with William Bundy, Princeton, N.J., February 26, 1988, and Nicholas Katzenbach, Princeton, N.J., December 7, 1988. For a critical view of

the nongroup, see Chester Cooper, *The Lost Crusade: America in Vietnam* (New York: Dodd, Mead, 1970), 414.

45. Clark Clifford with Richard Holbrooke, *Counsel to the President: A Memoir* (New York: Random House, 1991), 394.

46. Ibid., 386; and Joseph Califano, *The Triumph and Tragedy of Lyndon Johnson: The White House Years* (New York: Simon and Schuster, 1991), 10. For similar sketches of LBJ by his advisers, see Rowan, *Breaking Barriers*, 190, 196, 229, 236, 276; and Bill Moyers, "The Final Word," *Among Friends of LBJ*, June 15, 1982, 9. See also Robert Dallek, *Lone Star Rising* (New York: Oxford University Press, 1991), 352.

47. "The Talk of the Town," *New Yorker*, October 13, 1986, 35.

48. Robert A. Caro, *The Years of Lyndon Johnson: Means of Ascent* (New York: Alfred A. Knopf, 1990), 35–53.

49. Kearns, *Johnson*, 251.

50. Caro, *Means of Ascent*, 4.

51. *Time*, August 6, 1965, 17–18.

52. Ibid., 19.

53. Rusk, *As I Saw It*, 338.

54. Redford and McCulley, *White House Operations*, 66–67.

55. Art McCafferty memos to Komer, March 24, 25, 1966, LBJP, NSFCFVN, box 29.

56. See, for example, James Bishop, *A Day in the Life of President Johnson* (New York: Random House, 1967), 78.

57. *Time*, January 8, 1968, 9–16.

58. *Time*, February 9, 1968, 10–11.

59. Lewis Sorley, *Thunderbolt: General Creighton Abrams and the Army of His Times* (New York: Simon and Schuster, 1992), 251.

60. See Rostow to LBJ, September 12, 14, 1966, James Brown to LBJ, September 11, 1966, LBJP, NSFCFVN, box 35.

61. Califano, *Triumph and Tragedy*, 150; Volney Warner oral history interview, U.S. Army Military History Institute Library, Carlisle Barracks, Pa.

62. *Time*, May 20, 1966, 10.

63. *Time*, May 24, 1968, 17.

64. Clifford, *Counsel to the President*, 442–443.

65. Quoted in C. L. Sulzberger, *Seven Continents and Forty Years* (New York: Quadrangle, 1977), 443.

66. *Time*, August 6, 1965, 19.

67. Adm. Thomas Moorer oral history interview, LBJ Library.

68. *Time*, August 6, 1965.

69. George McGovern, *Grassroots* (New York: Random House, 1977), 104–105.

70. Lady Bird Johnson diary entry, March 7, 1965, in Lady Bird Johnson, *A White House Diary* (New York: Holt, Rinehart, Winston, 1970), 248.

71. LBJ to Mr. and Mrs. Charles R. Knack, August 24, 1967, LBJP, AF, Harry McPherson, box 29.

72. Henry Fowler oral history interview, LBJ Library.

73. Stephen Rosenfeld, "Fathers, Sons and War," *Washington Post*, April 19, 1985.

74. Henry Fowler oral history interview.

75. Tom Johnson notes on meeting, August 9, 1967, LBJP, TJNM, box 1.

76. Powell Allen Moore oral history interview, Richard H. Russell Library, Athens, Ga. I am grateful to Professor Frank Mitchell of the University of Southern California for bringing this document to my attention. See Dallek, *Lone Star Rising*, 42, for Johnson's lifelong tendency to seek sympathy.

77. William S. White, *The Making of a Journalist* (Lexington: University Press of Kentucky, 1986), 216.

78. Bundy quoted in Michael Charlton and Anthony Moncrief, *Many Reasons Why: The American Involvement in Vietnam*, 2d ed. (New York: Hill and Wang, 1989), 120.

79. John Roche oral history interview, LBJ Library; McPherson to LBJ, June 13, 1967, LBJP, AF, McPherson, box 29.

80. Robert Komer, *Bureaucracy at War* (Boulder, Colo.: Westview Press, 1986), 82–85; Bundy quoted in Charlton and Moncrief, *Many Reasons Why*, 122.

81. Cooper, *Lost Crusade*, 413–414; Moyers to LBJ, n.d., LBJP, AF, Bill Moyers, box 7.

82. Moyers to LBJ, n.d., LBJP, AF, Moyers, box 7; Komer, "A Strategic Plan for 1967 in Vietnam," November 29, 1966, LBJP, NSFRKF, box 5; Rostow to LBJ, November 30, 1966, LBJP, NSFMPWR, box 1.

83. Komer, *Bureaucracy at War*, 70–71, 94.

84. Ibid.

85. Cooper, *Lost Crusade*, 413–414.

86. William Bundy oral history interview, LBJ Library.

87. Cooper, *Lost Crusade*, 413–414.

88. William Bundy oral history interview.

89. Henry Fowler oral history interview.

2. NO MORE MACARTHURS

1. William C. Westmoreland, *A Soldier Reports* (New York: Dell, 1978), 207; for another account of this meeting, see Paul Miles, interview with Westmoreland, January 7, 1971, Paul Miles Papers, U.S. Army Military History Institute, Carlisle Barracks, Pa., box 29.

2. T. Harry Williams, *Americans at War: The Development of the American Military System* (New York: Collier Books, 1962), 143.

3. Lawrence J. Korb, *The Joint Chiefs of Staff: The First Twenty-Five Years* (Bloomington: Indiana University Press, 1976), 132; Edward Lutwak, *The Pentagon and the Art of War* (New York: Simon and Schuster, 1984), 86.

4. Ernest R. May, "The U.S. Government, a Legacy of the Cold War," *Diplomatic History* 16 (Spring 1992): 273. For the Korean War command system, see Roy K. Flint, "Problems of Command: The Joint Chiefs, MacArthur, and the Korean War," unpublished paper in possession of the author; and D. Clayton James, *Refighting the Last War: Command and Crises in Korea* (New York: Free Press, 1992), 55, 97–98, 176, 217.

5. Quoted in Stephen Ambrose, *Eisenhower the President* (New York: Simon and Schuster, 1984), 223–225, 428–429, 495–496, 515; and Korb, *Joint Chiefs of Staff*, 109.

6. Quoted in Forrest Pogue, *George C. Marshall*, 4 vols. (New York: Viking, 1963–1987), 4: 423.

7. Quoted in John Lewis Gaddis, *Strategies of Containment* (New York: Oxford University Press, 1982), 25n.

8. Thomas M. Coffey, *Iron Eagle: The Turbulent Life of General Curtis LeMay* (New York: Crown Publishers, 1986), 355.

9. Ibid.

10. Gregory Palmer, *The McNamara Strategy and the Vietnam War* (Westport, Conn.: Greenwood Press, 1978), 13, 131–143; and Jack Raymond, *Power at the Pentagon* (New York: Harper and Row, 1964), 280–285.

11. Hanson Baldwin, "The McNamara Monarchy," *Saturday Evening Post*, March 9, 1963, 8–9; Raymond, *Power at the Pentagon*, 280; William Franke to Hanson Baldwin, March 7, 1963, Hanson Baldwin Papers, Yale University Library, New Haven, Conn., box 22; Arleigh Burke to John McCain, March 18, 1963, ibid., box 9; Baldwin, "The Changing Role of the Military Professional," unpublished ms. in ibid., box 5 [4].

12. "The Management Team," *Time*, February 5, 1965, 22–23B.

13. Ibid.; "Joint Chiefs Wear a Different Hat," *Business Week*, July 30, 1966, 68–72; John P. McConnell, "Some Reflections on a Tour of Duty," *Air University Review* (September–October 1969): 4.

14. Coffey, *Iron Eagle*, 422.

15. David Halberstam, *The Best and the Brightest* (New York: Random House, 1972), 282.

16. JCS memo to secretary of defense, September 9, 1964, and memo for the record, September 14, 1964, LBJP, NSFCFVN, box 6; *The Senator Gravel Edition: The Pentagon Papers*, 4 vols. (Boston: Beacon Press, 1971), 3: 563–564.

17. Jack Valenti to LBJ, November 14, 1964, NC 19/CO 312, Vietnam, CCF, LBJP, White House Confidential File, box 71; James Thomson memo for the record, November 24, 1964, LBJP, NSF, Bundy Files, box 24.

18. Brian VanDeMark, *Into the Quagmire: Lyndon Johnson and the Escalation of the Vietnam War* (New York: Oxford University Press, 1991), 124–125, 127.

19. Halberstam, *Best and the Brightest*, 564.

20. Clark Clifford with Richard Holbrooke, *Counsel to the President: A Memoir* (New York: Random House, 1991), 406–407.

21. Bruce Palmer, *The Twenty-Five-Year War* (Lexington: University Press of Kentucky, 1985), 41.

22. See especially Larry Berman, *Planning a Tragedy* (New York: W. W. Norton, 1982); VanDeMark, *Into the Quagmire*; and William Conrad Gibbons, "The 1965 Decision to Send U.S. Ground Forces to Vietnam," paper given at the International Studies Association, April 16, 1987.

23. Berman, *Planning a Tragedy*, 111–112; Stanley Resor oral history interview, LBJ Library; Harold Brown oral history interview, LBJ Library. Brown observed that the president wanted to be sure that if there was trouble later everyone was implicated in the decision, and he went around the room asking each person his view to get him on record.

24. Halberstam, *Best and the Brightest*, 595.

25. See, for example, Gen. Victor Krulak to Gen. Wallace Greene, July 19, 1965, Victor Krulak Papers, Marine Corps Historical Center, Washington, D.C., box 1.

26. Korb, *Joint Chiefs of Staff*, 160.

27. Gen. Earle Wheeler oral history interview, LBJ Library.

28. Palmer, *Twenty-Five-Year War*, 28; Gen. Harold Johnson oral history interview, U.S. Army Military History Institute, Carlisle Barracks, Pa.

29. Halberstam, *Best and the Brightest*, 595.

30. Hanson Baldwin, "We Must Choose—(1) 'Bug Out' (2) Negotiate (3) Fight," *New York Times Magazine*, February 21, 1965, 9, 62–63. Baldwin later claimed that Wheeler, Harold Johnson, and Greene had all told Lyndon Johnson it would take one-half million to a million men and at least five years just to prevent North Vietnam from taking over the South. See Hanson Baldwin oral history interview, U.S. Naval Academy Library, Annapolis, Md., 710–711. Also Hanson Baldwin, letter to the editor of *Army* (September 1975): 2; and Greene to Baldwin, September 24, 1975, Hanson Baldwin oral history interview. See also Greene handwritten notes, Wallace Greene Papers, Marine Corps Historical Center, Washington, D.C., Box 24. Presumably speaking for Johnson's civilian advisers, William Bundy later admitted that "we didn't have any such figure as 500,000 in mind." Their estimate was in the neighborhood of 250,000 to 300,000. Michael Charlton and Anthony Moncrief, *Many Reasons Why: The American Involvement in Vietnam* (New York: Hill and Wang, 1989), 120.

31. Report of Ad Hoc Study Group, "Intensification of the Military Operations in Vietnam: Concept and Appraisal," July 14, 1965, LBJP, NSFCFVN, box 20.

32. Record of meeting with Joint Chiefs of Staff, July 22, 1965, LBJP, MNF, box 1; also McGeorge Bundy, handwritten notes on meeting, July 22, 1965, McGeorge Bundy Papers, LBJ Library, box 1.

33. Ibid.; see also Jack Valenti, *A Very Human President* (New York: W. W. Norton, 1975), 330–354; McGeorge Bundy, notes on meeting, July 22, 1965, McGeorge Bundy Papers, box 1.

34. Hanson Baldwin, "Military Disappointed," *New York Times*, July 29, 1965.

35. Record of meeting with advisers (immediately after meeting with JCS), July 22, 1965, LBJP, MNF, box 1.

36. See Korb, *Joint Chiefs of Staff*, 163, 179, for the argument that the chiefs should have resigned. For Harold Johnson's change of mind, see Lt. Gen. Harold G. Moore and Joseph L. Galloway, *We Were Soldiers Once . . . and Young* (New York: Random House), 16.

37. Earl H. Tilford, Jr., "Setup: Why and How the U.S. Air Force Lost in Vietnam," *Armed Forces and Society* 17 (Spring 1991): 339.

38. Andrew Goodpaster oral history interview, LBJ Library.

39. Stephen Peter Rosen, "Vietnam and the American Theory of Limited War," *International Security* 7 (Fall 1982): 96.

40. Bundy to LBJ, November 5, 1965, LBJP, NSFMPMB, box 5; Bundy to LBJ, November 10, 1967, LBJP, PAFDB, box 81.

41. Henry Brandon, *Anatomy of Error* (Boston: Gambit, 1969), 164; Halberstam, *Best and the Brightest*, 248, 633; Andrew Krepinevich, *The Army and Vietnam* (Baltimore: Johns Hopkins University Press, 1965), 34–35.

42. Richard Rusk and Dean Rusk, *As I Saw It* (New York: W. W. Norton, 1990), 452–453.

43. Clifford, *Counsel to the President*, 460.

44. Quoted in Robert A. Caro, *The Years of Lyndon Johnson: The Path to Power* (New York: Alfred A. Knopf, 1982), 494.

45. Martin Van Creveld, *Command in War* (Cambridge: Harvard University Press, 1985), 236–238, 244–245.

46. For McNamara and the impact of the missile crisis, see James G. Nathan,

"The Tragic Enshrinement of Toughness," in Thomas G. Paterson, ed., *Major Problems in American Foreign Policy*, vol. 2: *Since 1914* (New York: D. C. Heath, 1984), 570–571. For Johnson's populist observations regarding the military, see Doris Kearns, *Lyndon Johnson and the American Dream* (New York: Harper and Row, 1976), 262. Also Carl Rowan, *Breaking Barriers: A Memoir* (New York: Harper Perennial, 1991), 266, 271.

47. Rosen, "Vietnam," 96.

48. Quoted in Nathan, "Tragic Enshrinement of Toughness," 569.

49. Air Force Chief of Staff McConnell admitted this in "Some Reflections on a Tour of Duty," 87. For the effect on strategic thinking of the postwar emphasis on management skills, see Tilford, "Setup," 331–332.

50. Korb, *Joint Chiefs of Staff*, 18–24.

51. "Management Team," 22–23.

52. Ibid.; Lutwak, *Pentagon and the Art of War*, 86; Lawrence B. Tatum, "The Joint Chiefs of Staff and Defense Policy Formulation," *Air University Review* (May–June 1966): 40–44.

53. Westmoreland later observed that he spoke with Johnson only on several occasions during the war and usually visited with McNamara no more than twice a year. Charlton and Moncrief, *Many Reasons Why*, 139, 142.

54. In a cable of June 2, 1966, Wheeler urged Westmoreland to press for a single-strike bombing attack into Cambodia as a way of getting authorization for regular strikes. "Of course, this will not satisfy your need," he advised; "however, it would get our foot in the door, a situation I have found most useful in other areas." The cable is in BMF, WW/CBSLR, Record Group 407, box 15. See also Westmoreland's comments in Charlton and Moncrief, *Many Reasons Why*, 143.

55. JCS Memorandum-652-65, memorandum for the secretary of defense, "Concept for Vietnam," August 27, 1965, LBJP, NSF, National Security Council Histories, Deployment of Major U.S. Forces to Vietnam, vol. 7, document 36a.

56. *Pentagon Papers (Gravel)*, 4: 301.

57. Notes on meetings, December 17, 18, 1965, LBJP, MNF, box 1.

58. Wallace M. Greene, "The Bombing 'Pause': Formula for Failure," *Air Force Magazine* (April 1976): 36–39.

59. William Bundy oral history interview, LBJ Library.

60. See, for example, Westmoreland history notes, November 29, 1965, and December 29, 1965, WWP, USAMHI, box 27, recounting briefings of McNamara and Ambassador Henry Cabot Lodge, Jr., and especially Wheeler comments as reported in McGeorge Bundy notes on meetings, December 6, 7, 1965, McGeorge Bundy Papers, box 1.

61. McGeorge Bundy handwritten notes, December 6, 7, 21, 1965, February 18, 19, 1966, McGeorge Bundy Papers, box 1.

62. Earl H. Tilford, Jr., to author, January 1992.

63. For example, at a top-level meeting on September 13, 1965, McNamara, Rusk, and the president turned down a JCS proposal to bomb SAM sites, airfields having IL 28s, and targets near the Chinese border. McNamara warned that striking these targets would represent a significant escalation and believed such a step should be deferred until the administration got a better feel for North Vietnamese use of the aircraft and possible Chinese reactions. Notes on meeting, September 13, 1965, LBJP, PAFDB.

64. Mark Clodfelter, *The Limits of Air Power: The American Bombing of North Vietnam*

(New York: Free Press, 1989), 84–88; Earl H. Tilford, Jr., *Setup: What the Air Force Did in Vietnam and Why* (Maxwell Air Force Base: Air University Press, 1991), 108–111.

65. Author interview with Adm. Thomas Moorer, Washington, D.C., July 14, 1987.

66. Volney Warner oral history interview, U.S. Army Military History Institute, Carlisle Barracks, Pa.

67. Mark Perry, *Four Stars* (Boston: Houghton Mifflin, 1989), 156–158; Harold Johnson oral history interview; Harold Johnson cable to Westmoreland, October 20, 1967, BMF, WW/CBSLR, box 19. Charles F. Brower IV, "The Westmoreland 'Alternate Strategy' of 1967–1968," *Naval War College Review* 44 (Spring 1991): 20–51, argues that as early as March 1967, Westmoreland himself was profoundly dissatisfied with the attrition strategy and proposed an alternative strategy that at least implicitly recognized the weakness of his own approach.

68. Krulak to Greene, July 19, 1965, Victor Krulak Papers, box 1.

69. Quoted in Jack Shulimson, *Expanding War* (Washington, D.C.: Government Printing Office, 1982), 14–15. See also Victor Krulak, "Conflict of Strategies," *U.S. Naval Institute Proceedings* (November 1984), 85–86; Krulak to McNamara, May 9, 1966, Victor Krulak Papers, box 1; Westmoreland, *Soldier Reports*, 165; Wheeler to Westmoreland, September 12, 1966, BMF, WW/CBSLR, box 16. The army response is articulated in Westmoreland history notes, December 8, 1965, WWP, USAMHI, box 27; historical briefing, January 29, 1967, ibid., box 28; and Harold Johnson to Westmoreland, September 28, 1967, ibid., box 31. Greene probably exaggerates the extent to which the JCS were "interested" in his proposals. According to Neil Sheehan, Wheeler and Harold Johnson firmly supported Westmoreland and the army, and McDonald and McConnell were not the least inclined to buck the leadership. Neil Sheehan, *Bright Shining Lie* (New York: Random House, 1988), 632–633.

70. Westmoreland to Wheeler, January 23, 1967, BMF, WW/CBSLR, box 17.

71. Hanson Baldwin to Hobart Lewis, July 2, 1969, Baldwin Papers, box 5 [4]; and R. W. Apple to Baldwin, January 8, 1966, ibid., box 8.

72. Greene to author, February 6, 1988.

73. Adm. David McDonald oral history interview, U.S. Naval History Division, Washington, D.C.

74. Westmoreland, *Soldier Reports*, 161; for contemporary complaints, see Westmoreland to Adm. U. S. Grant Sharp, January 23, 1967, BMF, WW/CBSLR, box 17; and Westmoreland history notes, September 18, 1965, and January 16, 1966, WWP, USAMHI, box 27.

75. To Robert Cushman, May 25, 1957, Victor Krulak Papers, box 1.

76. See especially Westmoreland's comments in Charlton and Moncrief, *Many Reasons Why*, 143.

77. See, for example, Westmoreland to Waters, February 2, 1966, and Wheeler to Westmoreland and Sharp, April 1, 1967, BMF, WW/CBSLR, boxes 14 and 17; and Sharp to Wheeler, February 16, 1967, and Wheeler to Westmoreland and Sharp, February 18, 1967, ibid., box 17.

78. Notes on NSC meeting, June 22, 1966, LBJP, MNF, box 1. See also McGeorge Bundy memo for the president, September 12, 1965, LBJP, PAFDB, box 2.

79. See, for example Rostow draft agenda for Tuesday Lunch, July 26, 1966, LBJP, NSF, MPWR, box 9. In September 1966, State Department officials opposed

JCS recommendations to bomb certain targets for fear of jeopardizing talks set to begin between Rusk and top Soviet officials. See Rostow to LBJ, September 12, 1966, ibid., box 10.

80. Sharp to Wheeler, December 24, 1966, BMF, WW/CBSLR, box 17; see also Clodfelter, *Limits of Air Power*, 73–115; and Hanson Baldwin, "Gradualism in Vietnam," *New York Times*, July 2, 1966, copy in Hanson Baldwin Papers, box 97.

81. McNamara to LBJ, October 14, 1966, LBJP, NSF, NSCM, box 2.

82. Harold Johnson to Westmoreland, October 20, 1967, BMF, WW/CBSLR, box 19.

83. Benjamin Read and McGeorge Bundy comments at LBJ Library conference on the war in Vietnam, March 1991.

84. Clifford, *Counsel to the President*, 527. On Johnson as the man in the middle, see Robert Dallek, *Lone Star Rising* (New York: Oxford University Press, 1991), 110, 430, 447.

85. "I don't want loyalty. I want loyalty," Halberstam reports him saying. "I want him to kiss my ass in Macy's window at high noon and tell me it smells like roses." Halberstam, *Best and the Brightest*, 434.

86. David Dileo, *George Ball, Vietnam and the Rethinking of Containment* (Chapel Hill: University of North Carolina Press, 1991), 168. Those who left government, LBJ observed, should exercise the "utmost restraint" in telling how it worked to preserve the "candid, cordial and informal relationships" essential to its effective operation.

87. Quoted in Henry L. Trewhitt, *McNamara* (New York: Harper and Row, 1971), 237.

88. George Ball oral history interview, LBJ Library. For McNamara and Harriman, see Rudy Abramson, *Spanning the Century: The Life of W. Averell Harriman, 1891–1986* (New York: Morrow, 1992), 642–643. For McNamara's difficulties dealing with the war at the time and later, see especially Paul Hendrickson, "Divided against Himself," *Washington Post Magazine*, June 12, 1988, 20–31.

89. Quoted in Barry Rubin, *Secrets of State: The State Department and the Struggle over U.S. Foreign Policy* (New York: Oxford University Press, 1984), 99; and Rusk, *As I Saw It*, 435, 474.

90. The Napoleon quotation is in Westmoreland History File, Westmoreland Papers, LBJ Library, box 18. Westmoreland privately expressed great frustration with the "amazing lack of initiative" and "amazing lack of boldness" shown by Washington in planning the war. See Historical Briefing, February 3, 1967, WWP, USAMHI, box 28. The comment to McNamara is in Historical Briefing, October 17, 1966, ibid., box 27.

91. Miles interview with Westmoreland, January 7, 1971, Paul Miles Papers.

92. Westmoreland "historical briefing," July 12, 1967, WWP, USAMHI, box 29.

93. Wheeler to Westmoreland, June 2, 1966, to Westmoreland and Sharp, February 13, 1967, to Sharp and Westmoreland, March 6, 1967, BMF, WW/CBSLR, boxes 15, 16, 17.

94. Barry Zorthian oral history interview, LBJ Library.

95. Greene to author, May 9, 1988.

96. Gen. Leonard Chapman oral history interview, Marine Corps Historical Center, Washington, D.C.; *New York Herald-Tribune*, August 22, 23, 1966; *Time*, August 19, 1966, 9. Interestingly, the army filed away newspaper reports of the

Greene study to be used later to understand and analyze marine proposals to the Joint Chiefs. See Gen. Creighton Abrams to DCSOPS, August 8, 1966, Creighton Abrams Papers as Vice Chief of Staff, U.S. Army Military History Institute, Carlisle Barracks, Pa.

97. Krulak to Greene, ca. February 1, 1967, Victor Krulak Papers, box 1.

98. Krulak, "Conflict of Strategies," 85–87.

99. Krulak to McNamara, January 4, 1967, Victor Krulak Papers, box 1.

100. Komer, "A Strategic Plan for 1967 in Vietnam," November 29, 1966, LBJP, NSFRKF, box 5; Rostow to LBJ, November 30, 1966, LBJP, NSFMPWR, box 1; "Strategic Guidelines for 1967 in Vietnam," December 10, 1966, enclosed with Komer memorandum for LBJ, December 10, 1966, LBJP, NSFRKF, box 7.

101. Wheeler to Sharp and Westmoreland, February 18, 1967, March 6, 1967, BMF, WW/CBSLR, box 17.

102. Neil Sheehan et al., *The Pentagon Papers as Published by the New York Times* (New York: Bantam Books, 1971), 567.

103. Ibid., 534.

104. David Lilienthal journal, March 21, 1967, in David Lilienthal, *The Journals of David Lilienthal*, 7 vols. (New York: Harper and Row, 1964–1983), 6: 418. It is now clear that McNamara's "dissent" began earlier and went deeper than portrayed in the *Pentagon Papers*. He appears to have concluded after the battle of the Ia Drang valley in November 1965 that the war could not be won militarily, and as early as May 1966 he spoke of a political settlement in which the NLF would play a central role. See especially the memoranda by W. Averell Harriman of conversations with McNamara, May 14, 30, August 31, November 26, 1966, in W. Averell Harriman Papers, Manuscript Division, Library of Congress, Washington, D.C., box 486, and May 28, 1966, ibid., box 520.

105. Sheehan, *Pentagon Papers*, 584.

106. McNamara draft presidential memorandum, "Future Actions in Vietnam," May 19, 1967, LBJP, NSFCFVN, boxes 74–75.

107. Sheehan, *Pentagon Papers*, 538–539.

108. Wheeler to Sharp, May 26, 1967, BMF, WW/CBSLR, box 18. Katzenbach's "no committee" actually proposed a review in a memo of April 24, 1967, in *Pentagon Papers (Gravel)*, 4: 438.

109. Lilienthal journal, March 2, 1967, *Lilienthal Journals*, 6: 402–404; Eisenhower's observations come from author interview with Andrew Goodpaster, July 2, 1988.

110. Lilienthal journal, March 21, 1967, *Lilienthal Journals*, 6: 421.

111. Notes on discussion with the president, April 27, 1967, LBJ Library, Paul Warnke–John McNaughton Papers, box 2. Westmoreland's very different account of the same meeting is in Historical Briefing, April 27, 1967, WWP, USAMHI, box 28.

112. Rostow memos, May 19, 20, 1967, LBJP, NSFCFVN, boxes 74–75. Katzenbach note to author, March 8, 1991, recounts Johnson's fear of a ranging review with many people and departments involved.

113. Sheehan, *Pentagon Papers*, 539; for Johnson's laconic discussions of these events, see Lyndon Baines Johnson, *Vantage Point: Perspectives on the Presidency* (New York: Holt, Rinehart, Winston, 1971), 370.

114. Baldwin to Col. C. M. Peeke, September 9, 1966, Hanson Baldwin Papers, box 13; and unpublished article, ibid., box 29. Also *New York Times*, July 13, 24, 1967.

115. Robert Ginsburgh memo for the record, August 14, 1967, LBJP, NSF, NF Col. Ginsburgh, box 3.

116. Walter Isaacson and Evan Thomas, *The Wise Men* (New York: Simon and Schuster, 1986), 675.

117. Phil Goulding, *Confirm or Deny* (New York: Harper and Row, 1970), 178–180.

118. For the preparations, see Wheeler to Westmoreland, August 10, 1967, BMF, WW/CBSLR, box 18.

119. John M. Shaw, "The August 1967 Stennis Subcommittee Hearings on the Air War over North Vietnam," unpublished paper in possession of the author, is an excellent, thoughtful analysis of the hearings and their impact. Wheeler's eagerness to play by the rules and support the president is evident in Rostow to LBJ, August 9, 1967, LBJP, NSFMPWR, vol. 37, box 2.

120. Perry, *Four Stars*, 163–164. Perry's source for the story is an unnamed "former JCS flag rank officer." His account has been confirmed by a senior officer close to one of the deceased members of the JCS but denied by Gen. Wallace Greene and Adm. Thomas Moorer. Rumors of a resignation en masse actually first surfaced in late 1967 when McNamara's departure from the administration was announced. See *New York Times*, November 29, December 2, 4, 1967.

121. Johnson appears to have been furious with both McNamara and the Joint Chiefs. David Halberstam claims that McNamara's testimony, which had not been cleared by the White House, led Johnson to consider removing him. See *Best and the Brightest*, 644–645. "Buz, your generals almost destroyed us with their testimony before the Stennis committee," the president complained to Wheeler on October 17. "We were murdered on the hearings." Tom Johnson notes on meetings, October 17, 1967, LBJP, TJNM, box 1.

122. *Public Papers of the Presidents of the United States, Lyndon Baines Johnson, 1967* (Washington, D.C.: GPO, 1968), 2: 816–817.

123. McNamara deposition for the Westmoreland trial, copy in LBJ Library, 113, 176, 322. Record of meeting, LBJ, McNamara, Wheeler, Rusk, and Rostow, August 19, 1967, LBJP, MNF, box 2.

124. *Washington Post*, December 29, 1967.

125. Notes on Tuesday Lunch, September 5, 1967, LBJP, MNF, box 2.

126. *New York Times*, September 1, 1967. For Johnson's more hawkish tone, see Tom Johnson notes on meetings, August 16, 24, December 4, 1967, LBJP, TJNM, box 1.

127. Notes on meeting, September 12, 1967, LBJP, MNF, box 2.

128. *Pentagon Papers (Gravel)*, 4: 210–214; George Christian, notes on meeting, October 11, 1967, LBJP, AF, Christian, box 1. McConnell sought a special meeting with the president to secure authority to hit the MIG bases at Phuc Yen.

129. McNamara to LBJ, November 1, 1967, LBJP, NSFCFVN, box 75.

130. Johnson handwritten notes on McNamara to LBJ, November 1, 1967, in ibid.

131. Clifford, *Counsel to the President*, 455.

132. Jim Jones notes on meeting, November 2, 1967, LBJP, MNF, box 2; Bundy to LBJ, November 10, 1967, LBJP, PAFDB, box 81; for Katzenbach's views, see Katzenbach to LBJ, November 16, 1967, quoted in Larry Berman, *Lyndon Johnson's War: The Road to Stalemate in Vietnam* (New York: W. W. Norton, 1989), 106–107; see also "Carnegie Endowment Proposals," December 5, 1967, copy in Matthew B. Ridgway Papers, U.S. Army Military History Institute, Carlisle Barracks, Pa., box 34A; and Wil-

liam Depuy to Westmoreland, October 19, 1967, William Depuy Papers, U.S. Army Military History Institute, Carlisle Barracks, Pa., folder WXYZ(67).

133. McPherson to LBJ, October 27, 1967, LBJP, AF, McPherson, box 53.

134. Bundy to LBJ, November 10, 1967, LBJP, PAFDB, box 81.

135. Westmoreland to Abrams, November 17, 1967, WWP, USAMHI, box 34.

136. See Johnson memorandum for the record in *Vantage Point*, 600–601. A perfunctory "review" did take place in January right before the Tet offensive. When Senator Edward Kennedy in a speech of January 25 proposed a shift to an enclave strategy along the lines proposed by the Carnegie Foundation group, Johnson asked the Joint Chiefs to respond. See Harold Johnson to LBJ, February 1, 1968, Earle Wheeler to LBJ, February 3, 1968, and Cyrus Vance to LBJ, January 31, 1968, all in LBJP, NSFCFVN, box 102. Predictably, these officials supported the existing strategy.

137. Clifford, *Counsel to the President*, 457. Also, Carl Bernstein, "On the Mistakes of the War," *Time*, February 11, 1991, 72.

138. The rumors are reported in *New York Times*, November 28, 29, 30, 1967. Those members of the JCS still alive today freely admit that individually and as a group, sometimes half seriously, sometimes half jokingly, they talked of resigning. But as Robert Ginsburgh, liaison between the JCS and the NSC, observed, resigning was "not the military way of doing things," and the JCS concluded that it was "better to stay in there fighting" than to leave. Should they leave, they feared, they would merely be replaced by others who would do what the president wanted. Author interview with Adm. Thomas Moorer, Washington, D.C., July 14, 1987, and Robert Ginsburgh, June 10, 1988, and Wallace Greene letter to author, February 6, 1988.

139. Trewhitt, *McNamara*, 275, 287, 297. See also Hendrickson, "Divided against Himself," 20–31.

140. McDonald to Baldwin, July 20, 1967, Hanson Baldwin Papers, box 8 [5], and David McDonald oral history interview.

141. Quoted in Halberstam, *Best and the Brightest*, 646–647.

142. Handwritten note on Ginsburgh memorandum, May 23, 1968, LBJP, NSF, Subject File, "Press Appointments."

143. Author interviews with Moorer, July 14, 1987, and with Ginsburgh, June 10, 1988.

144. See especially Phil Goulding to Wheeler, copy in WWP, USAMHI, box 30, and Rostow to LBJ, February 4, 1968, with enclosures, LBJP.

145. Rostow memo to LBJ, September 13, 1967, with attachments, LBJP, NSF, NF, Col. Ginsburgh memos, box 3.

146. Margy and Bob McNamara to Joint Chiefs of Staff, April 12, 1968, John P. McConnell Papers, Air Force Historical Research Center, Maxwell Air Force Base, Ala.

147. Tom Johnson notes on NSC meeting, November 29, 1967, LBJP, TJNM, box 1.

3. THE "OTHER WAR"

1. Russell F. Weigley, *The American Way of War* (Bloomington: Indiana University Press, 1973), 153–163; Brian Linn, *The U.S. Army and Counterinsurgency in the Philippine War, 1899–1902* (Chapel Hill: University of North Carolina Press, 1989), 163–170;

Lester D. Langley, *The Banana Wars: An Inner History of American Empire, 1900–1934* (Lexington: University Press of Kentucky, 1983), 192–216; Larry E. Cable, *Conflict of Myths: The Development of American Counterinsurgency Doctrine and the Vietnam War* (New York: New York University Press, 1986), 3–110.

2. Cable, *Conflict of Myths*, 5–6; D. Michael Shafer, *Deadly Paradigms: The Failure of U.S. Counterinsurgency Policy* (Princeton, N.J.: Princeton University Press, 1988), 199–204, 238–239.

3. Douglas Blaufarb, *The Counterinsurgency Era: U.S. Doctrines and Performance* (New York: Free Press, 1977), 22.

4. Quoted in Thomas W. Scoville, *Reorganizing for Pacification Support* (Washington, D.C.: U.S. Army Center of Military History, 1982), 16.

5. McGeorge Bundy, notes on meeting, November 30, 1965, McGeorge Bundy Papers, box 1.

6. The freewheeling Lansdale quickly tangled with Lodge, Porter, and Barry Zorthian and soon found himself isolated, powerless, and deeply frustrated. See Komer Special Annex to Report to LBJ, April 19, 1966, LBJP, NSFCFVN, box 31. See also Zalin Grant, *Facing the Phoenix* (New York: W. W. Norton, 1991), 254; and Cecil B. Currey, *Edward Lansdale: The Unquiet American* (Boston: Houghton Mifflin, 1988), 291–325.

7. Blaufarb, *Counterinsurgency Era*, 222–225; *The Senator Gravel Edition: The Pentagon Papers*, 4 vols. (Boston: Beacon Press, 1971), 2: 526–533.

8. Quoted in Jack Valenti, *A Very Human President* (New York: W. W. Norton, 1975), 133; also Lady Bird Johnson diary, March 11, 1966, in Lady Bird Johnson, *A White House Diary* (New York: Holt, Rinehart, Winston, 1975), 370–371; Merle Miller, *Lyndon: An Oral Biography* (New York: G. P. Putnam, 1980), 464–467; McGeorge Bundy, notes on meeting, April 6, 1965, McGeorge Bundy Papers, boxes 18–19.

9. Quoted in Scoville, *Pacification Support*, 22.

10. Notes on cabinet meeting, January 11, 1966, LBJP, MNF, box 1.

11. Memorandum to Bundy, Lodge, et al., from William Porter and Leonard Unger, January 13, 1966, LBJ Library, Paul Warnke-John McNaughton Papers, box 1.

12. *Pentagon Papers (Gravel)*, 2: 548–554.

13. U. Alexis Johnson, *The Right Hand of Power* (Englewood Cliffs, N.J.: Prentice-Hall, 1984), 398–400.

14. Grant, *Facing the Phoenix*, 276.

15. William Colby, *Lost Victory: A First-Hand Account of America's Sixteen-Year Involvement in Vietnam* (Chicago: Contemporary Books, 1989), 235–237.

16. McGeorge Bundy notes, January 11, 1966, McGeorge Bundy Papers, box 2.

17. McGeorge Bundy to LBJ, February 16, 1966, LBJP, VNRF, box 1.

18. Military civic action programs are described in "Military Civic Actions in Vietnam," March 24, 1966, LBJP, NSFCFVN, box 29.

19. Report of Management Survey Team, December 29, 1965, LBJP, NSFCFVN, box 24.

20. Westmoreland to James L. Collins, January 1966, BMF, WW/CBSLR, box 14. See also R. C. Bowman to Robert Komer, March 28, 1966, LBJP, NSFCFVN, box 29; and Grant, *Phoenix*, 254.

21. Robert Komer, *Bureaucracy at War* (Boulder, Colo.: Westview Press, 1986), 89–92; R. C. Bowman memo to Komer, March 28, 1966, LBJP, NSFCFVN, box 29.

22. Bundy to LBJ, February 3, 1966, LBJP, NSFRKF, box 6.

23. *Pengagon Papers (Gravel)*, 2: 564; McGeorge Bundy to LBJ, February 16, 1966, LBJP, VNRF, box 1.

24. *Pentagon Papers (Gravel)*, 2: 564.

25. Chester Cooper memorandum to LBJ, March 3, 1966, LBJP, NSFRKF, box 6.

26. NSAM 343 can be found in *Pentagon Papers (Gravel)*, 2: 567–568.

27. Colby, *Lost Victory*, 206.

28. Walter Guzzardi, "Management of the War: A Tale of Two Capitals," *Fortune* (April 1967): 137.

29. Quoted in Scoville, *Pacification Support*, 28.

30. Komer to Porter, Letter 8, May 11, 1966, 9, July 27, 1966, 17, September 21, 1966, LBJP, NSFRKF, box 4.

31. Komer to Porter, Letter 9, July 27, 1966, ibid.

32. Komer to Porter, Letter 11, August 10, 1966, 9, July 27, 1966, in ibid.

33. Komer to Porter, Letter 16, September 12, 1966, in ibid.

34. Komer to Porter, Letter 9, July 27, 1966, in ibid.

35. Lodge weekly telegram to president, April 20, 1966, LBJP, NSFMPWR, box 7.

36. Komer memo for LBJ, July 1, 1966, LBJP, NSFCFVN, box 34; Lodge weekly telegram to president, July 27, 1966, LBJP, NSFMPWR, box 9.

37. Guzzardi, "Management of the War," 137.

38. For background on the PROVN study, see Volney Warner oral history interview, U.S. Army Military History Institute, Carlisle Barracks, Pa. The report was so controversial that the army's deputy chief of staff for operations refused to sign it. See also Grant, *Phoenix*, 267.

39. *Pentagon Papers (Gravel)*, 2: 576–577.

40. Ibid., 581.

41. Lodge weekly telegram to president, August 31, 1966, LBJP, NSFMPWR, box 10. Presidential adviser Maxwell Taylor drew very different conclusions from the Westmoreland "concept." See Taylor to president, August 30, 1966, LBJP, NSFCFVN, boxes 35–36.

42. Hubert Humphrey to LBJ, September 16, 1966, LBJP, NSFCFVN, box 35; W. Averell Harriman, memorandum of conversation with Nathan, September 13, 1966, W. Averell Harriman Papers, box 520.

43. *Pentagon Papers (Gravel)*, 2: 573–575.

44. Westmoreland historical briefing, October 17, 1966, WWP, USAMHI, box 27.

45. Rostow to LBJ, August 31, 1966, LBJP, NSFMPWR, box 10; *Pentagon Papers (Gravel)*, 2: 589–590.

46. Leonard Unger to Dean Rusk, October 2, 1966, LBJP, NSFMPWR, box 11; *Pentagon Papers (Gravel)*, 2: 594–597. Also McNamara to LBJ, October 14, 1966, LBJP, NSFNSCM, box 2.

47. *Pentagon Papers (Gravel)*, 2: 594–597. Also McNamara to LBJ, October 14, 1966, LBJP, NSFNSCM, box 2.

48. Wheeler to Sharp and Westmoreland, October 17, 1966, BMF, WW/CBSLR, box 16. See also summary notes of 565th NSC Meeting, October 15, 1966, LBJP, NSFNSCM, box 2.

49. Rostow to LBJ, October 6, 1966, and Komer memo, October 16, 1966, LBJP,

NSF, National Security Council histories, Manila conference, and president's Asian trip, box 45.

50. *Pentagon Papers (Gravel)*, 2: 601–602.

51. Blaufarb, *Counterinsurgency Era*, 238.

52. Colby, *Lost Victory*, 207.

53. Westmoreland to Wheeler, December 12, 1966, BMF, WW/CBSLR, box 17.

54. John Paul Vann memo for the record, January 14, 1967, John Paul Vann Papers, U.S. Army Military History Institute, Carlisle Barracks, Pa.

55. Quoted in Blaufarb, *Counterinsurgency Era*, 239.

56. Vann memo, n.d., John Paul Vann Papers.

57. Vann memo for the record, "Seminar on Vietnam Planning and Operations," n.d., John Paul Vann Papers.

58. Lansdale memorandum, "The Battleground in 1967," n.d., John Paul Vann Papers.

59. National Security Action Memorandum No. 362, May 9, 1967, Paul Warnke-John McNaughton Papers, box 7.

60. Wheeler to Westmoreland, February 14, 28, 1967, BMF, WW/CBSLR, box 17.

61. Blaufarb, *Counterinsurgency Era*, 240; also William Leonhart to LBJ, June 7, 1967, LBJP, NSFKLF, box 15.

62. Blaufarb, *Counterinsurgency Era*, 240; *Pentagon Papers (Gravel)*, 2: 615–623; James K. McCollum, "The CORDS Pacification Organization in Vietnam: A Civilian-Military Effort," *Armed Forces and Society* 10 (Fall 1983): 112–113.

63. *Newsweek*, March 27, 1967, 25, 28; Hugh Sidey, "A Burgeoning Boss Picks an Old Hand," *Life*, March 24, 1967, 32B; "Quartet at the Top," *Time*, March 24, 1967, 14.

64. Neil Sheehan, *Bright Shining Lie* (New York: Random House, 1988), 653–654; Colby, *Lost Victory*, 209.

65. *Newsweek*, March 27, 1967, 25.

66. Blaufarb, *Counterinsurgency Era*, 240.

67. Ellsworth Bunker second weekly telegram to LBJ, May 10, 1967, LBJP, DSDUF.

68. Blaufarb, *Counterinsurgency Era*, 241.

69. Leonhart to LBJ, June 7, 1967, LBJP, NSFKLF, box 15.

70. Leonhart to LBJ, June 3, 1967, ibid.; McPherson to LBJ, June 13, 1967, LBJP, AF, McPherson, box 29; notes on cabinet meeting, July 19, 1967, LBJP, TJNM, box 1.

71. "Project TAKEOFF–Action Program," n.d., LBJP.

72. Bunker eighth weekly telegram to LBJ, June 21, 1967, LBJP, NSFCFVN, box 104.

73. Blaufarb, *Counterinsurgency Era*, 209.

74. "Project TAKEOFF–Action Program," n.d., LBJP; Bunker fourth weekly telegram to LBJ, May 25, 1967, LBJP, DSDUF.

75. McCollum, "CORDS," 116–117; Blaufarb, *Counterinsurgency Era*, 243–245.

76. "Project TAKEOFF–Action Program," LBJP.

77. Bunker weekly telegrams, September 13, 1967, October 4, 1967, December 7, 1967, and December 31, 1967, LBJP, NSFCFVN, boxes 104–105.

78. Komer, *Bureaucracy at War*, 33.

79. Leonhart memo to LBJ, September 14, 1967, LBJP, NSFKLF, box 15.

80. Bunker thirty-first weekly telegram, December 13, 1967, LBJP, NSFCFVN, box 105.

81. *New York Times*, December 1, 1967.

82. Warner, "Bearing the Brunt at Con Thien," *Reporter*, October 19, 1967, 21.

83. Bunker thirty-third, thirty-fourth, and thirty-sixth weekly telegrams, January 2, 13, 24, 1968, LBJP, NSFCFVN, box 105.

84. Bunker fourth weekly telegram, May 24, 1967, and ninth weekly telegram, June 28, 1967, ibid., box 104.

85. David Lilienthal journal, November 8, 1967, David Lilienthal, *The Journals of David Lilienthal*, 7 vols. (New York: Harper and Row, 1964–1983), 6: 507.

86. Colby, *Lost Victory*.

87. Sheehan, *Bright Shining Lie*, 668.

88. Blaufarb, *Counterinsurgency Era*, 278.

89. Dave Dickens, "An Evaluation of Australian and New Zealand Army Joint Operations in South Vietnam," research essay, Victoria University, Wellington, New Zealand, 1991, chap. 3.

90. Blaufarb, *Counterinsurgency Era*, 242.

91. McPherson to LBJ, June 13, 1967, LBJP, AF, McPherson, box 29.

92. Andrew Krepinevich, *The Army and Vietnam* (Baltimore: Johns Hopkins University Press, 1986), 232.

93. Komer, *Bureaucracy at War*, 104–106.

4. THE NOT-SO-SECRET SEARCH FOR PEACE

1. Quoted in George C. Herring, *The Secret Diplomacy of the Vietnam War: The "Negotiating Volumes" of the Pentagon Papers* (Austin: University of Texas Press, 1983), xvi.

2. This chapter makes no effort to discuss all the peace initiatives that were undertaken during the war. It deals merely with those that seem most revealing of U.S. war management. For a fuller discussion, see Herring, *Secret Diplomacy*, passim, and undated memorandum in LBJP, NSFCFVN, box 94.

3. David Kraslow and Stuart H. Loory, *The Secret Search for Peace in Vietnam* (New York: Random House, 1968), 97–98; Walter Johnson, ed., *The Papers of Adlai E. Stevenson*, 8 vols. (Boston: Little, Brown, 1972–1979), 8: 661.

4. Kraslow and Loory, *Secret Search*, 98–99.

5. U Thant "lied like a sailor," Rusk later wrote. "I never had much respect for U Thant's integrity." Dean Rusk as told to Richard Rusk, *As I Saw It* (New York: W. W. Norton, 1990), 463.

6. Dean Rusk oral history interview, LBJ Library. Schoenbaum, *Rusk*, 434; the Seaborn missions are discussed in Herring, *Secret Diplomacy*, 4–44.

7. "Chronology of U Thant Suggestion that DRV and US Representatives Meet in Rangoon to Discuss Restoration of Peace in Vietnam," n.d., LBJP, NSFCFVN, box 94.

8. Stevenson to Johnson, February 17, 1965, Johnson, ed., *Stevenson Papers*, 8: 702–704.

9. Ibid., 663.

10. "Chronology of U Thant Suggestion."

11. *New York Times*, February 17, 18, 21, 25, 1965.

12. *New York Times*, November 17, 21, 1965.

13. William Bundy oral history interview, LBJ Library. For the accounts of Soviet officials, see Dean Rusk oral history interview. For one effort to determine what had happened, see "Chronology of U Thant Suggestion."

14. Kraslow and Loory, *Secret Search*, 126–131.

15. William Bundy oral history interview, LBJ Library.

16. Weiss memo, December 7, 1965, and Richard Dudman notes, n.d., Richard Dudman Papers, Manuscript Division, Library of Congress, Washington, D.C.

17. Kraslow and Loory, *Secret Search*, 134–135; *St. Louis Post-Dispatch*, December 17, 1965.

18. James Wechsler column, *New York Post*, December 21, 1965.

19. *New York Times*, December 19, 20, 1965.

20. Notes of meeting, December 18, 1965, LBJP, MNF, box 1.

21. Herring, *Secret Diplomacy*, 64.

22. Record of meeting in president's office, May 16, 1965, LBJP, MNF, box 1.

23. For the background, see memorandum, "Negotiating and International Actions Concerning Vietnam," July 24, 1965, LBJP, NSFCFVN, box 213; and McGeorge Bundy to LBJ, July 27, 1965, ibid., box 74.

24. See, for example, McGeorge Bundy to LBJ, July 27, 1965, ibid., box 74.

25. Herring, *Secret Diplomacy*, 74–75.

26. During this same period, a small nongroup in the State Department began preparing a formal paper to elaborate the U.S. position should formal negotiations materialize. See Robert Komer to Jack Valenti, March 29, 1966, LBJP, NSFCFVN, box 29.

27. The documentation for these conversations is in Herring, *Secret Diplomacy*, 95–108.

28. Ibid., 106–107.

29. Bundy to LBJ, September 12, 1965, LBJP, PAFDB, box 2.

30. *The Pentagon Papers (The Senator Gravel Edition)*, 4 vols. (Boston: Beacon Press, 1971), 4: 33.

31. William Bundy's oral history interview has extensive background information on the Christmas bombing pause. See also McGeorge Bundy memorandum for LBJ, "Once More on the Pause," November 27, 1965, LBJP.

32. Lyndon Baines Johnson, *The Vantage Point: Perspectives on the Presidency* (New York: Holt, Rinehart, Winston, 1971), 237. Johnson told Harriman that with people like Mansfield and Fulbright thinking that there can be peace "we ought to give it the old college try." Harriman notes on telephone conversation with LBJ and memorandum for the record, December 28, 1965, W. Averell Harriman Papers, box 474.

33. *Time*, January 14, 1966, 20.

34. The fourteen points are in Herring, *Secret Diplomacy*, 144–145.

35. Summary notes of NSC meeting, January 29, 1966, LBJP, NSFNSCM, box 2.

36. William Bundy oral history interview, LBJ Library. For other positive comments on the results of the peace offensive, see Harriman, notes on conversation with

McGeorge Bundy, January 22, 1966, W. Averell Harriman Papers, box 474; Harriman to Chester Bowles, January 25, 1966, ibid., box 560; and Harriman, "summary report" on mission, n.d., ibid., box 559.

37. For PINTA, see Herring, *Secret Diplomacy*, 116–158.

38. See, for example, McGeorge Bundy, notes on meeting, July 28, 1965, McGeorge Bundy Papers, box 1. Also Rusk, *As I Saw It*, 459. "It's like a prizefight," Johnson said in July 1965. "Our right is our military power, but our left must be our peace proposals. Every time you move troops forward, you move diplomats forward." Brian VanDeMark, *Into the Quagmire* (New York: Oxford University Press, 1991), 202.

39. For the Ronning missions, see Herring, *Secret Diplomacy*, 159–207; and Chester Ronning, *A Memoir of China in Revolution: From the Boxer Rebellion to the People's Republic* (New York: Pantheon, 1974).

40. Rudy Abramson, *The Life of W. Averell Harriman: Spanning the Century, 1891–1986* (New York: Morrow, 1992), 637–643; author interview with William Bundy, February 26, 1988; Walter Isaacson and Evan Thomas, *The Wise Men: Six Friends and the World They Made* (New York: Simon and Schuster, 1986), 663–664.

41. See, for example, Rostow memos to LBJ, June 15, 21, 1966, LBJP, NSFMPWR, box 8, and Rostow to LBJ, July 15, 1966, Files of Walt Rostow, meetings with the president, box 1.

42. See, for example, memorandum, September 30, 1966, W. Averell Harriman Papers, box 499; memorandum of meeting, August 11, 1966, ibid., box 520; Harriman to Rusk and LBJ, August 18, 1966, ibid., box 499; Harriman notes on meeting with Fulbright, August 24, 1966, ibid., box 462.

43. LBJ to Ralph Yarborough, ca. January 9, 1967, LBJP, NSFMPWR, box 12.

44. *Time*, November 25, 1966, 16.

45. Author interviews with William Bundy and with Chester Cooper, Austin, Tex., March 8, 1991.

46. MARIGOLD is covered in detail in Herring, *Secret Diplomacy*, 211–370, and in Kraslow and Loory, *Secret Search for Peace*, 3–88.

47. Cooper, *Lost Crusade*, 334.

48. William Bundy oral history interview, LBJ Library. Even the normally skeptical Rusk and Rostow were convinced at this point that MARIGOLD had promise. See Rostow handwritten note to LBJ, December 2, 1966, LBJP, NSFMPWR, boxes 11–12.

49. Author interview with Ben Read, Washington, D.C., November 16, 1988.

50. Cooper, *Lost Crusade*, 334–336; Kraslow and Loory, *Secret Search*, 30–31.

51. Author interview with Benjamin Read.

52. Kraslow and Loory, *Secret Search*, 50–51.

53. Chester Cooper oral history interview, LBJ Library.

54. See Kraslow and Loory, *Secret Search*, 63–64, and Herring, *Secret Diplomacy*, 295. Records of the meetings where these issues were discussed remain closed to researchers, and it is impossible to determine precisely what happened. In a column in the *Washington Post* on December 30, 1966, Joseph Kraft reported that the December bombings were also the result of a political tradeoff. McNamara had rejected JCS proposals in late 1966 for a major expansion of the bombing, but the Chiefs insisted on taking the issue directly to the president, presenting their case in Austin on December 6. When Johnson seemed to lean in their direction, McNamara enlisted the support of

Rusk, and the two secretaries were able to bring the president around. As was his custom, however, he tossed the Chiefs a few bones in the form of targets around Hanoi, and these may have been the strikes that were connected to MARIGOLD. In a memo to LBJ, January 6, 1967, LBJP, NSFMPWR, box 12, Rostow reported McNamara's admission that Kraft had at least part of the story right.

55. Herring, *Secret Diplomacy*, 296–314.

56. Johnson, *Vantage Point*, 251–252.

57. Nicholas deB. Katzenbach oral history interview, LBJ Library.

58. W. Averell Harriman oral history interview, LBJ Library.

59. Janos Radvanyi, *Delusion and Reality: Gambits, Hoaxes, and Diplomatic One-Upmanship in Vietnam* (South Bend, Ind.: Gateway Editions, 1978), 197–203.

60. Wallace Thies, *When Governments Collide: Coercion and Diplomacy in the Vietnam Conflict, 1964–1968* (Berkeley: University of California Press, 1980), 148n, 337–342.

61. *Washington Post*, February 2, 1967; Estabrook's "tip" on MARIGOLD came from Denmark's permanent representative to the UN, suggesting how difficult it was to keep secrets. Robert H. Estabrook, "Journalists and Policymakers: A 1950s and 1960s Retrospective," *SHAFR Newsletter* 23 (December 1992): 15.

62. See Alsop column, February 3, 1967, and *Washington Post* editorial, February 11, 1967.

63. *New York Times*, February 10, 1967. See also Walter Lippmann column, *Washington Post*, February 9, 1967, and statement by Senator Charles Percy (R-IL), *Washington Post*, February 9, 1967.

64. SUNFLOWER is covered in detail in Herring, *Secret Diplomacy*, 371–518, and Kraslow and Loory, *Secret Search*, 197–212.

65. For the Guthrie–Le Chang talks, see Herring, *Secret Diplomacy*, 416–426, 433.

66. Cooper, *Lost Crusade*, 353–354.

67. The letter to Ho is in Herring, *Secret Diplomacy*, 440–441.

68. William Bundy oral history interview, LBJ Library.

69. Notes on NSC meeting, February 8, 1967, LBJP, NSFNSCM, box 2.

70. Herring, *Secret Diplomacy*, 374; Cooper, *Lost Crusade*, 355–356.

71. For the actual document, see Rusk cable to Bruce and Cooper, February 7, 1967, in Herring, *Secret Diplomacy*, 436–438. The statement in the cable was as follows: if North Vietnam would "agree to an assured stoppage of infiltration into South Vietnam, we will stop the bombing of North Vietnam and stop further augmentation of U.S. forces in South Vietnam."

72. Benjamin Read oral history interview, LBJ Library.

73. These events are chronicled in Chester Cooper oral history interview, and in Cooper, *Lost Crusade*, 357–361.

74. Cooper, *Lost Crusade*, 362; Harold Wilson, *The Labour Government, 1964–1970: A Personal Record* (London: Weidenfeld, Nicolson, Joseph, 1971), 354–356.

75. Wilson, *Labour Government*, 354–356.

76. Rusk, *As I Saw It*, 471.

77. Cooper, memorandum of conversation with Rusk, August 23, 1966, W. Averell Harriman Papers, box 451.

78. Walt Rostow oral history interview, LBJ Library, 82; Dean Rusk oral history interview, LBJ Library.

79. Harrison Salisbury, *Behind the Lines: Hanoi, December 23, 1966–January 7, 1967* (New York: Harper and Row, 1967), passim; *New York Times*, December 26, 27, 31, 1966.

80. See Salisbury notes on interview with Pham Van Dong, January 2, 1967, and Rusk memorandum for LBJ, January 14, 1967, LBJP, DSDUF, box 2; also Harrison Salisbury oral history interview, LBJ Library.

81. Harrison Salisbury oral history interview.

82. Rusk memorandum for LBJ, January 14, 1967, and Rostow to president, January 19, 1967, LBJP, DSDUF, box 2.

83. Rostow to LBJ, January 23, 1967, LBJP, NSFCFVN, boxes 74–75.

84. See Harry Ashmore, "The Public Relations of Peace," *Center Magazine* (October–November 1967): 4–11, 63–69.

85. Harriman memorandum of conversation with LBJ, January 30, 1967, W. Averell Harriman Papers, box 475.

86. Herring, *Secret Diplomacy*, 432.

87. Arthur M. Schlesinger, Jr., *Robert Kennedy and His Times* (New York: Ballantine, 1979), 824–828.

88. Author interview with Katzenbach, December 7, 1988. Walt Rostow later described the meeting as "cool" but "restrained," "not warm" but "orderly," and said the press had exaggerated the tension. Walt Rostow oral history interview.

89. *Washington Post*, February 7, 1967, and February 10, 1967.

90. "The Swinging Senator," *Nation*, February 20, 1967, 226–227.

91. Cooper to Harriman, July 17, 1965, "Organizing for Negotiations," W. Averell Harriman Papers, box 451.

92. See especially Harriman memoranda, May 14, 30, November 26, 1966, W. Averell Harriman Papers, box 486, and Harriman memoranda, May 28, October 10, 1966, ibid., box 520.

93. Cooper to Harriman, July 17, 1967, W. Averell Harriman Papers, box 451, and Harriman memorandum of conversation with McNamara, August 22, 1967, ibid., box 486.

94. Tom Johnson notes on meetings, October 3, 16, 1967, LBJP, TJNM, box 1.

95. So called by Benjamin Read because Pennsylvania was his home state. Author interview with Benjamin Read.

96. Notes of Tuesday Lunch meeting, September 12, 1967, LBJP, MNF, box 2.

97. Tom Johnson notes on meeting, August 8, 1967, LBJP, TJNM, box 1; Herring, *Secret Diplomacy*, 532. Read later commented that Kissinger carried out his assignment with "complete fidelity" (author interview with Read). Kissinger's most recent biographer does not disagree, but he does find in Kissinger's handling of PA an example of what would become a pattern in his diplomacy, "his attempt to mediate a dispute by finding a semantic formulation to finesse differences" (Walter Isaacson, *Kissinger: A Biography* [New York: Simon and Schuster, 1992], 122).

98. Harriman memorandum of conversation with McNamara, August 22, 1967, W. Averell Harriman Papers, box 486. See also Tom Johnson notes on meetings, August 8, September 26, October 3, 4, 5, 16, 1967, LBJP, TJNM, box 1.

99. Herring, *Secret Diplomacy*, 730–732.

100. Notes on Tuesday Lunch, September 12, 1967, LBJP, MNF, box 2.

101. Katzenbach to LBJ, September 26, 1967, LBJP, NSF, Rostow Files, box 9; Tom Johnson notes on meetings, September 26, October 4, 5, 16, 1967, LBJP, TJNM, box 1.

102. Tom Johnson notes on meetings, October 4, 5, 16, 17, 18, 23, 1967, LBJP, TJNM, box 1.

103. Tom Johnson notes on meetings, September 26, 1967, ibid.

104. *New York Times*, October 1–3, 1967; *Time*, October 6, 1967; *Newsweek*, October 9, 1967, 24; TRB, *New Republic*, October 14, 1967, 4.

105. *Time*, February 17, 1967, 18.

106. Quoted in Neil Sheehan et al., *The Pentagon Papers as Published by the New York Times* (New York: Bantam Books, 1971), 570.

107. Memorandum of conversation, Harriman and Thanat, January 6, 1966, W. Averell Harriman Papers, box 559.

108. In late 1965, North Vietnam had gained an edge on the United States by being the first belligerent to announce a holiday truce. The following year, therefore, Johnson dispatched his friend James Rowe to the Vatican to persuade the pope to issue his Christmas appeal for peace early enough so that the president could respond by announcing a holiday truce. Rowe easily secured such a promise from the pope, but Hanoi once again beat the United States to the punch, announcing its own holiday truce while the presidential emissary was en route back to Washington. See James H. Rowe oral history interview, James H. Rowe, Jr. Papers, Franklin D. Roosevelt Library, Hyde Park, New York. I am indebted to F. Kevin Simon for bringing this document to my attention.

5. "WITHOUT IRE"

1. Quoted in Bruce Russett and Alfred Stefan, *Military Force and American Society* (New York: Harper and Row, 1973), 170.

2. Michael Howard, *The Causes of Wars* (Cambridge: Harvard University Press, 1983), 104; Richard J. Barnet, *The Rockets' Red Glare: War, Politics and the American Presidency* (New York: Simon and Schuster, 1990), 157–162.

3. Barnet, *Rockets' Red Glare*, 216–233; Michael Leigh, *Mobilizing Consent: Public Opinion and American Foreign Policy* (Westport, Conn.: Greenwood Press, 1976), esp. 99–106; Allan M. Winkler, *The Politics of Propaganda: The Office of War Information, 1942–1945* (New Haven: Yale University Press, 1978); Richard W. Steele, "News of the 'Good War': World War II News Management," *Journalism Quarterly* 62 (Winter 1985): 707–716.

4. Leigh, *Mobilizing Consent*, 99–134.

5. Richard J. Barnet, *Roots of War* (Baltimore: Penguin Books, 1973), 245.

6. Michael Walla, "Selling the Marshall Plan at Home: The Committee for the Marshall Plan to Aid European Recovery," *Diplomatic History* 10 (Summer 1986): 247–265.

7. Barnet, *Rockets' Red Glare*, 308–317; Mason E. Horrell, "MacArthur, Correspondents and Controversy: Censorship in the Korean War," M.A. thesis, University of Kentucky, 1991; Daniel Lykins, "Total War to Cold War: The Advertising Council and the Creation of the Cold War Consensus," M.A. thesis, University of Kentucky, 1990.

8. Robert E. Osgood, *Limited War*, 279–284.

9. Moyers to LBJ, October 3, 1964, LBJP, AF, Moyers, box 10.

10. Bundy to LBJ, February 9, 1965, LBJP, NSFCFVN, box 13.

11. The rise of the antiwar movement is splendidly chronicled in Charles De-Benedetti, Charles Chatfield, assisting author, *An American Ordeal: The Antiwar Movement of the Vietnam Era* (Syracuse: Syracuse University Press, 1990).

12. See various items in LBJP, NSFMPMB, box 18.

13. "Arthur Dean Committee" folder, LBJP, NSFCFVN, box 195.

14. Lady Bird Johnson diary entry, April 21, 1965, in Lady Bird Johnson, *A White House Diary* (New York: Holt, Rinehart, Winston, 1970), 469.

15. Arthur Sylvester to Gen. Wallace M. Greene, May 27, 1965, Wallace M. Greene Papers.

16. See above, chap. 4.

17. Harriman to LBJ, May 15, 1965, W. Averell Harriman Papers, box 474. Curiously, Harriman saw this "opportunity" after being shouted down while trying to give a speech at Cornell University. See Rudy Abramson, *Spanning the Century: The Life of W. Averell Harriman, 1891–1986* (New York: Morrow, 1992), 638.

18. Valenti to Bundy, April 23, 1965, LBJP, NSFCFVN, box 13.

19. Moyers to LBJ, May 27, 1965, LBJP, AF, Moyers, box 11.

20. Melvin Small, *Johnson, Nixon and the Doves* (New Brunswick: Rutgers University Press, 1988), 45–47; Joseph G. Morgan, "The Vietnam Lobby: The American Friends of Vietnam," Ph.D. dissertation, Georgetown University, 1992, 371–379.

21. Clark Clifford with Richard Holbrooke, *Counsel to the President: A Memoir* (New York: Random House, 1991), 386.

22. Quoted in William M. Hammond, *Public Affairs: The Military and the Media, 1962–1968* (Washington, D.C.: Government Printing Office, 1988), 151.

23. Brian VanDeMark, *Into the Quagmire: Lyndon Johnson and the Escalation of the Vietnam War* (New York: Oxford University Press, 1991), 54.

24. Ibid., 67–69, 76, 78, 110, 113.

25. Hammond, *Military and Media, 1962–1968*, 11–65; Clarence R. Wyatt, "Paper Soldiers: The American Press and the Vietnam War," Ph.D. dissertation, University of Kentucky, 1990, 320.

26. Hammond, *Military and Media, 1962–1968*, 67–85; Barry Zorthian oral history interview, LBJ Library; State Department to Embassy Saigon, June 6, 1964, LBJP, NSFCFVN, box 198.

27. Hammond, *Military and Media, 1962–1968*, 87–132; Wyatt, "Paper Soldiers," 321–331.

28. McGeorge Bundy to LBJ, May 12, 1965, LBJP, NSFMPMB, box 3.

29. Greenfield memo for Bundy, n.d., LBJP, NSFMPMB, box 3; Hammond, *Military and Media, 1962–1968*, 133–148.

30. Hammond, *Military and Media, 1962–1968*, 181; Small, *Johnson, Nixon and the Doves*, 25, 43.

31. Alsop to McGeorge Bundy, February 16, 1965, Joseph Alsop Papers, Manuscript Division, Library of Congress, box 71; and Alsop to Patrick O'Donovan, June 24, 1965, ibid., box 72.

32. Kathleen J. Turner, *Lyndon Johnson's Dual War: Vietnam and the Press* (Chicago:

University of Chicago Press, 1985), 61–62, 106, 138–139. See also Robert Kintner oral history interview, LBJ Library.

33. Quoted in VanDeMark, *Into the Quagmire*, 185.

34. Notes on meeting, July 21, 1965, LBJP, MNF, box 1.

35. Quoted in Larry Berman, *Planning a Tragedy: The Americanization of the Vietnam War* (New York: W. W. Norton, 1982), 119.

36. Bundy memorandum for LBJ, June 30, 1965, LBJP, NSF, National Security Council Histories: Deployment of Major U.S. Forces to Vietnam, July 1965, box 43.

37. VanDeMark, *Into the Quagmire*, 163–164.

38. Gordon Chase memorandum for the record, August 4, 1965, "August 3 Dinner Meeting on Information Problem," LBJP, VNRF, box 1.

39. Bill Moyers, "One Thing We Learned," *Foreign Affairs* 46 (July 1968): 662.

40. Memorandum of conversation, Rusk and Harold Holt, April 28, 1965, "National Security File, 1963–1969" (microfilm publication) (Frederick, Md., 1988), "Asia and the Pacific," reel 1, frame 152.

41. Quoted in William Conrad Gibbons, "The 1965 Decision to Send U.S. Ground Forces to Vietnam," paper given at the International Studies Association, April 16, 1987.

42. Record of meeting, July 19, 1965, LBJP, NSFCFVN, box 15; Turner, *Dual War*, 149; Busby to LBJ, July 21, 1965, LBJP, AF, Busby, box 3; VanDeMark, *Into the Quagmire*, 175, 207; Valenti to LBJ, July 22, 1965, LBJP, Office of the President Files, "Valenti," box 12.

43. Quoted in Doris Kearns, *Lyndon Johnson and the American Dream* (New York: Harper and Row, 1976), 251.

44. Quoted in Michael Charlton and Anthony Moncrief, *Many Reasons Why: The American Involvement in Vietnam*, 2d ed. (New York: Hill and Wang, 1989), 115.

45. Notes on National Security Council meeting, July 27, 1965, LBJP, MNF, box 1.

46. Ibid.

47. James Greenfield and William Jorden memorandum for Moyers, August 13, 1965, LBJP, NSFCFVN, boxes 196–197.

48. Gordon Chase memorandum for the record, August 4, 1965, "August 3 Dinner Meeting on Information Problem," LBJP, VNRF, box 1.

49. Ibid.

50. Greenfield and Jorden memo for Moyers, August 13, 1965, LBJP, NSFCFVN, boxes 196–197.

51. Gordon Chase memorandum for the record, "August 4 Luncheon Meeting on the Information Problem," LBJP, VNRF, box 1; agenda for Tuesday Lunch, August 17, 1965, LBJP, NSFMPMB, box 19.

52. Harriman to Rusk, August 10, 1965, W. Averell Harriman Papers, box 474.

53. Press release, November 5, 1965, Richard Dudman Papers, box 13.

54. Moyers memorandum, n.d., LBJP, NSFCFVN, box 194; Benjamin Read to Bromley Smith, August 10, 1965, ibid.; Chester Cooper to Bundy, August 18, 1965, ibid., box 195.

55. See various memoranda, LBJP, NSFCFVN, box 23.

56. *New York Times*, September 9, 1965.

57. Cooper memorandum, September 10, 1965, LBJP, NSFCFVN, box 22; Small, *Johnson, Nixon and the Doves*, 46–48; Morgan, "Vietnam Lobby," 383–391.

58. Memorandum for the record, August 4, 1965, LBJP, NSFCFVN, boxes 196–197; Greenfield and Jorden memorandum for Moyers, August 13, 1965, ibid.; Cooper to Moyers, August 13, 1965, ibid., box 222.

59. Hammond, *Military and Media, 1962–1968*, 185–191; memorandum of discussion in Moyers office, August 10, 1965, LBJP, NSFCFVN, boxes 196–197.

60. Hammond, *Military and Media, 1962–1968*, 190; Harriman memorandum of conversation with Sulzberger, August 20, 1965, W. Averell Harriman Papers, box 474.

61. Greenfield and Jorden to Moyers, August 13, 1965, LBJP, NSFCFVN, boxes 196–197; Gordon Chase memorandum for Douglas Cater, August 23, 1965, ibid.; memorandum for the record, August 4, 1965, ibid.; Public Affairs Policy Committee meeting, September 13, 1965, ibid., box 195.

62. Greene to Lemuel Shepherd, November 22, 1965, Greene Papers, box 24.

63. Notes on Public Affairs Policy Committee meetings, November 1, 8, 15, 1965, LBJP, NSFCFVN, box 195.

64. Dan Ropa to Bundy, November 4, 1965, LBJP, NSFCFVN, box 24.

65. *New York Times*, November 29, 1965.

66. LBJP, NSFCFVN, box 23.

67. Greenfield to Rusk, November 4, 1965, LBJP, NSFCFVN, box 24.

68. David Lilienthal journal, December 29, 1965, in David Lilienthal, *The Journals of David Lilienthal*, 7 vols. (New York: Harper and Row, 1964–1983), 6: 180.

69. Redmon to Moyers, December 27, 1965, LBJP, AF, Moyers, box 11; Cooper memorandum for the record, Public Affairs Policy Committee meeting, November 29, 1965, LBJP, NSFCFVN, box 195; Greenfield to Rusk, November 4, 1965, ibid., box 24.

70. See above, chap. 3.

71. *Time*, June 17, 1966, 9.

72. Jorden to Rostow, June 1966, LBJP, NSFCFVN, box 33; Dixon Donnelly memorandum, August 23, 1966, LBJP, NSFKLF, box 17; Peter Rosenblatt to Komer, November 22, 1966, ibid., box 15.

73. See, for example, Moyers memoranda, April–May 1966, LBJP, AF, Moyers, box 12.

74. Donnelly to Komer, October 18, 1966, LBJP, NSFKLF, box 17.

75. Jorden to Rostow, April 19, 1966, LBJP, NSFCFVN, box 29.

76. Turner, *Dual War*, 157–158; Maxwell Taylor estimated that he gave more than 140 speeches on Vietnam. The audiences included groups such as the American Poultry and Hatchery Association. John M. Taylor, *General Maxwell Taylor: The Sword and the Pen* (New York: Doubleday, 1989), 328.

77. Hammond, *Military and Media, 1962–1968*, 249.

78. Wheeler to Westmoreland, February 1, 1966, BMF, WW/CBSLR, box 20; William Westmoreland, *A Soldier Reports* (New York: Dell, 1980), 214.

79. Telephone message relayed to Rostow from LBJ Ranch, December 5, 1966, LBJP, NSFCFVN, box 38.

80. Gen. Harold Johnson to Westmoreland, May 6, 1966, and Westmoreland to Johnson, September 27, 1966, BMF, WW/CBSLR, box 26.

81. Wheeler to Westmoreland, November 11, 1966, ibid.

82. Summary notes for 581st NSC meeting, February 7, 1968, LBJP, NSFNSCM, box 3. Kintner later lamented that he never convinced Johnson that a "sentence or two of critical comment meant nothing." The major weakness of the Johnson presidency, he concluded, was the excessive attention paid the press. Robert Kintner oral history interview, LBJ Library.

83. Harold Johnson memorandum for the record, July 20, 1966, Harold Johnson Papers, box 127.

84. Turner, *Dual War*, 157.

85. See, for example, Moyers to Arthur Krock, September 15, 1966, LBJP, AF, Moyers, box 12; Rostow to LBJ, May 9, 1966, LBJP, NSFMPWR, box 12.

86. Memoranda of conversations, Harriman and Moyers, July 9, 1966, Harriman and LBJ, July 6, 1966, W. Averell Harriman Papers, box 474.

87. Kintner memorandum for Rusk, July 11, 1966, LBJP, NF, box 5; Andrew Goodpaster memorandum for LBJ, July 15, 1966, copy in LBJP, NSFMPWR, box 9.

88. LBJ memorandum, July 7, 1966, LBJP, NSFCFVN, box 34; LBJ to Lodge, July 12, 1966, LBJP, NSFMPWR, box 9.

89. HHS to BKS, August 18, 1966, LBJP, NSFCFVN, box 35.

90. For the limited impact of AFV activities, see Morgan, "American Friends of Vietnam," 391. For White House concerns, see Moyers to LBJ, May 3, 1966, Redmon to Moyers, June 9, 1966, LBJP, AF, Moyers, box 12; Harris survey press release, June 13, 1966, copy in W. Averell Harriman Papers, box 520.

91. Rostow proposals, May 1, 1966, LBJP, NSFMPWR, box 2.

92. Turner, *Dual War*, 161–164.

93. Ibid.

94. Wyatt, "Paper Soldiers," 353–357.

95. Hanson Baldwin to Clifton Daniel, February 3, 1966, January 31, 1967, Hanson Baldwin Papers, box 11; Neil Sheehan to Baldwin, May 5, 1966, ibid., box 14.

96. Alsop to Moyers, January 11, 1966, LBJP, AF, Moyers, box 7.

97. Redmon to Moyers, September 7, September 27, 1966, LBJP, AF, Moyers, box 12.

98. Lilienthal Journal, December 16, 1966, *Lilienthal Journals*, 6: 327.

99. Redmon to Moyers, September 27, 1966, LBJP, AF, Moyers, box 12.

100. Lilienthal Journal, October 4, 1966, *Lilienthal Journals*, 6: 296.

101. Eisenhower memorandum, September 16, 1966, LBJP, NSFMPWR, box 10.

102. Pearson to LBJ, December 5, 1966, Drew Pearson Papers, LBJ Library, box G265; Komer, "A Strategic Plan for 1967 in Vietnam," November 29, 1966, LBJP, NSFRKF, box 5; Rostow to LBJ, November 30, 1966, LBJP, NSFMPWR, box 1.

103. Diary entry, January 5, 1967, Johnson, *White House Diary*, 469.

104. For the mood of 1967, see George C. Herring, *America's Longest War: The United States and Vietnam, 1950–1975*, rev. ed. (New York: Alfred A. Knopf, 1986), 170–175, 181–182; Small, *Johnson, Nixon and the Doves*, 96–120; Hammond, *Military and the Media*, 291–314.

105. Notes on meeting, November 4, 1967, LBJP, MNF, box 2; notes on meeting with Bob Thompson, August 21, 1967, LBJP, AF, George Christian, box 3.

106. Notes on meeting, August 19, 1967, LBJP, MNF, box 2.

107. Notes on meeting, September 5, 1967, ibid.

108. Small, *Johnson, Nixon and the Doves*, 110–117.

109. Ibid., 102–106; Charles DeBenedetti, "Lyndon Johnson and the Antiwar Opposition," in Robert A. Divine, ed., *The Johnson Years, Volume Two: Vietnam, the Environment, and Science* (Lawrence: University Press of Kansas, 1987), 40–42; notes on meeting with congressional leaders, October 31, 1967, LBJP, PAFDB.

110. Small, *Johnson, Nixon and the Doves*, 104.

111. Alsop to LBJ, November 3, 1967, Joseph Alsop Papers, box 130.

112. See, for example, the elaborate itinerary arranged for Hanson Baldwin by MACV in Hanson Baldwin Papers, box 96.

113. Small, *Johnson, Nixon and the Doves*, 108.

114. Turner, *Dual War*, 203.

115. Tom Johnson notes on meeting, July 13, 1967, LBJP, TJNM, box 1; Westmoreland to Wheeler, November 7, 1967, BMF, WW/CBSLR, box 20.

116. Memorandum to Mission Council, n.d., "Vietnam, the Media, and Public Support for the War [Microfilm Collection]" (Frederick: University Publications of America, 1985), reel 2.

117. Memorandum to members of Mission Council, n.d. (ca. August 1967), LBJP, NSFKLF, box 16; Hammond, *Military and Media*, 321.

118. Rostow to LBJ, August 15, 1967, LBJP, NSF, NF, box 7; Christian to LBJ, August 22, 1967, LBJP, AF, Fred Panzer, box 427; Kaplan to Rostow, 2 memoranda, October 9, 1967, LBJP, NSFCFVN, box 99.

119. See the extensive documentation in LBJP, NSFCFVN, box 102.

120. For the November Wise Men's meeting, see Larry Berman, *Lyndon Johnson's War: The Road to Stalemate in Vietnam* (New York: W. W. Norton, 1989), 85–92; Clifford, *Counsel to the President*, 454–455.

121. For the Douglas committee, see Douglas to Alsop, August 22, 1967, Joseph Alsop Papers, box 76; Abbott Washburn memo, September 29, 1967, LBJP, NSF, NF, Roche, box 7; *Washington Post*, October 19, 1967; Rusk to diplomatic posts, October 26, 1967, "Vietnam, the Media, and Public Support for the War," reel 2; Paul Douglas, *In the Fullness of Time* (New York: Harcourt, Brace, Jovanovich, 1971), 608; Douglas to Dean Acheson, November 29, 1967, Dean Acheson Papers, Yale University Library, New Haven, Conn., box 9.

122. Wheeler to Westmoreland, October 31, 1967, Westmoreland to Sharp, November 3, 1967, BMF, WW/CBSLR, box 20; Tom Johnson notes on meeting, November 21, 1967, LBJP, TJNM, box 1; OASD(PA) memo for the record, December 11, 1967, LBJP, NSFCFVN, box 98.

123. See especially R. W. Apple, Jr., "Vietnam: The Signs of Stalemate," *New York Times*, August 7, 1967, and summaries and citations of other articles in Hammond, *Military and Media*, 297, 316.

124. For Johnson's obsession, see William Bundy oral history interview, LBJ Library, and Tom Johnson notes on meeting, October 3, 1967, LBJP, TJNM, box 1. Rostow to Bunker, September 22, 1967, LBJP, DSDUF, box 4, requests evidence of progress.

125. Rostow memo, October 13, 1967, LBJP, NSFKLF, box 16; Wheeler to Sharp and Westmoreland, November 9, 1967, BMF, WW/CBSLR, box 20.

126. Saigon cable 7867, October 7, 1967, LBJP, NSFCFVN, box 99.

127. Turner, *Dual War*, 201.

128. Itinerary, Hanson Baldwin Papers, box 96; Baldwin articles, *New York Times*, November 23, December 3, 6, 17, 1967.

129. See extensive documentation in LBJP, NSFCFVN, box 100.

130. Kaplan to Rostow, October 9, 1967, LBJP, NSFCFVN, box 99.

131. See, for example, MACV, J-2, Order of Battle Branch, Report, ca. September 22, 1967, "Vietnam, the Media, and Public Support for the War," reel 2.

132. Barry Zorthian memorandum, November 1, 1967, LBJP, NSFCFVN, box 152; Zorthian to Otis Hays, USIA, December 12, 1967, ibid., box 100.

133. Berman, *Lyndon Johnson's War*, 74–75; *Time*, October 13, 1967, 25.

134. Tom Johnson notes on LBJ conversation with Chalmers Roberts, October 16, 1967, Tom Johnson notes on meeting, October 3, 1967, LBJP, TJNM, box 1.

135. Tom Johnson notes on meeting, October 17, 1967, ibid.

136. *Time*, November 17, 1967, 23.

137. *Public Papers of the Presidents of the United States, Lyndon Baines Johnson, 1967*, vol. 2 (Washington, D.C.: Government Printing Office, 1968), 1045–1055.

138. Turner, *Dual War*, 204; *Time*, November 24, 1967, 7.

139. Rostow memorandum, November 16, 1967, "Vietnam, the Media, and Public Support for the War," reel 1.

140. Berman, *Lyndon Johnson's War*, 104–105.

141. Westmoreland record of White House meeting, November 22, 1967, WWP, USAMHI, box 29; Westmoreland to Abrams, November 23, 1967, ibid., box 34.

142. Marshall Wright memorandum, January 3, 1968, LBJP, NSFCFVN, box 100; Hammond, *Military and Media*, 334–340; Berman, *Lyndon Johnson's War*, 107–108.

143. Berman, *Lyndon Johnson's War*, 107–108; Fred Panzer to Jim Jones, December 28, 1967, LBJP, Confidential File, box 73; Wheeler to Westmoreland, January 27, 1967, BMF, WW/CBSLR, box 23.

144. See above, note 50.

6. "FIGHTING WHILE NEGOTIATING"

1. Lyndon Baines Johnson, *The Vantage Point: Perspectives on the Presidency* (New York: Holt, Rinehart, Winston, 1971), 399.

2. See Rostow to LBJ, January 30, 1968, Vance response attached to Rostow to LBJ, February 1, 1968, Harold Johnson to LBJ, February 1, 1968, Wheeler to LBJ, February 3, 1968, all in LBJP, NSFCFVN, box 102.

3. Notes on meeting with JCS, January 29, 1968, LBJP, TJNM, box 2.

4. Notes on meetings with congressional leaders, January 30, 31, 1968, notes on discussions with correspondents, February 2, 9, March 2, 1968, LBJP, TJNM, box 2. This was not the first time Johnson had spoken of asking the military to "sign in blood." In 1965, he had asked Gen. Bruce Palmer and Cyrus Vance to "sign in blood" that the United States had given no aid to a particular political faction in the Dominican Republic. Bruce Palmer, Jr., *Intervention in the Caribbean: The Dominican Crisis of 1965* (Lexington: University Press of Kentucky, 1989), 61–62.

5. Don Oberdorfer, *Tet!* (Garden City: Doubleday, 1971) is the classic account, but see also James J. Wirtz, *The Tet Offensive: Intelligence Failure in War* (Ithaca: Cornell University Press, 1991), a more recent study that focuses on the intelligence failure.

6. George C. Herring, *America's Longest War: The United States and Vietnam, 1950–1975* (New York: Alfred A. Knopf, 1986), 191–192.

7. Townsend Hoopes, *The Limits of Intervention* (New York: McKay, 1970), 145.

8. Earle Wheeler oral history interview; Harry McPherson oral history interview, LBJ Library.

9. Secretary of State to Embassy Saigon, February 1, 1968, LBJP, NSF, National Security Council Histories, March 31st [1968] Speech, vol. 8, box 49; Tom Johnson notes on meeting, February 6, 1968, LBJP, TJNM, box 2.

10. Tom Johnson notes on meetings, February 6, 9, 1968, LBJP, TJNM, box 2.

11. Gordon Hill memorandum for the record, February 26, 1968, LBJP, NSFCFVN, box 98; William M. Hammond, *Public Affairs: The Military and the Media, 1962–1968* (Washington, D.C.: Government Printing Office, 1988), 366–367.

12. Tom Johnson notes on meetings, February 6, 13, 1968, LBJP, TJNM, box 2.

13. Herbert Y. Schandler, *Lyndon Johnson and Vietnam: The Unmaking of a President* (Princeton, N.J.: Princeton University Press, 1977), 92–98.

14. Tom Johnson notes on meeting, February 9, 1968, LBJP, TJNM, box 2.

15. Tom Johnson notes on meetings, February 7, 9, 11, 12, 1968, LBJP, TJNM, box 2; Schandler, *Johnson and Vietnam*, 92–104.

16. Westmoreland memorandum, n.d., "The Origins of the Post-1968 Plans for Additional Forces in RVN," WWP, LBJ Library, box 19.

17. Ibid.; Westmoreland to Townsend Hoopes, November 17, 1970, ibid.

18. "I am fed up to the teeth," he complained on February 6, 1968, specifically protesting the way the United States applied rigid restrictions on its own actions for humanitarian reasons while the North Vietnamese placed munitions in civilian residential areas to protect them against American bombing. Tom Johnson notes on meeting, February 6, 1968, LBJP, TJNM, box 2.

19. Tom Johnson notes on meeting, February 28, 1968, ibid.

20. Notes on meeting, February 27, 1968, LBJP, MNF, box 2; Clark Clifford with Richard Holbrooke, *Counsel to the President: A Memoir* (New York: Random House, 1991), 484–485; Joseph Califano, *The Triumph and Tragedy of Lyndon Johnson: The White House Years* (New York: Simon and Schuster, 1991), 263–264.

21. Rostow to LBJ, February 27, 1968, LBJP, NSFMPWR, box 6; Clifford, *Counsel*, 484–485.

22. Paul Warnke oral history interview, LBJ Library; Herring, *America's Longest War*, 195–196.

23. Ibid.

24. Clifford, *Counsel*, 493–494.

25. Memorandum, "Public Affairs," March 3, 1968, Clark Clifford Papers, LBJ Library, box 1.

26. Clifford, *Counsel*, 494–496.

27. Ibid.; Tom Johnson notes on meeting, March 4, 1968, LBJP, TJNM, box 2.

28. Tom Johnson notes on meetings, March 4, 6, 11, 12, 19, 1968, LBJP, TJNM, box 2.

29. Schandler, *Johnson and Vietnam*, 232–234.

30. Westmoreland to Wheeler, March 2, 1968, BMF, WW/CBSLR, box 21; *Time*, March 22, 1968, 25.

31. Rostow to LBJ, March 11, 1968, LBJP, PAFDB, box 94; Richard Moose to

Rostow, March 4, 1968, Marshall Wright and Lou Schwartz memoranda, March 18, 19, 1968, LBJP, NSFCFVN, box 100.

32. Westmoreland to Wheeler, March 2, 1968, BMF, WW/CBSLR, box 21.

33. Tom Johnson notes on meetings, March 6, 1968, LBJP, TJNM, box 2.

34. Wheeler to Westmoreland, March 8, 1968, Westmoreland to Wheeler, March 8, 1968, BMF, WW/CBSLR, box 21.

35. Notes on meetings, March 19, 20, 22, 1968, LBJP, MNF, box 2; McPherson to LBJ, March 23, 1968, LBJP, NSF, National Security Council Histories, March 31st [1968] Speech, vol. 4, box 48; Harriman to Rusk, March 29, 1968, W. Averell Harriman Papers, box 500.

36. Earle Wheeler oral history interview.

37. Notes on meetings, March 19, 20, 1968, LBJP, MNF, box 2; Clifford, *Counsel*, 507.

38. Tom Johnson notes on meeting, March 26, 1968, LBJP, TJNM, box 2; Herring, *America's Longest War*, 206–208; the March 31 speech is in *Public Papers of Lyndon B. Johnson, 1968–1969*, 2 vols. (Washington, D.C.: Government Printing Office, 1970), 1: 469–476.

39. McPherson to LBJ, April 4, 1968, LBJP, AF, McPherson, box 53.

40. Clark Clifford oral history interview, LBJ Library.

41. Rostow to LBJ, September 16, 1968, LBJP, NSFMPWR, box 6.

42. Tom Johnson notes on meetings, April 6, 8, 1968, LBJP, TJNM, box 3; Bunker memorandum, "Viet-Nam Negotiations: Dangers and Opportunities," April 8, 1968, W. Averell Harriman Papers, box 521; Rostow to LBJ, April 3, 1968, LBJP, NSF, Rostow Files, box 6.

43. Harriman memorandum, "General Review of the Last Six Months," December 10, 1968, W. Averell Harriman Papers, box 521; Clifford, *Counsel*, 534–536.

44. Clifford, *Counsel*, 461.

45. Dean Rusk as told to Richard Rusk, *As I Saw It* (New York: W. W. Norton, 1990), 417.

46. Harriman memorandum, "General Review of the Last Six Months," December 14, 1968, W. Averell Harriman Papers, box 521.

47. Clifford, *Counsel*, 476.

48. LBJ note, November 21, 1968, LBJP, NSF, Rostow Files, box 6.

49. *Time*, May 3, 1968, 14; June 28, 1968, 12–13.

50. William Bundy oral history interview, LBJ Library.

51. Clifford, *Counsel*, 527.

52. Harriman memorandum of telephone conversation with LBJ, April 11, 1968, W. Averell Harriman Papers, box 475; notes on meeting, May 6, 1968, LBJP, MNF, box 3; Tom Johnson notes on meetings, May 7, 8, 1968, LBJP, TJNM, box 3; Harold Johnson notes on meetings, May 6, 8, 1968, Harold Johnson Papers, box 127.

53. Ibid.

54. Ibid.

55. Clifford, *Counsel*, 538.

56. Andrew Goodpaster oral history interview, LBJ Library.

57. Gen. Dwight Beach to Adm. U. S. Grant Sharp, April 12, 1968, WWP, USAMHI, box 32; Sharp to Wheeler, May 3, 1968, BMF, WW/CBSLR, box 22.

58. Raphael Littauer and Norman Uphoff, eds., *The Air War in Indochina* (Boston: Beacon Press, 1972), 277.

59. Frank Clay to Gen. and Mrs. Lucius Clay, May 15, 1968, Frank Clay Papers, U.S. Army Military History Institute, Carlisle Barracks, Pa.

60. Wheeler to Westmoreland, March 31, 1968, BMF, WW/CBSLR, box 21. Westmoreland explains the meaning of search and destroy and the reasons for dropping the name in a memorandum to Townsend Hoopes, June 28, 1969, WWP, LBJ Library, box 19.

61. Westmoreland to Wheeler, March 28, 1968, BMF, WW/CBSLR, box 21; Westmoreland to Wheeler, April 12, 1968, ibid., box 22; Beach to Sharp, April 12, 1968, WWP, USAMHI, box 32.

62. Rostow to LBJ, April 30, 1968, LBJP, DSDUF, box 2; Tom Johnson notes on meetings, May 14, 28, 1968, LBJP, TJNM, box 3; Westmoreland to Wheeler, May 14, 1968, Westmoreland to Sharp, May 26, 1968, Wheeler to Westmoreland, May 28, 1968, Beach to Sharp, May 29, 1968, BMF, WW/CBSLR, box 22; notes on meetings, May 25, 28, 1968, LBJP, MNF, box 3.

63. Tom Johnson notes on meetings, April 23, 30, May 14, 15, 21, 1968, LBJP, TJNM, box 3; notes on National Security Council meeting, May 22, 1968, LBJP, NSFNSCM, box 3; notes on meeting, May 25, 1968, LBJP, MNF, box 3.

64. Tom Johnson notes on meetings, April 23, May 14, 15, 21, LBJP, TJNM, box 3; notes on National Security Council meeting, May 22, 1968, LBJP, NSFNSCM, box 3; Harriman memorandum of conversation with Valerian Zorin, May 27, 1968, W. Averell Harriman Papers, box 553.

65. Lou Schwartz memoranda for Rostow, April 8, 10, 1968, Marshall Wright memorandum, April 29, 1968, LBJP, NSFCFVN, box 100; William Jorden memorandum for Harriman and Vance, April 29, 1968, LBJP, AF, Christian, box 12.

66. Schwartz memorandum for Rostow, May 20, June 3, 1968, Rostow to LBJ, June 3, 1968, LBJP, NSFCFVN, box 101; Westmoreland to Wheeler, April 23, 1968, BMF, WW/CBSLR, box 22; Ronald H. Spector, *After Tet: The Bloodiest Year* (New York: Free Press, 1992), 214–215.

67. Dixon Donnelly memorandum to Schwartz, June 17, 1968, LBJP, NSFCFVN, box 101.

68. Lewis Sorley, *Thunderbolt: Gen. Creighton Abrams and the Army of His Times* (New York: Simon and Schuster, 1992), 230, 233, 235; Jeffrey J. Clarke, *Advice and Support: The Final Years* (Washington, D.C.: Government Printing Office, 1988), 362–363; Spector, *After Tet*, 182–183.

69. Rostow to LBJ, May 24, 1968, LBJP, DSDUF, box 2; Robert Shaplen, *The Road from War: Vietnam, 1965–1970* (New York: Harper and Row, 1970), 216–217.

70. Clifford, *Counsel*, 546–547.

71. Harriman memorandum of phone conversation with Clifford, June 21, 1968, W. Averell Harriman Papers, box 447; Rostow to LBJ, June 24, 1968, LBJP, DSDUF, box 5; Adm. John McCain to Wheeler, July 18, 19, 1968, BMF, WW/CBSLR, box 23.

72. Harriman memorandum, "General Review of the Last Six Months," December 10, 1968, W. Averell Harriman Papers, box 521; Clifford, *Counsel*, 546–547; Tom Johnson notes on meeting, June 9, 1968, LBJP, TJNM, box 3.

73. Clifford, *Counsel*, 549.

74. William Bundy oral history interview, LBJ Library.

75. Harriman memorandum, "General Review of the Last Six Months," December 10, 1968, W. Averell Harriman Papers, box 521.

76. Chester Cooper, *The Lost Crusade: America in Vietnam* (New York: Dodd, Mead, 1970), 415.

77. Clifford, *Counsel*, 570–574.

78. Ibid., 571–572.

79. Tom Johnson notes on meeting, October 14, 1968, LBJP, TJNM, box 3.

80. Ibid.; Clifford, *Counsel*, 571–572.

81. Abrams to Wheeler, September 1, 1968, WWP, USAMHI, box 34; Tom Johnson notes on meetings, September 16, October 14, 1968, LBJP, TJNM, box 4; Bunker Weekly Report, October 19, 1968, LBJP, NSFCFVN, boxes 104–105.

82. Memorandum for the record, October 31, 1968, November 11, 1968, LBJP, PAFDB, box 115; notes on NSC meeting, October 31, 1968, LBJP, NSFNSCM, box 3.

83. Tom Johnson notes on meetings, October 14, 15, 22, 23, 25, 27, 28, 29, 30, 1968, LBJP, TJNM, box 4; notes on meetings, October 14, 31, 1968, LBJP, MNF, box 3; Walt Rostow oral history interview.

84. Clifford, *Counsel*, 568.

85. Tom Johnson notes on meeting, October 14, 1968, LBJP, TJNM, box 4; Sorley, *Abrams*, 253.

86. Tom Johnson notes on meetings, November 5, 11, December 3, 1968, LBJP, TJNM, box 4.

87. Clifford, *Counsel*, 550–553.

88. McPherson to Clifford, August 13, 1968, LBJP, AF, McPherson, box 53.

89. Herring, *America's Longest War*, 216–219.

90. Harriman notes, December 10, 1968, W. Averell Harriman Papers, box 556; Harriman notes on conversation with Rusk, December 14, 1968, ibid., box 500.

91. Ibid.

92. Johnson, *Vantage Point*, 566–567.

93. Chalmers Roberts, *First Rough Draft: A Journalist's Journal of Our Times* (New York: Praeger, 1973), 267.

94. Truong Nhu Tang, David Chanoff, and Doan Van Toai, *A Vietcong Memoir* (New York: Harcourt Brace Jovanovich, 1985), 86–87.

7. CONCLUSION

1. See, for example, Guenter Lewy, *America in Vietnam* (New York: Oxford University Press, 1978); Harry G. Summers, *On Strategy: The Vietnam War in Context* (Carlisle Barracks: Strategic Studies Institute, Army War College, 1981); and Andrew Krepinevich, *The U.S. Army in Vietnam* (Baltimore: Johns Hopkins University Press, 1986).

2. Wayne S. Cole, "American Entry into World War II: A Historiographical Appraisal," *Mississippi Valley Historical Review* 43 (March 1957): 615.

3. William Colby, "A Participant's Commentary on Vietnam," *Prologue* (Spring 1991): 62.

4. David Lilienthal oral history interview, LBJ Library.

5. For the "Caligula syndrome," see Larry Berman, *Planning a Tragedy: The*

Americanization of the Vietnam War (New York: W. W. Norton, 1983), 3–7. For an alternative view, see David Marshall Barrett, "The Mythology Surrounding Lyndon Johnson, His Advisers, and the 1965 Decision to Escalate the Vietnam War," *Political Science Quarterly* 103 (Winter 1988–89): 637–673; and "Doing 'Tuesday Lunch' at Lyndon Johnson's White House: New Archival Evidence on Vietnam Decisionmaking," *PS: Political Science and Politics* (December 1991): 676–679.

6. Joseph Califano, *The Triumph and Tragedy of Lyndon Johnson: The White House Years* (New York: Simon and Schuster, 1992), 11.

7. Memorandum of LBJ conversation with Ted Sell, November 12, 1968, LBJP, AF, Christian, box 1.

8. Ibid.; Tom Johnson notes on meeting with press, March 2, 1968, LBJP, TJNM, box 2.

9. Notes on meeting with Wheeler and Abrams, February 28, 1968, LBJP, TJNM, box 2; notes on meeting in cabinet room, April 8, 1968, LBJP, MNF, box 2.

10. Author interview with William Bundy.

11. The Goldwater-McNichols Act of 1986 and a presidential order signed January 14, 1987, by Ronald Reagan sought to correct the most obvious flaws in the command system by giving the Joint Chiefs of Staff a place in the chain of command between the secretary of defense and the field commander and by increasing the responsibilities and power of the chairman of the JCS. Gen. Colin Powell thus played a much more central role in the planning of strategy during the Persian Gulf War. His new status in the chain of command did not, however, ensure that he was consulted on major decisions or that there was an open and candid discussion of alternatives. See Bob Woodward, *The Commanders* (New York: Pocket Books, 1992), 283, 284, 297, 305.

12. Author interview with Robert Ginsburgh.

13. Quoted in Larry Berman, *Lyndon Johnson's War* (New York: W. W. Norton, 1989), i.

14. Wheeler speech given in Detroit, December 18, 1967, copy in LBJP, NSFCFVN, box 100.

15. Quoted in Robert Komer, *Bureaucracy at War* (Boulder: Westview Press, 1986), 2.

16. Stephen Peter Rosen, "Vietnam and the American Theory of Limited War," *International Security* 7 (Fall 1982): 83.

17. Bundy is quoted in Michael Charlton and Anthony Moncrief, *Many Reasons Why: The American Involvement in Vietnam*, 2d ed. (New York: Hill and Wang, 1988), 120; the military officers are quoted in Hanson Baldwin, "magaziner," December 16, 1965, Hanson Baldwin Papers, box 27; McPherson is quoted in Walter LaFeber, *America, Russia and the Cold War*, 5th ed. (New York: Alfred A. Knopf, 1985), 254; Westmoreland's statement is in an undated memorandum, WWP, LBJ Library, box 19.

18. Rosen, "Limited War," 83.

19. D. Michael Shafer, "The Vietnam Combat Experience: The Human Legacy," in D. Michael Shafer, *The Legacy* (Boston: Beacon Press, 1990), 84.

20. See, for example, Mark I. Gelfand's analysis of the administration's management of another "war" in "The War on Poverty," Robert A. Divine, ed., *Exploring the Johnson Years* (Austin, University of Texas Press, 1981), 126–146.

INDEX

Abrams, Creighton W., 18, 44, 170, 173, 175
Accelerated Pacification Campaign, 151, 170, 173, 175
Acheson, Dean G., 16, 56, 156
Agroville Program, 65
Air war. *See* Bombing of North Vietnam
Alsop, Joseph, 107, 128, 139, 142, 145, 161
American Friends of Vietnam, 126, 133, 134, 138
Anderson, Adm. George, 29, 40
Antiwar protest, 125, 126, 128, 130, 134, 141–142
Army of the Republic of Vietnam (ARVN), 74, 145, 147–148, 153, 155, 157
Arnett, Peter, 127, 142
Ashmore, Harry, 112–113
Aubrac, Raymond, 116–117

Baggs, William, 112–113
Baker, Russell, 94
Baldwin, Hanson, 29, 35, 54, 61, 145
Ball, George W., 13, 32, 48, 59, 98, 129, 136, 172
Bay of Pigs, 28

Bell, David, 68, 70
Black, Eugene, 125
Blaufarb, Douglas, 66, 87
Bombing halt (1968), 162, 167, 172
Bombing of Laos, 168
Bombing of North Vietnam: civil-military conflict over, 46; decision for, 32; escalation of, 102; in MARI-GOLD, 105–106; and PENNSYL-VANIA contact, 117; post-Tet debate on, 155, 168–169, 171; in Stennis hearings, 55–56; strategy for, 43–44
Bombing of South Vietnam, 168
Bombing pauses, 41, 96–102
Bradley, Gen. Omar, 137
Brown, George, 110
Buddhist crisis (1966), 73
Bundy, McGeorge: and bombing halt after Tet, 162; and bombing halt, December 1965, 99–100; on doves and hawks, 119–120; national security adviser, 7, 8; urges Johnson to take control of war, 37, 60; and Kennedy advisory system, 6; on limited war, 42; naming military operations, 137; and pacification, 67, 70; and peace moves, 99; and public support for war, 1965,

129, 130; resignation from government, 10; and Vietnam Public Affairs Committee, 12, 132

Bundy, William: and bombing pause, 101; "break point" in war, 42; coordination of war effort, 21; despair after Tet, 157; on escalation (1967), 52; on Harriman "peace shop," 104; on La Pira peace move, 94; on LBJ management style, 22–23; on limited war, 184; and SUNFLOWER peace contact, 109; and troop request (1965), 32; and Tuesday Lunch, 15; on U Thant peace initiative, 94; on Vietnam War, 20–21

Bunker, Ellsworth, 59, 80, 82, 83, 86, 147, 165

Busby, Horace, 130, 139

Burke, Adm. Arleigh, 29

Byroade, Henry, 101

Califano, Joseph, 16, 157, 181

Cambodia, 51, 157

Cam Ne incident, 133

Canada, 102

Carnegie Endowment, 59

Carver, George, 59

Cedar Falls operation, 79

Censorship, 124, 127–128, 143

Chicago Sun-Times, 92

Chieu Hoi, 72–73, 81, 84

China, Peoples Republic of, 131

Christian, George, 14, 18, 143

Civil-military conflict, 33, 35, 38, 41, 45–47, 51–57, 61

Clifford, Clark M.: bombing halt after Tet, 162; and bombing of North Vietnam, 32, 155, 169; and JCS post-Tet proposals, 158; and Kosygin peace initiative, 171; and LBJ Camranh Bay trip, 19; LBJ cuts out of cable traffic, 172; in LBJ "kitchen cabinet," 15–16; on LBJ leadership style, 48; on LBJ personality, 16; and McNamara October 1967 proposals, 59; on PENNSYLVANIA peace initiative, 118; and public relations after Tet, 154; and

South Vietnamese, 175; strategy after Tet, 165–166; task force headed by, 158–161

Colby, William, 79, 82, 86, 180

Collins, Gen. J. Lawton, 137

Columbia Broadcasting System (CBS), 133

Commercial import program, 69

Committee for Peace with Freedom in Vietnam (Douglas Committee), 144

Committee for the Marshall Plan, 123, 144

Cooper, Chester, 15, 22, 70, 104, 106, 110, 114

Cooper, John Sherman, 118

CORDS. See United States Civil Operations, Revolutionary Development Support

Credibility gap, 127, 128, 143, 145, 162

Cuban missile crisis, 5, 28, 38, 39, 180

Dean, Arthur, 125, 133

Dean, John Gunter, 113

Dean, Sir Patrick, 151

De Gaulle, Charles, 103

Democratic National Committee, 126

DePuy, Gen. William, 79, 144

D'Orlandi, Giovanni, 104

Douglas, Paul, 144

Douglas Committee. See Committee for Peace with Freedom in Vietnam

Dudman, Richard, 95

Dulles, Allen, 125

Eisenhower, Dwight D., 13, 27, 54, 140, 144, 173

Estabrook, Robert, 107, 114

Evans, Rowland, 114

Fanfani, Amintore, 94

"Five-o-clock follies," 127

Forrestal, James V., 26

Fortas, Abe, 15, 59, 118

Four Points, 97, 99, 102, 113

Fowler, Henry, 19, 23

Freedom House, 134

Frye, Bill, 92

Fulbright, J. William, 68, 95, 97, 98, 103, 113, 118

Gandhi, Indira, 103
Geneva Conference (1954), 98, 99
Ginsburgh, Col. Robert, 11
Goldberg, Arthur, 95, 162
Goldwater-McNichols Act, 219n.11
Goodpaster, Gen. Andrew, 34, 166, 167
Government of Vietnam (GVN), 65–66, 85, 131, 175–176
Great Society, 130
Greene, Gen. Wallace, 45, 50, 129, 134
Greenfield, James A., 128, 132, 133, 135
Gronouski, John, 106
Guam Conference (March 1967), 54, 80
Gullion, Edmund, 98–99
Guthrie, John, 108

Halberstam, David, 34, 48, 127
Harkins, Gen. Paul D., 30
Harriman, W. Averell: as ambassador for peace, 102–103; and antiwar protests, 138; and bombing halt after Tet, 162; and Kosygin peace initiative, 171; and La Pira contact, 95; MARIGOLD peace initiative, 106, 107; named negotiator, 151; and *New York Times*, 134; and peace offensive (1966), 100; "peace shop" of, 103–104; and Rusk, 165; strategy after Tet, 165–166; and U.S. response to peace signals
Helms, Richard, 14, 154
Ho Chi Minh, 91, 93, 94–95, 101, 108, 112
Ho Chi Minh Trail, 157
Honolulu Conference (February 1966), 68, 135
Hoopes, Townsend, 158
Hop Tac Program, 66
Hue, battle for, 153
Humphrey, Hubert H., 136, 166, 172–173

Ia Drang, battle of, 42, 44
Interdepartmental Regional Groups (IRG), 13

Johnson, Gen. Harold K., 31, 34, 36, 44, 47, 50, 73
Johnson, Lady Bird, 125, 140, 186
Johnson, Louis, 26
Johnson, Lyndon Baines: advisory system of, 6–16; and bombing halt of 1968, 172–174; and bombing of North Vietnam, 46, 169; and bombing pause, 41–42, 100–101; as commander-in-chief, 16–20; and CORDS, 80; decisions on war (1967), 53–54, 61; and divisions among advisers, 62, 165–166; and doves, 141–142; and escalation, 31, 42; as "flypaper president," 137; and Gen. Greene, 50; and Harriman, 103; and Ho Chi Minh, letter to, 108–109; intensifies military pressure in South Vietnam, 174; Johns Hopkins speech, 96, 125; and Joint Chiefs of Staff, 31–36, 40, 57–58, 153; and Khe Sanh, 152–153; kitchen cabinet of, 15; and Krulak, 50; names Komer to direct pacification in Washington, 71; leadership assessed, 179, 180–183; leadership style, 47–48, 180–182; loyalty, standards for, 48; and McGeorge Bundy, 10; and McNamara, 7–8, 59, 61, 101; and McNamara October 1967 proposals, 58–59; names McNamara to World Bank, 61; management style of, 22–23; March 31, 1968 speech, 151–152, 163–164; and MARIGOLD, 106–107; middle-of-the-road approach of, 167, 171; and military, 17, 38, 39, 49, 57, 163, 181–182; and pacification, 63, 67, 71, 74, 77; peace offensive, 100–102; and PENNSYLVANIA contact, 117; personality, 16–17, 149; and population security strategy, 161; and post-Tet debate on ground forces, 156; post-Tet mood of, 162–163; public relations activities of, 136–138; public relations offensive of 1967, 141–150; and public support for war, 125, 127–128, 129, 135–136; and Robert

Kennedy peace contact, 114; and Rostow, 11; San Antonio speech, 117; under siege in White House, 141; and South Vietnamese, 67, 176; speaking tour (1966), 139; speeches on Vietnam, 125, 154; stalemate, concerns about, 145; and Stennis hearings, 56; on U Thant and La Pira initiatives, 96; Vietnam War, absorption in, 19; Vietnam War, frustration with, 115; Vietnam War, resentment toward, 17; war in "cold blood," 131, 185; war decisions of 1965, 32–36; as war leader, xi, 37; war message of, 1–2, 5–6; and Westmoreland, 25, 43, 49, 182; and Westmoreland 1965 troop request, 32; and Westmoreland 1968 troop request, 160–161; and withdrawal from presidential race, 116–117, 163

Joint Chiefs of Staff. See United States Joint Chiefs of Staff

Joint U.S. Public Affairs Office (JUSPAO), 69, 79

Jorden, William, 167

Junior Chamber of Commerce, 133

Kahn, Herman, 5

Kaplan, Harold, 136, 143, 146

Katzenbach, Nicholas DeB.: and Ashmore-Baggs contact, 113; and bombing of North Vietnam, 109; and ground strategy, 59; in Johnson advisory system, 12; and MARIGOLD, 106; and non-group, 15; and PENNSYLVANIA contact, 115, 117; post-Tet despair of, 157; post-Tet strategy of, 165; and Robert Kennedy contact, 114; trip to Vietnam, 76

Kennedy, Edward M., 152, 161

Kennedy, John F., 6, 27–28, 30, 65

Kennedy, Robert F., 11, 95, 103, 111, 113

Khe Sanh, battle of, 37, 152, 154

King, Martin Luther, Jr., 141

Kintner, Robert, 136, 147

Kissinger, Henry A., 5, 116, 207 n.97

Komer, Robert: on bureaucracy, 180; and coordination of war effort, 21; and CORDS, 81–82; urges information campaign, 140; urges NSAM to integrate strategy, 51; and pacification, 71–72, 74–75, 85; and President's Vietnam Group, 12; Project Takeoff, 83; proposes War Cabinet, 22

Korean War, 4, 5, 27, 38, 41, 90, 124, 129, 140, 167, 180, 183, 186

Kosygin, Alexei, 108–111, 171

Kraft, Joseph, 136, 142

Krulak, Victor, 45, 50

Lansdale, Edward, 67, 80

Laos, 51, 157, 174

LaPira, Giorgia, 94–95

La Pira peace initiative, 94–96, 99

Lathram, L. Wade, 78

Le Chang, 108

Le Duc Tho, 99

LeMay, Gen. Curtis, 28, 29, 30, 40

Leonhart, William, 83, 86

Lewandowski, Januscz, 104–105, 106

Lilienthal, David, 52–53, 135, 140, 180

Limited war: and American military experience, 3; commander-in-chief in, 16; history of, 3; public support for, 124, 148–149; strategies for, 4–5, 36

Limited war theory, 5, 9, 39, 126, 130–131, 149, 180

Lippmann, Walter, 136

Lodge, Henry Cabot, Jr., 50, 67, 69, 73, 74, 77, 104–106, 130, 144,

Look magazine, 94

Lovett, Robert M., 125

MacArthur, Gen. Douglas, 27, 38, 41, 49, 124

McCloy, John, 125

McConnell, Gen. John P., 29, 33, 35, 42, 58, 61–62

McDonald, Adm. David, 29, 35, 45, 61

McGovern, George, 19, 136

McNamara, Robert S: and bombing after

Tet, 155; and bombing of North Vietnam, 44, 47; and bombing pause of December 1965, 41–42, 99; censorship, 139; and crisis management, 39; and Cuban missile crisis, 28; and Department of Defense, 28; disenchantment with war, 52; dissent of, 48, 197 n.104; DPM of May 1967, 52–53; electronic barrier, 47, 76; influence wanes, 11; and JCS, 29, 31, 62; JCS August 1965 "Concept for Vietnam," 41; and Krulak effort to change strategy, 50–51; and LBJ, 7, 9; and limited war, 6, 121; loyalty, concept of, 48; management of war, 37–38; and MARIGOLD, 106; MAYFLOWER bombing pause, 97; and military, 29; and NSAM 341, 13; and pacification, 67, 75, 76–77; and PENNSYLVANIA peace contact, 114–118; and press, 143; proposals of October 31, 1967, 58; and public support of war, 130; resignation of, 61; after Tet, 157–158; speeches on Vietnam, 125; and Stennis hearings, 55–57; and Vietnam War, 10; and Westmoreland ground strategy, 43; and Westmoreland 1965 troop request, 32
McNaughton, John, 41, 52, 53
McPherson, Harry: and bombing halt after Tet, 162; on expansion of war, 21; and JCS post-Tet request, 158; and La Pira contact, 95; on limited war, 184; on pacification, 83, 87; and strategy, 60; on Tet impact in U.S., 154; urges coordination of fight-talk effort, 161
Mai Van Bo, 98–99, 113, 116–117, 118
Manac'h, Etienne, 113
Manila Conference (1966), 77, 139
Mansfield, Mike, 97–98, 118
March on Pentagon, 141–142, 146
Marcovich, Herbert, 116–117
MARIGOLD peace initiative, 104–108, 112, 114, 118, 184

MASHER, operation, 137
"maximum candor" press policy, 127–128, 134
MAYFLOWER bombing pause, 97–98, 125
Military Assistance Command, Vietnam (MACV). *See* United States Military Assistance Command, Vietnam
Mobilization of reserves, 52
Mohr, Charles, 68
Moorer, Adm. Thomas, 19, 44, 61
Morton, Rogers, 114
Morton, Thruston B., 148
Moyers, Bill, 10, 22, 130, 136

Nathan, Robert, 74
Nation, 114
National Liberation Front of South Vietnam (NLF), 64, 65, 66, 86–87, 145–146, 153
National Student Association, 134
National Security Action Memorandum (NSAM) 341, 13, 68
National Security Council (NSC). *See* United States National Security Council
Newsweek, 2, 113, 142
New York Times: and La Pira contact, 95; and LBJ, 2, 139; and MARIGOLD, 107; and military, 29–30, 57; and Robert Kennedy peace contact, 113–114; on San Antonio formula, 118; and U Thant peace contact, 93–94
Ngo Dinh Diem, 30, 65–66
Ngo Dinh Nhu, 65–66
Nguyen Cao Ky, 66
Nguyen Duy Trinh, 108
Nguyen Van Thieu, 66, 175–176
Nitze, Paul, 15, 158, 165
Nixon, Richard M., 172, 173
Non Group, 15, 22, 164
North Vietnam: and MAYFLOWER bombing pause, 97, 98, 101; and NLF, 65; offensive planned by, 118; and peace moves, 120; and PINTA

initiatives, 101–102; and U.S. peace offensive, 100, 101; U.S. underestimation of, 42
North Vietnamese Army (NVA), 145–146, 153
Novak, Robert, 114
Nuclear Test Ban Treaty, 28

O'Neill, Thomas P., 148
One-War Concept, 170, 173, 179
Osgood, Robert E., 4–5, 124

Pacification: assessment of progress, 87–88; defined, 64; disorganization of U.S. effort, 69–70; early efforts at, 65; LBJ commitment to, 63; management of, 63–88; problems of, 83
Palmer, Gen. Bruce, 32
Paris negotiations, 176
Peace initiatives, 89, 184
Peace offensives, 96–102, 135
Pearson, Drew, 140
PENNSYLVANIA peace initiative, 90, 114–120
Pham Van Dong, 94, 95, 108, 112
Phase A-Phase B proposal for deescalation, 104, 108–111, 116
PINTA peace initiative, 101–102
Poland, 106–107
Population security strategy, 152, 159, 161, 170
Porter, William, 70, 71–72, 73, 74
Powell, Gen. Colin, 219n.11
Powers, Gen. Thomas, 28
President's Vietnam Group, 12
Press, government relations with, 127–128, 134, 139, 141, 143, 144–145, 170
Private peace initiatives, 111–114
Program for the Pacification and Long-Term Development of Vietnam (PROVN), 73–74, 201n.38
Project Takeoff, 83, 84, 86
Pueblo incident, 156
Public opinion, 122–124, 132, 159–160, 185

Public opinion polls, 125, 128, 129, 135, 138, 139–140, 141, 144, 148
Public relations campaign, 1967, 141–150
Public relations, post-Tet policies, 161–162, 168

Raborn, Adm. William, 10
Radvanyi, Janos, 107
Rangoon, 101
Rapacki, Adam, 106, 107
Rayburn, Sam, 37
Read, Benjamin, 105–106, 110
Redmon, Hayes, 135
Reedy, George, 93
Resor, Stanley, 129
Reston, James, 136
Revolutionary Development Program, 66, 69, 72, 81, 84, 85
Ridgway, Gen. Matthew, 137
Roche, John, 21
ROLLING THUNDER. *See* bombing of North Vietnam
Roosevelt, Franklin D., 26, 37, 48, 122, 123
Ronning Chester, 102
Rostow, Walt Whitman: and bombing of North Vietnam, 169; and LBJ, 10–11; on Kissinger, 116; and McNamara May 1967 DPM, 54; named national security adviser, 10; and non-group, 15; urges NSAM to better integrate strategy, 51; and PENNSYLVANIA contact, 117; in post-Tet period, 165–166; urges President to rally country, 139, 154; on private peace moves, 111; and Robert Kennedy contact, 114; and Tuesday Lunch, 14
Rowan, Carl, 39
Rowe, James H., 208n.108
Rusk, Dean: and bombing of North Vietnam, 46, 169; and bombing pause of December 1965, 99–101; and Clifford, 165; on fighting while negotiating, 151; fourteen points of, 100; in Johnson administration,

11–12; and La Pira peace initiative, 94–96; and LBJ, 7–9; and limited war, 6; loyalty, concept of, 48; and McNamara, 38; and peace initiatives, 91; and PENNSYLVANIA initiative, 117; on private peace initiatives, 111; post-Tet bombing halt, 162; speeches on Vietnam, 125; SUNFLOWER, 109; and U Thant peace initiative, 92–94; on war in "cold blood," 2
Russell, Richard, 20

Safer, Morley, 133, 134
Salisbury, Harrison, 107, 108, 111–112
San Antonio formula, 117, 118, 141
SANE, 142
Schelling, Thomas, 5
Seaborn, Blair, 92
Search and destroy strategy, 43, 44, 159–160, 168, 170
Senior Interdepartmental Group (SIG), 13, 68
Sevareid, Eric, 94, 99
Sharp, Adm. U.S. Grant, 40, 47, 169
Sheehan, Neil, 82, 86, 127
Six-Day War, 53, 60
South Vietnam, elections in (1967), 115
South Vietnam, political disarray in (1966), 102
South Vietnamese: and CORDS, 84; and pacification, 86; and Paris negotiations,
South Vietnamese government. *See* Government of Vietnam
Soviet Union, 97, 108, 131
Spock, Dr. Benjamin, 142
Stalemate, perception of war as, 138, 145
State Department. *See* United States Department of State
Stennis, John, 55
Stennis Committee hearings, 55–56
Stevenson, Adlai E., 91–94
St. Louis Post-Dispatch, 95
Strategic Hamlet Program, 65–66
Students for a Democratic Society (SDS), 142

SUNFLOWER peace initiative, 107–111, 118
Sylvester, Arthur, 133, 134, 139

Taylor, Maxwell, 12–13, 29, 59, 68, 69, 70, 118, 154
Teach-ins, 126
Tet Offensive, 148, 150, 151–158
Thant, U, 91–94, 100
Time, 2, 19, 40, 100, 118, 147
Truman, Harry S., 37, 124, 144
Truman-MacArthur controversy, 180, 183
Tuesday Lunch, 8–10, 14–15, 44, 104, 116, 164

Unger, Leonard, 105–106
United Kingdom, 109
United Nations, 97–98
United States Agency for International Development (AID), 69, 75, 79, 86
United States Army, 44, 73–74, 87–88
United States Central Intelligence Agency (CIA), 75, 79, 123, 142
United States Civil Operations, Revolutionary Development Support (CORDS), 64, 80–81, 86–88
United States Department of State: and Ashmore-Baggs peace contact, 113; and Defense Department, 12; and MARIGOLD, 105; and pacification, 75, 79; and peace initiatives, 91; and public opinion, 123; public relations activities of, 136; and public relations policies, 154; and Robert Kennedy peace contact, 113–114; responsibility for war in, 21–22; and Salisbury peace contact, 112
United States Federal Bureau of Investigation (FBI), 142
United States Information Agency (USIA), 69, 75
United States Joint Chiefs of Staff: August 1965 "Concept for Vietnam," 41; and bombing after Tet, 155; and bombing halt, 1968, 173; in chain of command, 40, 219n.11; and civilian

control, 49–50; creation of, 26; and
escalation of war, 30; and expansion
of war after Tet, 155–157; and expansion of war (1967), 51; frustration
with limits on war, 31; impact of war
on, 61; and Khe Sanh, 153; and LBJ,
183; and MacArthur in Korea, 27;
and McNamara 1967 DPM, 53; military criticism of, 54; and mobilization
of reserves, 34; and pacification, 75;
proposals of October 1967, 58; resignation of, 56, 57, 199 n.138; and
Stennis hearings, 55–57; and troop
decision of 1965, 33–36; unified recommendations on war, 31; Vietnam
strategy of, 39–40; and Westmoreland's request for 44 battalions, 32
United States Marines, 44–45, 133
United States Military Assistance Command, Vietnam (MACV), 75, 81, 84,
143–145, 154, 167–168
United States National Security Council
(NSC), 6, 7, 13–14, 164
United States Office of Civil Operations
(OCO), 78–81
United States Office of War Information
(OWI), 122, 123, 143
U Thant peace initiative, 91–94, 98, 118

Valenti, Jack, 139
Vance, Cyrus, 12, 42, 167
Vann, John Paul, 78, 80
Vatican, 208 n.108
Vietnam Coordinating Committee, 68
Vietnam Documents and Research
Notes, 146
Vietnam Information Group, 143, 149,
161–162
Vietnamization, 60, 151, 163
Vietnam Public Affairs Committee, 12,
132, 136
Vietnam Public Affairs Working Group,
136
Vu Huu Binh, 101

Walt, Gen. Lewis, 183
Warnke, Paul, 15, 158, 165

Washington Post, 15, 107
Weiss, Peter, 95
Westmoreland, Gen. William C.: named
Army Chief of Staff, 161; and bombing of Cambodia and North Vietnam,
169; and civilian interference, 45; and
CORDS, 81, 82, 85; on escalation,
1967, 52; and LBJ, 25, 49, 182; on
limited war, 184; National Press Club
speech, 147; and pacification, 70;
post-Tet offensive conducted by, 161;
and public relations, 143; recalled to
Washington, October 1967, 59; on restrictions, 40, 45, 46; and strategy,
195 n.67; troop request after Tet, 155;
troop request (1965), 32; troop request
(1967), 51; and Tuesday lunch, 14
Wheeler, Gen. Earle G.: as Army Chief
of Staff, 29; and bombing pause, 42;
and bombing of North Vietnam, 43,
117–118, 169; as chairman, JCS,
30–31; and escalation, 42, 51–52,
137; on "fog of war," 183; "foot-in-
the-door" approach, 41, 49–50; impact of war on, 61; influence rises, 11;
and McNamara May 1967 DPM, 53;
and non-group, 15; post-Tet report of
156–158; and public relations, 168;
Tet impact in U.S., 154; and Tuesday
lunch, 14, 40; and unified recommendations from JCS, 33; and Wise Men,
59
White, William S., 20
WHITE Wing, operation, 137
Why Vietnam?, 132
Williams, G. Mennen, 100
Wilson, Harold, 108–111
Win, Ne, 91
Wise Men, 59–60, 125, 130, 144, 162,
163
Women's Strike for Peace, 142

XYZ peace contact, 98–99

Young Democrats, 126, 133, 134

Zorthian, Barry, 50